90 Days to the Data Mart

Alan Simon

WILEY COMPUTER PUBLISHING

John Wiley & Sons, Inc.
New York • Chichester • Weinheim • Brisbane • Singapore • Toronto

Publisher: Robert Ipsen
Editor: Robert M. Elliott
Managing Editor: Micheline Frederick
Text Design & Composition: Benchmark Productions, Inc.

Designations used by companies to distinguish their products are often claimed as trademarks. In all instances where John Wiley & Sons, Inc., is aware of a claim, the product names appear in initial capital or ALL CAPITAL LETTERS. Readers, however, should contact the appropriate companies for more complete information regarding trademarks and registration.

This book is printed on acid-free paper. ♾

This publication is designed to provide accurate and authoritative information in regard to the subject matter covered. It is sold with the understanding that the publisher is not engaged in professional services. If professional advice or other expert assistance is required, the services of a competent professional person should be sought.

Library of Congress Cataloging-in-Publication Data:
Simon, Alan R.
    90 days to the data mart / Alan Simon.
      p. cm.
    Includes index.
    ISBN 0-471-25194-1 (pbk. : alk. paper)
    1. Data marts. I. Title.
  QA76.9.D34S56 1998
  005.74'068'4--dc21   98-52000
                                            CIP

Printed in the United States of America.
10 9 8 7 6 5 4 3 2 1

Preface

This is a book about data marts, intended for those who practice information technology (IT) in the real world under any of the following conditions:

♦ You have to fight to get IT projects funded in a corporate environment, with intense scrutiny on budget requests.

♦ Executive sponsors are leery of project failure rates and want as much of a guarantee of success as you can possibly give.

♦ It seems that every time you turn around, pitfalls and problems are waiting to ambush you and your team.

Wary of surprisingly high data warehouse project failure rates—particularly for large, complex efforts—corporate executive sponsors are turning an eye toward smaller-scale efforts that have come to be known as *data marts*.

A tremendous amount of hype and confusion is associated with data marts today, and vendors that tout data marts as a quick, easy, "safe" answer to data warehousing woes don't help the situation. As much as possible, this book puts aside the data mart hype and vague generalizations to help you figure out what you really need to do to rapidly develop data marts.

This book discusses topics that are rarely seen in print but are essential to data mart project success, such as the following:

♦ How to tell, at any point in the data project, if you're in trouble

♦ How a data mart team should be composed at each phase of your project and what each team member's roles and tasks should be

♦ How to analyze archived historical data that will be brought into the data mart—specifically, that each tape-based or disk-based set of data must be evaluated individually because of the likelihood of data structure changes over time

♦ How to quickly analyze external data sources, depending on whether your organization is currently using that data (e.g., after it is loaded into flat files)

♦ How to build a data mart team culture conducive to rapid development and with minimized interference from corporate politics

It also addresses many more subjects that will be of concern to you when you are rapidly developing a data mart.

A final note: The book assumes you have a basic understanding of the concepts and principles of data warehousing. Readers with little or no familiarity with data warehousing are urged to consult one of the many texts available that discuss this area as a prerequisite to this book's subject matter. Similarly, references are made throughout the book to concepts and architectural models such as client/server computing and Web-enabled environments, as well as basic database management techniques. Readers not familiar with these subjects also should consult appropriate texts for explanations.

Contents

Contents

A Road Map To Rapid
Data Mart
Development

This Book's Audience

This book will be of interest to anyone involved with a data mart project; the contents are especially appropriate for individuals filling one of the following roles:

♦ Data mart project sponsor (from either an information technology or a business organization)

♦ Data mart project manager

♦ Data mart chief architect or designer

This book will refer to "your project" or "your team;" thus, anyone playing one of the leadership roles listed above—*regardless of whether that role is business oriented or technology oriented*—will benefit from the broad perspective presented in the chapters that follow. Indeed, one of the most valuable aspects of this book is that individuals from the business side and the information technology (IT) side can gain an appreciation of the tasks that need to be performed by all team members from both sides. As the inevitable project problems occur, this understanding will help the team move through them without dissension.

In addition to those leaders of a data mart effort listed above, anyone involved in a data mart project—database developer, quality assurance specialist, user, or trainer, for example—can gain an understanding of "the big picture."

This Book Is Guaranteed to Be Hype-Free

Chances are that you've been exposed to (and probably overwhelmed by) the data mart mania that has taken hold in the past few years. This means that you've probably puzzled over the following:

- The "Is it a data mart or data warehouse?" question
- The "backlash" against data warehousing that promotes the "data warehousing has failed; the only thing left is data marts" philosophy
- The ROLAP versus MOLAP debate (i.e., relational online analytical processing versus multidimensional online analytical processing) that is discussed in Chapter 3

To counteract the hype in the world of data warehousing and data marts, Chapters 1 and 2 presents a down-to-earth, guaranteed-no-hype discussion of data marts. Where there are gray areas between the concepts of data warehousing and data marts, guidelines are presented. The purpose of Chapter 2, however, is to give you a context for what you will build in around 90 days.

About the "90 Days"

It is absolutely realistic to expect to successfully build and deploy a data mart in 90 days. Many people have done it. However, 90 days is *not* a magic time frame. If, say, 90 days is the average duration from start to deployment for a given set of functionality (which we'll call X), it stands to reason that for a broader set of functionality—say 1.5 or 2 times X, or whatever the multiplier is—your project is likely to take somewhat longer. You could, of course, attempt to adjust the duration by adding members to your team, and in some situations that will help. However, the dependencies among the various tasks may make it counterproductive to simply throw people into a project with the expectation that additional staff will shorten a development cycle. This is discussed further in Chapter 2.

The important thing to note about the 90 days is that to increase your chances of successful development and deployment, your data mart should include about 90 days' worth of functionality in terms of what it will take to successfully roll out an environment to a group of end users. Some data mart projects will take longer, and some will take less time. What determines the end-to-end duration of your project? A combination of factors that is discussed in Chapters 2 and 3 and then presented, in detail, throughout the week-by-week chapters and the decision points with which you'll be faced. To give you a preview, these include the basic architecture under which you'll be developing your environment (i.e., "classical" one-way data extractions versus application-embedded "push" technology), data volumes, and the quality of your source data, among other factors.

To help reduce the volatility from one project to another, though, the approach presented in this book requires you to accomplish a number of prerequisite steps (these are discussed in Chapter 3). Once these prerequisites have been completed (in some situations, they may take one or two months; in others, nine months or longer), enough common ground has been established to avoid unanticipated problems once the development and deployment clock starts running. The caveat is this: If you start your actual project work without making sure that all of the prerequisites have been accomplished, your project is at risk!

An Approach and a Philosophy— Not a Methodology

It's very important to understand that the material presented in this book is *not* a methodology, but rather an approach and, in many ways, a philosophy. What's the distinction?

Though you can define methodology in a number of ways, in this book it is considered a set of interrelated steps and groups of steps that, when combined, gives you a blueprint to take you toward your objective. Your objective is a data mart that is up and running and is being used by the community for which it was intended.

The problem with methodologies is that there are so many of them. Nearly every large information technology organization has a methodology that represents its officially approved way to develop applications. Further, most consulting organizations have their own methodologies that they use on their clients' projects.

Some methodologies work well; others don't. Some methodologies work in certain situations (i.e., a certain project size or complexity) but not in others (such as a much larger, more complex project). And occasionally your organization and the consulting firm hired to develop an application face a "methodology clash."

The information in this book is intended to "overlay" any methodology with a methodology-neutral approach. That is, you can take the techniques, tactics, and tools presented in this book and either use them exactly as they are presented or tailor them to your particular methodology.

For example, Cambridge Technology Partners uses a Rapid Applications Development (RAD) methodology that is oriented toward very rapid delivery of business solutions. When doing rapid data mart solutions for our clients, it tailors the standard RAD methodology with specific tools and tactics that are needed for a data mart environment (i.e., those that have to with source systems analysis, source-to-target data mappings, and so on).

Another organization that uses a different methodology can just as easily take the approach presented in this book and tailor its standard methodology. A specific example follows.

During the first two weeks of a data mart project, in which the scope of the effort is being determined and various points of functionality prioritized, the book's approach calls for the creation of three matrices: One that maps each piece of functionality to the "facts" needed to support that functionality, a second that maps those facts back to the source(s) from which data will need to be drawn to create each fact, and a third that converges these two matrices, mapping functionality components to the sources. (These are described in detail, with examples, in the chapters for Weeks 1 and 2).

Suppose that your organization's standard methodology also calls for a scoping exercise at the very beginning of the project, but instead of matrices your methodology calls for graphical representation of data facts using entity-relationship (ER) diagramming. Additionally, your methodology calls for drawing and labeling functionality in the form of business processes, using process flow diagrams.

It is relatively straightforward to create the "missing links" between the methodology-neutral approach presented in this book and your methodology. Specifically, you need to augment your diagramming techniques with mapping between the business processes and the data facts (entities) needed for each process and a diagramming technique for data sources, showing how each maps to one or more facts (entities).

Remember that the approach, the concepts, and the principles—not the specific techniques—presented in the following chapters are most important. Although these techniques *do* work, you do not need to scrap this approach simply because you already have a standard methodology with a different set of techniques. You may adapt to suit your environment.

A Technology- and Product-Neutral Approach

Another philosophy of this book's approach is that it is technology and product neutral, which means you can use it for the following:

♦ Both ROLAP and MOLAP data marts

♦ A project in which middleware tools (i.e., one or more products to do the extraction, transformation, data quality assurance, and loading functions) are used or in which you will be doing those middleware functions by custom coding (e.g., in SQL, COBOL, SAS, or another 4GL)

♦ A ROLAP solution with a Web-enabled front-end or a ROLAP solution with a "fat client" front end

♦ Any data mart situation, regardless of the technology or products you select

It is true that each product and technology has unique steps that don't apply on an alternate path. However, whether you select a multidimensional database or a relational database for your data mart, you still have to do conceptual data modeling. Regardless of the desktop tool you are providing your users, you still must train them, create standard screens, handle metadata, and perform other tasks common to that tool.

Where appropriate, this book lists specific steps that you need to do for a particular technology and product, but in most cases, the discussion is as generic as possible, focusing more on the processes than the specific techniques.

An Approach for All Classes of Business Intelligence Processing

In general, you create a data mart to do one or more of the following classes of business intelligence processing:

♦ *Basic querying and reporting.* "Tell me what happened."

♦ *OLAP.* "Tell me what happened and why."

♦ *Executive Information Systems (EIS) delivery.* "Tell me lots of things, but don't make me work too hard to get the answers."

♦ *Data mining.* "Tell me what might happen, and tell me something interesting, even though I'm not really sure what questions to ask."

The book's approach applies to a data mart that is created for any of these purposes (or any combination of purposes). The only caveat is that the more of the above business intelligence classes you include in your environment, the more screen development, tool setup and configuration, training, and other tool-oriented tasks and steps you'll need to do. As a result, the duration of your project will likely increase. It won't affect the overall flow of the approach, but it will extend your completion date slightly.

Flexibility and Recovery as Fundamental Principles

This book does not offer a "cookbook" set of steps to be performed sequentially, according to a well-defined, formal, immutable "branching logic." In fact, a great deal of the value of this book's approach is in the strategies and tactics, all grounded in real-world projects, that you can use to get the project back on track when problems occur. Flexibility is a key element to IT development success, and data marts are no exception.

From Concept to Use ... It's All Here

It's one thing to successfully construct a data mart; it's another to actually deploy it and have your user community using it as part of their work processes. In addition to the requirements, design, and construction of data mart, this book covers the entire data mart story, end to end, from concept to its use.

When This Book's Approach Will Work

The book's rapid data mart development approach works very well for *most* data mart projects.

In Chapter 1, a number of figures show examples of data mart environments. The architectures of these data mart environments are similar in the following ways:

♦ Data is periodically extracted from one or more sources (including, in some cases, a data warehouse).

♦ After the middleware functions (transformation, quality assurance, and movement) occur, the data is loaded into the data mart.

♦ The data mart is an "architectural end point"—no further movement of data occurs, nor is the data mart intended to be a component of a distributed data warehousing environment in which integration with other data marts occurs.

Basically, this approach works if your objective is to develop an environment with a relatively straightforward and simple architecture. However, this approach is not appropriate and should not be used in any environment that could be categorized as architecturally complex. Examples include the following:

♦ A data mart that is really an operational data store (ODS) or an environment in which changes to one or more data sources must be propagated to a separate informational database in real time (or near real time). Increasingly, ODSs will be part of an overall enterprise environment in which applications use messaging to transmit new or changed data; that is, the applications are "warehouse enabled." The need to either develop warehouse-enabled applications or retrofit existing applications with a messaging capability precludes a rapid development approach because of the end-to-end, source-to-target architectural complexity needed to successfully implement an ODS.

♦ Integrated "enterprise" data marts. The latest trend in data marts is to build a series of data marts that integrate in a bottom-up manner to develop a data warehousing environment as contrasted with a single-database, monolithic data warehouse. To successfully accomplish bottom-up component integration requires an intensive, detailed architectural effort that absolutely cannot be done (nor should be done) rapidly. The last two chapters of this book discuss the emerging area of enterprise data marts in more detail, presenting examples of a recommended approach and discussion of other techniques that are likely to fail.

♦ A data mart with sensitive contents. Any data mart needs to have security requirements identified, designed, and implemented. In most cases, granting users permission to perform various functions—such as read, update, and delete—with different database elements in the data mart is sufficient. If, however, a data mart's contents (and the way they are used) are particularly sensitive, it is likely that intensive security engineering will need to be performed. Rapid design and development is not desirable in these situations.

♦ Data warehouse environments that incorporate unstructured information (images, drawings, video, etc.) to complement traditional data types (numeric information, dates, and character strings). If you choose this path for your data mart, the complexities of an integrated, multimedia environment will require extensive design of your database that is far more extensive than can be handled in the time allotted in this book's approach.

♦ A hybrid OLAP (HOLAP) data mart with a combination of multidimensional database structures (for precalculated summary information) and relational tables for detailed data. If you build this type of data mart, you need to devote a great deal of time to your database architecture. This type will preclude rapid design and development.

♦ Any data mart that will contain large volumes of data (100 gigabytes or more). Even though such an environment may not be architecturally complex, the sheer volume of data will introduce complexity to the environment that will require careful evaluation of server hardware, intensive stress testing for database performance, and testing of various user interaction models (number of simultaneous users with various mixes of queries). A separate effort, dedicated exclusively to designing, prototyping, and testing the very large database environment, needs to be included in the development life cycle and will preclude rapid design and development.

T I P In some situations, you will know even before you start a data mart project that rapid development will not be possible. For example, requirements to integrate a data mart with other existing data marts—or others under development in parallel with your effort— will almost always surface as project approval is being sought. You would, therefore, seek funding to embark on a development program that includes sufficient time for the architectural work necessary to accomplish this objective.

However, you might not learn that you will have out-of-the-ordinary security requirements or be dealing with very large databases until you have already begun your project. Some requirements surface during the scope; others show up as a result of work done during the design phase. In these situations, the phase in which the complexity is discovered can be completed and then a reevaluation of the project can be accomplished in which plans are made for the additional integration architecture, security engineering, or whatever else is needed.

Part One

Setting the Stage

Data Marts: Definition, Concepts, and Terminology

A Note to the Reader: Part of the problem with trying to define a data mart is that definitions usually compare a data mart with a data warehouse. A data warehouse is "too expensive," but a data mart is "cost-effective." A data warehouse "takes too long to build," whereas a data mart "can be built in a very short time."

Even attempts to get more specific usually compare the two. A data warehouse has "many subject areas" while a data mart contains "only one or two subjects." It is also said that a data mart has a subset of the contents of a data warehouse.

How can you build something at all—let alone rapidly—when defining it is so difficult?

This chapter takes a two-dimensional look at the concept of data marts. One dimension is the data source architecture—the way(s) it comes to be populated with its contents. The other dimension is its content model in comparison with a data warehouse.

Taking both dimensions into consideration makes two things become very apparent. First, data marts vary widely from one another in the combination of the data source architecture and the content model; any thought of an "automatic data mart blueprint" is wishful thinking.

Second, with the focus on these two characteristics, the actual definition of a data mart is fairly irrelevant. It turns out, after all, that you can build something even though it's difficult to define!

The Premise of the Data Mart

You develop a data mart for the same reason you develop a data warehouse: to provide a consolidation of data regardless of platform, geographic, application, and organizational barriers. And once you've consolidated that data, you have created an environment that will provide users with business intelligence.

So, what then is the difference between the two?

It's tempting to define a *data mart* as simply a "smaller-scale data warehouse," and in many environments, that definition is an accurate one. A development team may set out with a mission to build a data warehouse containing a given set of information, covering a certain period of time. Once it is completed, the objective may be to deploy the data warehouse to a number of organizations within the company.

But with a budget cut here, a technical challenge there, before long, the project has been scaled back: less information and for a shorter historical period. Further, only one organization will now use this environment, at least for the foreseeable future.

A failed project? Of course not; the team is now developing a data mart, not a data warehouse.

A Historical Perspective on Data Marts

When the term *data mart* first came into vogue, it was generally used to describe an environment that would receive a subset of a data warehouse's contents and then would be the primary point of data access for a subset of the organization's total user base (i.e., one or two departments). Basically, the data mart would serve the role of "retail data outlet," as follows:

♦ The content would be limited, but it would be tailored to the business intelligence needs of its small user community.

♦ The user community could be given a business intelligence tool different from the "standard" product (whatever it happened to be) that was used by others to directly access the data warehouse.

♦ It would be possible, if necessary, for the data mart to use a different database management product—perhaps even a different database management model—from that for the data warehouse. The data warehouse could be relationally based, for example, while the data mart's smaller subset of data could be stored in a multidimensional database (MDDB).

In short, the data mart would be related to—but independent from—the architecture, technology, products, and other properties of the data warehouse from which it received its contents. The guiding principles of the data mart would be the same as those for a data warehouse: subject oriented and nonvolatile (i.e., the database wouldn't be updated by user transactions).

Figure 1.1 illustrates a typical data warehouse-data mart architecture implemented according to this philosophy.

The Backlash

A funny thing happened in the world of data warehouses and data marts. Big data warehousing projects weren't quite as successful in many organizations as had been hoped. The premise of data warehousing is, after all, fairly straightforward: extract certain data at periodic intervals from internal applications; if necessary, augment it with externally provided data from service bureaus or other extraenterprise sources; perform a series of quality assurance checks and transformation processes; and then load your results into a target database, ready to be used by the organization's business community.

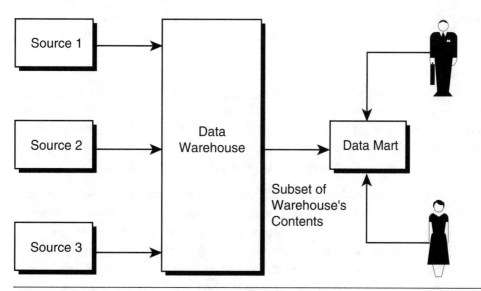

Figure 1.1 The original concept of the data mart.

Alas, more than a few data warehousing projects were overcome by a combination of the following:

♦ Technology challenges (e.g., scalability issues, such as handling very large databases)

♦ Procedural and methodology challenges (e.g., not doing well at determining the business value sought from the data warehouse and relating that value back to specific functionality and data needs)

♦ Organizational challenges (specifically, the cross-organization cooperation that is usually needed for a data warehousing environment and the negative impact of corporate politics)

As a result, they were only partially deployed; deployed but never used because of problems like data integrity, or canceled outright.

The business value of data warehousing—or more precisely, the business intelligence functions performed with the contents of a data warehouse—has really never been in doubt, and the results from most surveys of successfully completed and used data warehouses have shown an outstanding return on investment (ROI) in most cases.

Seeing projects fail that should have been "slam dunks" caused more than a few people to take notice, however, and what can only be described as a backlash against data warehousing started creeping into the discipline. Some people believe data warehousing is a good concept that just doesn't work in the real world.

The Shift

Interestingly, smaller-scale data warehousing efforts, the ones that were being developed in three to six months with scaled-back functionality, were usually successful. But how could those types of environments be easily distinguished in the marketplace (and the corresponding battle for product and consulting service dollars) from the very large, dump-everything-in-there attempts that usually failed?

Somewhere along the line, the phrase *data mart* was extended to refer not only to an environment sourced by a data warehouse, but to *any* smaller-scale effort with a relatively short time from concept to deployment. In the "brave new world" of data marts, such an environment could do its own data extraction, quality assurance, transformation, and the other necessary functions directly against source environments. Figure 1.2 shows a "new style" data mart environment that, at least visually, is indistinguishable from a data warehousing environment.

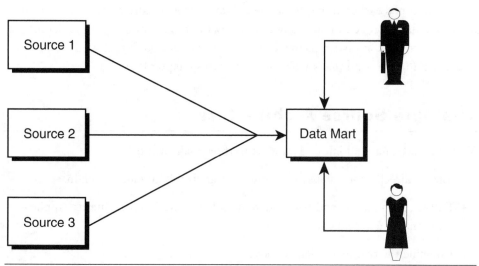

Figure 1.2 A data mart with direct access to source data.

Where Are We Today?

Today, data marts are good—they are *very* good—and most organizations are building at least one of them. Data warehouses are not "bad," but they have an image problem today. Surf around the Internet and check out vendor product literature, white papers, and other material relating to data marts. In many cases, the selling pitch is that developing a data warehouse will cost too much and it will probably fail, anyway. If you go the data mart route, you won't be sorry.

Under the old definition of a data mart, the distinguishing characteristic was that its contents would be provided from a data warehouse. If you saw any environment like that pictured in Figure 1.1, the system on the right side of the picture was a data mart, no doubt about it. The wording would likely vary from one definition to another, but a description of this type of environment would be a satisfactory definition for a data mart.

But how about with an environment like that shown in Figure 1.2 that, according to "the marketplace," is now defined as a data mart? How exactly would you define this environment? You could use phrases like "nonvolatile" and "subject oriented," but that's how you define a data warehouse (at least according to the classical definition).

Perhaps you could make a distinction between respective lengths of development—a data warehouse takes longer to build than a data mart—but where is the cutoff? Is it at the six-month point? The one-year point?

As mentioned earlier, trying to define a data mart is usually an exercise in futility. So maybe the approach to take is not to worry too much about a formal definition, but rather to look at distinguishing characteristics and models that would be classified as data marts. And that's what the rest of this chapter does.

The Data Source Architecture

You can load data load into a data mart in three main ways:

♦ Take it directly and exclusively from an organizational data warehouse

♦ Extract, manipulate, and consolidate data from one or more internal applications and/or external data sources

♦ Combine the two means listed above

The following sections discuss each of these methods

A Warehouse-Based Data Source

Figure 1.1 illustrates the model by which a data mart's contents are provided solely from a data warehouse somewhere in the organization. The data mart is "linked" to the data warehouse in terms of architecture, data flows, and data content.

It's important to note that even in warehouse-based data mart environments, you still need to extract data, verify the quality of that data, move it across platform barriers, and load it into the target database. You could, conceivably, need to perform data transformation services—for example, resummarizing the warehouse's contents to an even less granular level of detail.

In addition, all of the standard system development functions and processes—including business needs analysis, project plan development, tool and hardware selection, testing, and user training—still need to be done. Therefore, you should never consider data mart development to be an effortless prospect when you already have a data warehouse in place.

The primary advantage you gain from relying solely on a data warehouse for your data is that you can shortcut the process of hunting out the various candidate data sources, digging into their respective data environments to see what's there and what the quality looks like, and—perhaps most important—you can insulate yourself from a large part of the heterogeneity problem (i.e., dealing with many different platforms).

A disadvantage, though, to this approach is that your data mart is *extremely* dependent on the data warehousing environment. Changes in the warehouse may very well affect your data mart in terms of content, timing of data availability, and other factors. If your organization has a data warehousing environment that runs very smoothly, this cross-environment coupling won't affect you very much; one that is constantly dealing with problems can have an unfortunate and unpredictable impact on your data mart.

TIP Always make sure that at least one member of your data mart team is representing your needs and concerns on the data warehousing working group, management staff, or whatever type of data warehousing cross-organization structure is in place.

Applications and External Sources

The second way you can load data into your data mart is by going to the various applications within your enterprise and to various external sources to "get the data yourself." As shown in Figure 1.2, this model is conceptually identical to that of most data warehouses. A large portion of the approach discussed in this book focuses on the challenges you face in this area.

Chances are that most of your data mart efforts will be of this variety. The marketplace has come to recognize an environment with direct data feeds from one or more transactional data stores to an informational data store as either a data warehouse or data mart, as discussed earlier in this chapter. Therefore, your "build a data mart mission" will, increasingly, require you to go get your own data.

The Hybrid Approach

The third data source architecture model is a combination of the two previous approaches. For example, there may be a data warehouse in your organization that will provide most of the data you need for your data mart, but there are certain pieces of information that have been identified as necessary to include but are just not in the data warehouse.

One approach to this quandary is to submit a request to include that information in the data warehouse, wait for that to occur, and then acquire that data along with the rest of the contents you need for your data mart. However, there could be a tremendous time delay until this occurs. Your request could be one of dozens waiting to be serviced by the data warehousing support staff, and it could be lower on the queue than many others.

To overcome this data warehousing bottleneck, you could acquire your missing data yourself to supplement the data you will be receiving from the data warehouse. Several of the figures in the rest of this chapter show examples of this approach.

The Content Model

The other defining aspect of a data mart is its *content model*, which encompasses the guiding principles of what is to be stored within its domain. The following sections give some examples of methods of "content bounding" for a data mart and, for each method, examples for each of three approaches to the data source architecture described above.

When you look at the combination of the data source architecture and the content model, a clearer picture of just a data mart starts to emerge.

Geography-Bounded Data

Assume that you are a sales executive with a department store organization, responsible for a territory that covers the states of Arizona, Nevada, and Colorado. Among the responsibilities assigned to you and your staff is detailed analysis of sales and marketing activity in each of your 15 stores, as well as of each department in those stores. A key aspect of this analysis is information about your competitors, including not only other department store chains, but also the many specialty retailers that sell products found in one of the departments in your stores. You need to track promotional campaigns, pricing, and many other data points.

Figure 1.3 illustrates a model in which the data mart to support your activities would have its content provided exclusively from your corporate data warehouse. Note that the warehousing environment receives its contents from a variety of sources, including internal production applications as well as external syndicated data sources.

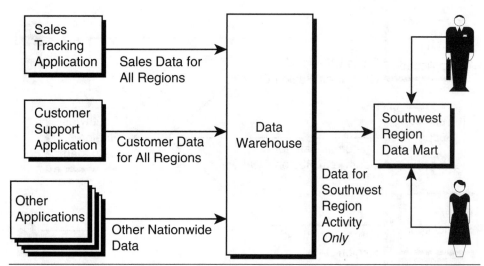

Figure 1.3 Geography-bounded data provided by a data warehouse to a data mart.

Note that your Southwest Region data mart receives detailed internal and competitive data for activity in *only* Arizona, Colorado, and Nevada. The management processes established in your company charter you with detailed analytical activity for stores and competitive activity within your region, but *not* within other regions. However, to see how your region is doing as compared to other regions within the company, your data mart does receive some high-level summary information (e.g., total sales by department by month and sales by square foot).

One of the primary limiting factors with the preceding model is the strain placed upon the data warehouse to deal with local, single-department competitors for the entire country. Although it's conceivable that this competitive data-collection mission could be accomplished by a data warehouse, it's unlikely to have the completeness desired by you and your counterparts in other regions or be able to add new competitors in a timely fashion.

Figure 1.4 illustrates the second approach to geography-bounded data marts, or those with no centralized data warehouse from which to receive your data. Note that in going to each of the internal data sources, your extraction processes focus exclusively on data for your region: sales data from stores in Pennsylvania, for example, are filtered out and don't traverse the pipeline from source to data mart.

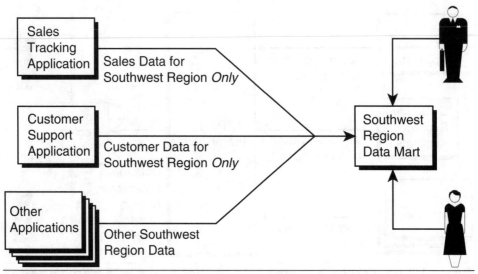

Figure 1.4 Geography-bounded data provided by a direct access to data sources.

The primary drawback to this data mart approach is the loss of "data acquisition leverage." If, say, your Southwest Region were the only region building a data mart and performing business intelligence processing, there would be no problems. However, if each one of your peers in the other five regions in the country is also building a data mart, acquiring much of the same internal data that you are, there will be a tremendous amount of redundancy in the data acquisition processes. So much redundancy would occur, in fact, that it is unlikely in today's lean IT organizations that all of your respective data mart needs could be supported by the available staff.

A third approach, then, is to acquire some of your data from a data warehouse and for supplemental information that is important only to you (or for other data not available in the warehouse) to handle the acquisition processes yourself. Figure 1.5 illustrates an example of this model.

The philosophy behind the approach in Figure 1.5 is to acquire "slices" of data from the data warehouse for everything that's available there. For locally oriented information, bring it into your environment yourself rather than try to route it through a centralized data warehousing environment.

Organization-Bounded Data

Now suppose that you work with a large manufacturing conglomerate. You are assigned responsibility for the research, development, manufacturing, marketing, sales, and customer support functions for a brand new product line in an area your company has never entered before. Additionally, as a result of a recent reorganization, you are in charge of a "virtual organization" that draws support in these areas from a core set of service providers across the corporation (and across the world).

To support this mission, you decide that a data mart dedicated to the Product X Organization is necessary. It will be one in which you can have a complete "command center" for all activities, from research and development through the rest of the functions listed above, to human resources, training, and other areas.

Figure 1.6 shows a model wherein you can access your information from a corporate data warehousing environment. Note the distinction between this environment and the single data warehouse showed in Figure 1.3. Given the broad, end-to-end range of functions in this scenario, it is highly unlikely that a single data warehouse could contain all the information related to research, development, sales,

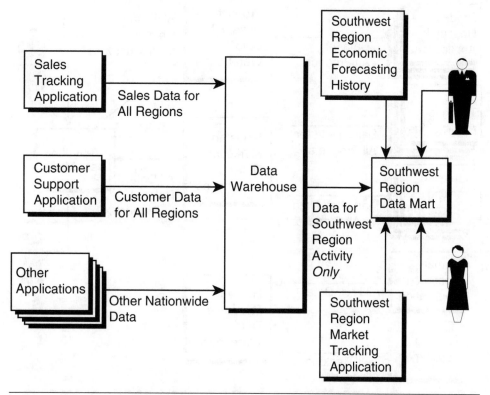

Figure 1.5 A geography-bounded data mart built from both a data warehouse and custom data acquisition.

marketing, human resources, and other functions. What is more likely, though, is that an organization with a great deal of experience in data warehousing has, over time, developed a suite of data warehouses related to each of these functions and can provide an environment from which you can pick and choose the information you need for your data mart.

What distinguishes the model shown in Figure 1.6 is that, just as with a single data warehouse as the source to your data mart, the data has already been "preconditioned." Unlike the approach discussed next, you don't have to go out to the various sources yourself to get the information you need.

Alternatively, in the absence of data warehousing sources, you would need to acquire the data yourself. As shown in Figure 1.7, this will require you to go to a very large number of corporate applications that perform all of the functions your

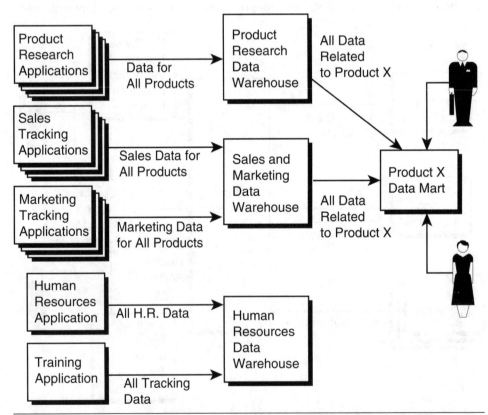

Figure 1.6 An organization-bounded data mart receiving its contents from multiple data warehouses.

organization does and extract *only* the data relevant to your organization and the products you are developing.

Finally, Figure 1.8 shows a hybrid approach for organization-bounded data mart development and support.

Function-Bounded Data

A discussion in the previous section dealt with a data warehouse organized by function. Is it accurate to classify that as a data warehouse, or is it really a data mart?

The answer: Call it whatever you want to! If you would rather describe the environment shown in Figure 1.6 as a *data mart* with its contents provided by other data marts, that's fine; if you prefer to call each of them a data warehouse, that's okay too.

Regardless of what term you use, you have a function-bounded set of data: content provided by multiple sources as related to a function, or set of functions, within the

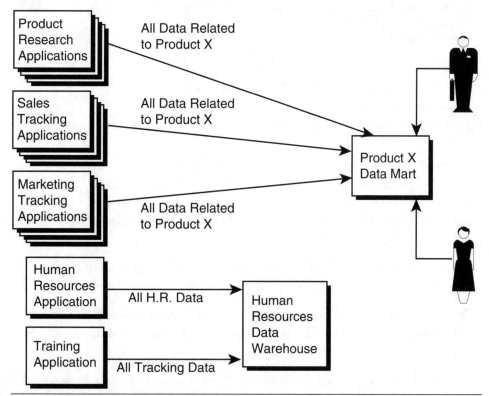

Figure 1.7 Organization-bounded data extracted from the sources to a data mart.

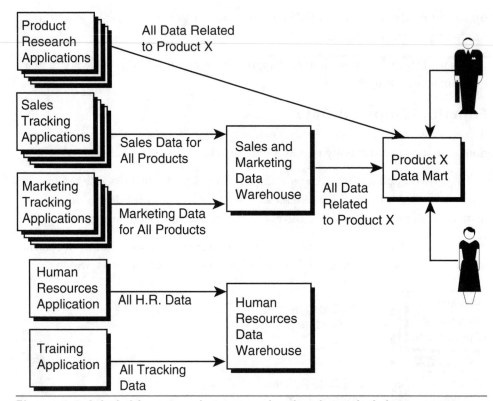

Figure 1.8 A hybrid approach to organization-bounded data marts.

company. Assume that you are the vice president in charge of shipping and distribution for a global chemical company. Your company's products are manufactured in many different plants, in many different stages, all over the world. You want a data mart for your organization to be able to analyze and make decisions about shipping and distribution for the entire company.

Figure 1.9 shows an environment in which your data mart would receive this information solely from a centralized data warehouse.

In contrast, Figure 1.10 illustrates an environment wherein you need to acquire the shipping and distribution data yourself from many different sources across the enterprise.

Figure 1.11 illustrates a hybrid environment for acquiring functionally bounded data.

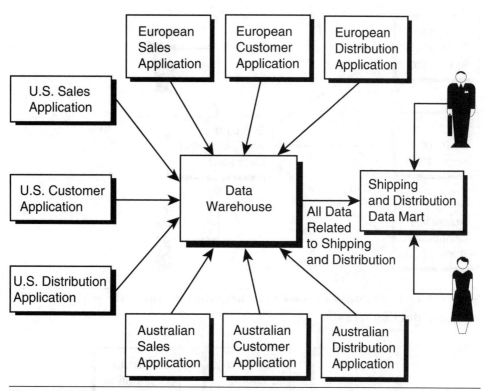

Figure 1.9 Function-bounded data provided by a data warehouse to a data mart.

Once again, as with the other data mart content models, your end result—the data mart—will contain a particular slice of the universe of available information. And the data acquisition model will often be guided by a "reality check" as to whether this universe of consolidated information could even have been built into a single data warehousing environment. If so, go get it from there. If not, you will need to acquire it yourself.

Other Data Mart Content Models

The following sections describe three other data mart content models that may be of interest to your organization. There are, in reality, many others, some of which may be very particular to your organization's needs. It is important to get a "fresh look" at the business needs of every data mart project rather than just trying to force-fit a canned solution.

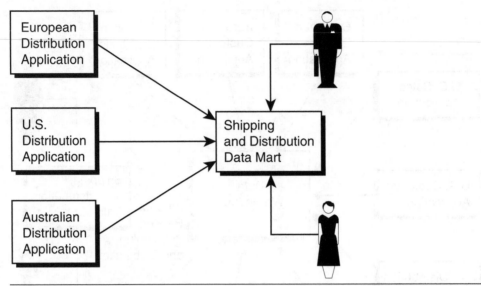

Figure 1.10 Function-bounded data acquired by the data mart from multiple data sources.

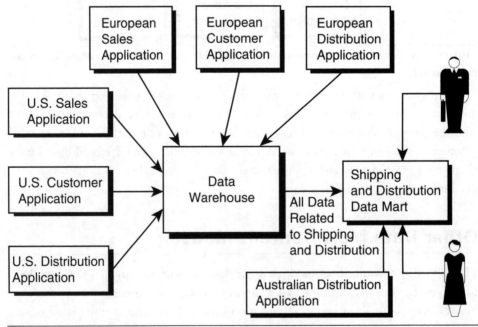

Figure 1.11 A hybrid approach to function-bounded data for a data mart.

Competitor-Bounded Data

You have a corporate mission: overtake the company directly ahead of you in market share within the next 18 months. You could, to aid this mission, develop a data mart that is competitor-bounded, one that contains every possible piece of information you can get about that competitor. Figure 1.12 provides an example of this.

A "Task-Defined" Data Mart

Another use for a data mart is to support a specific task (or set of related tasks), usually on a recurring basis. A common example is to support an annual budgeting process. For example, assume that your organization has a well-defined series of budgeting steps, covering a four-month process, consisting of the following:

♦ Setting and communicating organizational targets to different departments

♦ Collecting current year actual expenditures by department

♦ Readjusting the two prior years' actual expenditures according to new departmental alignments

♦ Collecting and consolidating forecasts of many types of expenditures—such as head count, office and administrative, and product development—from all departments

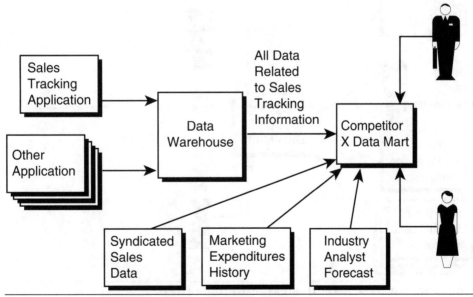

Figure 1.12 A competitor-bounded data mart.

♦ Providing analytical tools to budget analysts and senior management to use all of the consolidated inputs and do what-if analysis on budget allocations

Figure 1.13 illustrates a data mart created in support of this very specifically defined budgeting task, with data drawn, as appropriate, from various applications within the enterprise. Something unique about an environment like this one, as contrasted with the other examples in this chapter, is that the data mart has an operational mission rather than an informational or analytical one. In the example shown, information about spending targets and constraints is input directly into the data mart and integrated with the "secondhand" data obtained from applications in the enterprise (general ledger and head-count management) and archived data from past budgeting cycles.

The Answers to Specific Business Questions

A final model for discussion is building a data mart to answer specific business questions. It includes no ad hoc reporting and no multidimensional analysis—just a few standard reports dedicated to providing key business indicators, and the underlying data to those indicators, from which you can gauge the state of your business and adjust policies accordingly. Although this model of developing a data mart is

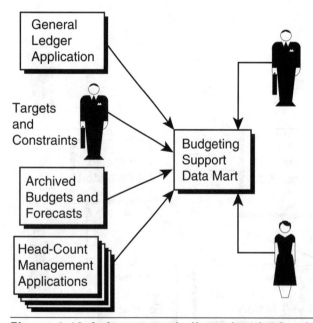

Figure 1.13 A data mart dedicated to budgeting.

usually very difficult to extend and evolve into additional capabilities because of its rigid nature, sometimes the business value from being able to answer these questions is so overwhelming that this is a valid approach to take.

Summary

It isn't the definition of a data mart (or lack thereof) that is important, but rather the attributes and characteristics that will guide you in your business analysis and subsequent development processes.

You can select your content in any one of many ways available to you, and as for how you get data into the data mart? Well, that all depends.

If you have sources available—data warehouses or other data marts—that you know can provide part or all of the information you need, then by all means, use them. If, however, no "pretreated data" is available, it is your responsibility to go to the various sources (after figuring out where they are) to acquire the data yourself.

The approach introduced in Chapter 2 and discussed in detail in the middle section of this book will guide you through these steps and processes.

Rapid Data Mart Development:
An Overview

A Note to the Reader: In a perfect IT world, you would develop a data mart in a very straightforward process. Every piece of data you might possibly need would already be waiting for you in a larger data warehouse, and it wouldn't be much different from ordering à la carte at a restaurant.

"I'll take an order of consumer goods product sales for all U.S. regions from column 1, but hold the Western and Midwest Regions. I'll also have an order of European customer sales activity, same as usual, but could you add data for 1991 this time?"

Alas, it isn't a perfect IT world, and you will likely find yourself tasked with building a data mart by having to go directly to the data sources yourself; no data warehouse, with a lot of the preliminary work done for you, is available.

Even if you could get all of your data mart's contents from an already existing, ready-to-serve-you data mart, you would still have to do the following:

♦ Work with your users to figure out what data they really need.

♦ Determine if the data warehouse's level of summarization is adequate for each group of data or if additional summarization rollups are needed.

> ♦ *Choose the hardware and software that will be needed for your data mart.*
>
> ♦ *Train your users.*
>
> ♦ *Perform many other tasks essential to getting your data mart up and running.*
>
> *The approach introduced in this chapter can be used in one of two ways: in an "as-is" manner or tailored to your organization's development methodology.*
>
> *This chapter presents a consolidated overview of the approach that is detailed in Part II of this book.*

A Phased Approach

Figure 2.1 illustrates the various phases of rapid data mart development.

Scope

The first two weeks of the data mart project are devoted to ensuring that the vision, mission, and scope of your effort are *quickly* determined. To be more specific, you and your team will do the following:

♦ Build and validate the business case for proceeding with subsequent data mart project phases (i.e., design, development, and deployment).

♦ Explore, evaluate, and decide upon the boundaries of your data mart: What business functionality will be supported, what facts (groups of data) are needed for the functionality, what data sources will be used to create the facts, who the users will be, what business units will be served, and so on.

♦ Conduct preliminary explorations into the candidate technologies of the data mart, particularly front-end tools but also data mart middleware products

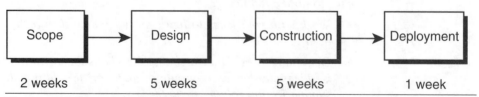

Figure 2.1 The phases of rapid data mart development.

(i.e., those that support the extraction, transformation, and movement of data) and the database management system (DBMS) upon which the data mart will be hosted.

By the time the scoping effort is completed, there will be consensus as to where you will be headed—and more important, why—during the following phases.

Design

The design phase will last for five weeks and will include a series of parallel tasks in multiple categories:

- ◆ Formalizing and finalizing the business functionality that will be delivered through the data mart

- ◆ Performing data analysis, modeling, and design

- ◆ Doing process analysis, modeling, and design

- ◆ Conducting systems and infrastructure research

- ◆ Evaluating and selecting products

- ◆ Developing a detailed project plan for the following construction phase

The key to success in the design phase is performing as many tasks as possible in parallel, carefully linking various deliverables and decision points from the threads of activity at critical junctures when necessary to form input for following activities.

Construction

The construction phase is exactly as it sounds: the actual building of the data mart. With a properly scaled data mart and a highly qualified team, construction can be accomplished in five weeks, even allowing for a midcourse correction (e.g., having to modify the database structure because of something that had been overlooked or because of initial user feedback).

All of the classical data warehousing steps—such as mapping source-to-target physical data, developing transformation, creating metadata, testing, and tuning—are included in the construction phase. Additionally, activities such as user training and infrastructure preparation will occur at the same time everything converges with deployment of the constructed data mart.

Deployment and Administration

The end of construction marks the availability of a completed data mart environment, but components still need to be deployed to their respective platforms. Rollout of client desktop tools for a moderately sized user communication—approximately 30 people—can be accomplished in one week if the importance of this phase isn't overlooked.

Caveat

There is one caveat to the phases discussed above: To accomplish them successfully and rapidly, you must have the data mart development team identified and trained and ensure that all contracts for external data sources have been approved. These prerequisites are discussed in detail in Chapter 3.

The Six Principles of Rapid Data Mart Development

This book's approach to rapid data mart development, and indeed every tactical step in every phase, is grounded in the six principles explained in the following sections. Even as you vary the book's approach to adapt it to your organization's specific development methodology and processes or tailor your deliverables as necessary, it's essential to keep these principles in mind.

Principle 1: Focus on Requirements, Not Data

Do *not* build a data mart solely to determine how your sales are doing month to month across the country or if your time to market for new products is better or worse since the last reorganization and the new production plant's opening. Also, do not build a data mart to collect organization-bound, function-bound, geographically-bound, or any other grouped subset of available data (see Chapter 1 for a discussion of these and other data mart content models), simply to have data available to support business questions.

It is true that a data mart, properly constructed, can answer specific questions or provide a collection of data from which business intelligence can be drawn. Unless you plan to do something further with the answers to those questions or the business intelligence gained from the conglomerated information, however, it may be a waste of time and resources to build the data mart.

Doing something further could mean active, functional processes and steps. For example, determining your month-to-month sales performance could cause you to either do nothing—stay the course—if results are trending upward according to your business plan, or take aggressive and authoritative action if problems exist.

In another example, analysts and managers could be empowered, upon discovering problem areas or potential opportunities as a result of OLAP activity against the contents of the data mart, to either put action plans in place themselves (as part of their job responsibilities) or to route the result to someone with authority to do so (i.e., their manager).

To put it simply, if you focus your up-front analytical and scoping efforts on data needs to the exclusion of functionality or push functionality in the background while you concentrate on facts, dimensions, hierarchy levels, and the other details of your data architecture you risk the following:

♦ Having to constantly defend your project, especially during any rough spots. The absence of specific business functionality will often put you, your team, and your project as a whole on a defensive stance, diverting your energies to meetings to justify and rejustify the business value your data mart will deliver.

♦ As you fight for adequate help from IT support organizations, finding yourself hard-pressed to make a stand to upper management on the basis of data needs if you don't have specific functionality needs (and corresponding direct business value) to justify your requests for database administrator (DBA) support and networking support. (And you will have to fight for these supporting functions because your high-value project may seem like one more nuisance to those running the IT infrastructure.)

♦ Developing and deploying a data mart that turns out not to be useful. When users try to take action based on the results of their queries and reports, there could be missing pieces of data that impede their ability to act.

By focusing on desired functionality first (see Figure 2.2) and then matching that functionality with appropriate data needs, you substantially reduce the risk of getting too far in the project and either having the business value questioned or delivering a data mart that doesn't provide the anticipated business value. This is a departure from the "data first" approaches and methodologies to database-oriented applications and environments in the mid 1980s wherein initial efforts would focus on the data models (entities, relationships, and attributes). Later, the process and functional models (e.g., data flow diagrams, process flow diagrams, state transition diagrams) would fill in the blanks.

With an emphasis on rapid development and deployment, focus first on the business value you are tasked with providing and the *actionable* processes and steps for which the data mart will provide support. Once there is consensus about these aspects, the data needs can be researched and analyzed with less questioning about its necessity.

Principle 2: Be Cautiously Daring

A data mart project is your chance to check out new products, try new technologies, and draw new users into the realm of data-driven analysis and decision-making. The key is to do so in a calculated manner, reducing your overall exposure and managing your risk.

Your corporate culture and experience will guide you in determining what is a manageable risk. For example, you may decide that developing your company's first intranet-based data mart is a good idea. However, if your company is behind the times when it comes to Internet technologies—without a browser user or a website— an intranet-based data mart may not be a good idea. The click-and-jump mode of browser applications could be the most appropriate medium for moving your end users into the world of OLAP, but do not assume that this daring move (for your organization) will be an easy one. Training, assimilation, and user support will be absolutely critical.

You can take chances and do some daring things on your data mart projects, but do so in a manner that manages your risk in the best way possible.

Principle 3: Be Flexibly Rigid

You must maintain an appropriate balancing act throughout your entire data mart project.

For example, *scope creep*—allowing additional requirements to sneak into a project's functionality after the requirements collection process has been completed— is highly undesirable. It can cause disruptive backtracking and discontent within project teams.

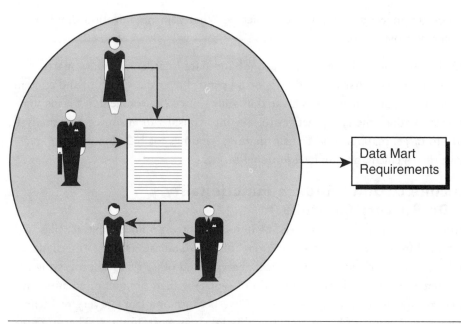

Figure 2.2 Driving data mart projects from function, not data.

However, you need to consider that there may be functionality items that had been overlooked, no matter how thorough your review and consensus-building processes were during the scoping phase of your project. Also, the level of granularity (detail) for a certain subject area (e.g., sales by product by territory) may need to be looked at again. Clearly, you want to avoid letting scope creep put your data mart project at risk. As requests for additional functionality come in during the design and development phases, put them into the "subsequent phase queue." However, neither methodology nor ego should stand in your way if something surfaces that is an absolute show-stopper.

Principle 4: Use Best Practices Adjusted for a Data Mart Project

In many ways, this book's approach to successfully and quickly developing a data mart is similar to that for developing a transactional client/server application. A multiphased approach, starting with the project scope, early consensus-driven involvement of the user community that is maintained throughout the project, an emphasis on quality assurance processes very early in the project, and many other facets of the project are simply "best practices" that your organization should follow on any project effort.

At the same time, though, the "secondhand data" nature of a data mart—particularly the fact that you had little or no control over the structure and content of your mart's data when it was created in your source environments—means that you need to adjust the best practices to take into consideration source data analysis, source-to-target mapping and transformation, windows for bulk loading of data, change management, and many additional facets.

Principle 5: Don't Reduce Functionality (Or Do So *Very* Carefully!)

In an interesting paradox, managers, analysts, and others who use extract files with data pulled from one or more applications' files or databases (sort of "quasi–data warehouses") to do reporting, statistical analysis, and other types of processing are very often extremely resistant to the idea of replacing their limited, often antiquated analytical capabilities with a data mart. Why? Because of a fear—a very real fear, in many organizations—of having functionality taken away from them. They are not interested in multidimensional analysis or drill-down if they can't get their familiar reports when their extract files are replaced by the data mart.

From the first days of your scoping phase, when you're beginning to gather functionality requirements from the user community, you need to pay careful attention to existing reports and queries users can make. Make sure the users tell you about all of their current reports and sources for their information.

In addition, note which reports the entire user community considers worthless. Not propagating that functionality into your data mart is probably okay, but be sure to get 100% consensus that its absence is acceptable.

Principle 6: Manage Risk!

Every week's chapter in Part II of this book contains a "You Know You're in Trouble When" section. These sections give examples of problems you may encounter and offer advice on dealing with them.

Ensuring that your project's risk is carefully managed must begin before your project begins. Chapter 3 discusses what you need to do before your the clock starts running on your project to managing your project risk.

Summary

You may need to tailor this book's approach to take specific deliverables and techniques of your organization's mandated development methodology into consideration. However, as long as you follow the basic premise of scoping activities leading to design, design preceding construction, and adhere to the six principles presented in this chapter, you will have set the foundation for successfully and rapidly developing your data mart.

Data Mart Project
Prerequisites

A Note to the Reader: Warning: Do not start your 90-day clock until you've dealt with and conquered all of the items covered in this chapter.

Some of these items are of the "greasing the wheel" variety, such as preselling the project to executive management. Others are prerequisites to tactical and functional activities that you will need to do throughout your data mart development (e.g., making sure you have appropriate project management processes in place). Still others are "pre-work," including early research and knowledge acquisition that will help you expedite activities later in the project, particularly during the design and product selection phase.

Introduction: The Three Categories of Data Mart Project Prerequisites

The activities you need to take care of before beginning your data mart fall into three main categories:

♦ Topics relating to technology and products

♦ People and organizational issues

♦ Methodology and business process matters

At least one facet of your data mart project (and often two or more) will be directly and positively affected by the research you accomplish, the discussions you have and agreements you reach, or the training and education you achieve. Conversely, the failure to accomplish any of the prerequisites before you begin your project will have a direct and adverse impact on at least one aspect of your data mart development.

The rapid data mart development approach is crafted so that there is a great deal of just-in-time completion of tasks that are prerequisites to others. The completion of each phase of development (scope, design, construction, and deployment) in the relatively brief time periods presented (two weeks, five weeks, five weeks, and one week, respectively) is absolutely dependent on having as little down time as possible between tasks.

Therefore, for example, failure to do early, predevelopment research on desktop tools your users might use to access the data mart and based on that research to create a shortlist of products to be given hands-on evaluation and testing will make it impossible to accomplish the two-week product selection called for in Weeks 3 and 4. That, in turn, will make it impossible to complete the detailed, product-specific functionality and process flow for the ways the tool will be used—an activity that is scheduled to be completed by Week 5. That delay will affect the Week 6 deliverable of the physical user interface design, and so on.

As a result, design would take longer than five weeks, which places your 90-day development cycle at risk. The cycle could last 120 days, 150 days, or perhaps 25 days if your project is canceled or indefinitely postponed because of a lack of accomplishment by you and your team. For longer, more complex data mart projects, 120 days becomes 150 days or 180 days, 150 days becomes nine months, and so on.

These prerequisites are tasks and processes that you need to do. Failure to complete them will place your project at risk, cost you more money than you would otherwise have to spend (especially if you're using outside consultants who are billing for time spent on your project), and in general, cause much unnecessary unpleasantness.

Technology and Products

Technology and product prerequisites focus on two main areas:

♦ Research and preevaluation of data mart products

♦ Research into your organization's standards and constraints in the context of the impact they will have on your data mart project

Data Mart Products

One of the great chicken-or-egg paradoxes of the data warehousing has been the way products and tools are selected for a given implementation. One school of thought is that product selection should be consistent with classical systems development methodologies: Concentrate first on requirements definition, systems analysis, and conceptual systems and application design. When those steps have been validated by all appropriate persons (e.g., the user community, the IT organization, executive management), *then* evaluate and select all appropriate products and tools for both development and eventual deployment to the user community.

The contrasting school of thought is that there is very little value in accomplishing requirements definition, analysis, and design in a product-neutral "vacuum." Proponents believe the most valuable way to draw out data warehousing requirements is to interactively work with users with a few pieces of data at a time, presenting concepts and possible deliverables visually and therefore expediting the overall development process. Doing so requires having your tools and products, especially the front-end analytical and information delivery one(s), already selected and in place. Though this approach is often derided, it's hard to argue with the power of interactive, visual development.

The method you use depends on your situation. For a very large, very complex data warehousing environment with massive amounts of functionality, very large and complex data management requirements, and a very specific business mission, there is a strong argument to be made for the first approach in which *all* product selection occurs as late as possible in the development cycle to avoid any unpleasant surprises.

However, the sequential and time-consuming nature of requirements, analysis, design, and product selection is not compatible with rapid data mart development and the just-in-time manner in which tasks provide output to their successors in a complex model of interwoven activities.

A solution to this quandary is to do early, preproject research into data mart projects—not just the front-end business intelligence tools (e.g., OLAP products, basic querying and reporting tools, or tools to build an executive information system), but also products responsible for data extraction, transformation, data movement, and the rest of the middleware functions. In addition, research into database management systems of all varieties, including multidimensional and relational, should be accomplished. This research should take the form of as many of the following activities as possible:

♦ Meeting with vendors and going on sales calls

♦ Going to data warehousing and data mart trade shows and conferences

♦ Engaging qualified outside consultants to discuss the advantages and disadvantages of various products under circumstances that are likely to be similar to your data mart environment

♦ Talking with others, both within your company and elsewhere, who have had experiences similar to those you envision for your data mart project

♦ Checking out websites (of the vendors, independent evaluation services, and others)

Other activities may also make sense for your given situation (for example, bringing a product in-house for a no-cost short-term evaluation period, provided you or someone else can spend time working with it).

TIP *Look within!* If your organization has pursued any kind of enterprise data warehousing architecture effort or study group within the past few years, chances are that some research has already been done into data warehousing and data mart products and their respective capabilities in the various categories. The information might be dated if the effort occurred more than six months ago, but a quick pass through any existing internal recommendations for tool selection standards that exist may save you some time.

Your objective in doing this research is a very straightforward one: You want to develop a shortlist of products so that when you begin your design phase, you can evaluate them in a rapid, hands-on manner. Though there is no magic number of products that should be on your shortlist, it's recommended that you select no more than the following:

♦ Three front-end business intelligence tools

♦ Two middleware tool products for extraction, transformation, and so on

♦ Two different relational DBMS products and one multidimensional database product

It's also recommended that your front-end tools include products from both the relational OLAP (ROLAP) and multidimensional OLAP (MOLAP) categories for two reasons. First, it's unlikely that you have enough information as you begin your project to guide you toward one solution or another. Second, you might implement a hybrid OLAP (HOLAP) solution that contains both relational and multidimensional components. There is no point in limiting yourself at this stage to one product family over the other only to later, in a crunch, have to go back and scramble to do basic research during your project while the clock is running.

TIP If you are inclined toward relational technology, select two ROLAP products and one MOLAP product (preferably a complementary one that can be used as part of a HOLAP solution) for your shortlist. Conversely, if your organization has already had success in implementing MOLAP-based data marts and has very little relational expertise, select two MOLAP products and one ROLAP product for your shortlist (again, looking for interoperability as part of a HOLAP environment as part of your selection criteria).

Your Organization's Standards and Constraints

Don't be fooled into thinking that you have free rein on your data mart project with respect to products, technology, and architecture. You may face one of the following scenarios:

♦ Your organization still has Microsoft Windows 3.11 as the standard desktop for all users, so finding yourself enamored with an OLAP product that runs on only Microsoft Windows95 will not get you anywhere.

♦ You believe in running your data mart's database on Microsoft Windows NT, but the corporate server standard is Unix.

♦ Later in your development effort you find that you need 10 hours every weekend to update the data mart's database. What support is available from the IT organization, and is this even doable?

The Impact of Corporate Standards on a Data Mart Project: A Firsthand Lesson

Here's a real-life example of how organizational standards can affect a data mart project. Several years ago your author was working with a client that was developing a sales and marketing data mart to replace the current environment that was, at the time, outsourced to a service bureau in another city. The company's goal was to bring its sales and marketing analysis in-house, and I worked on the database management architecture.

This client brought in two relational DBMS vendors to determine which one's product would be best for the way it planned to access data. Full-scale evaluations, each two weeks in length, were planned in concert with the vendors. They used actual data extracted from the current environment and SQL statements that were conceptually identical to the ones run in the existing managed querying and reporting environment.

One vendor's product performed reasonably well. The second vendor's product had significant problems handling queries in which four or more tables were joined; performance was very, very slow. The client selected the first vendor's product because it appeared to be more data mart-capable than the second.

However, the client had a corporate DBMS standard with the edict that all new application development was to be done with the second product, the one the company didn't select because of unacceptable performance! A long series of meetings, waiver requests, and pressure from the second vendor on the client's management to adhere to the standard followed. The argument put forth by the client to its management was that this data mart environment wasn't an application but a data mart, so the standard, which had been put in place with OLTP rather than analytical applications in mind, didn't even apply.

Much later, the client received permission to purchase the first DBMS product, which it had selected based on performance more suitable to the needs of the data mart.

The lesson is to find out what constraints you'll likely be facing as early as possible—*before* your project begins—and deal with them quickly and forcefully, if necessary, rather than waiting until project delays result.

These issues and questions, and many others like them, will present you with an environment into which your data mart architecture, product selection, method of user access to the data mart, and support functions must fit. If, for example, an application that is likely to be a source for your data mart is being retired and replaced by another one, what is the impact on your data mart? Do you need to plan for two different source-to-data mart models, one for the current application and one for its replacement, or is the current application now designated as "no touch" for any purposes? What is the impact if the replacement application is part of an outsourcing trend and will be hosted at another organization's location? How does that affect your data acquisition plans for your data mart?

People and Organizational Issues

You will need to spend significant time during your project preparation efforts on issues regarding people and organizations. These include the following:

♦ Forming your entire development team, which means evaluating and selecting a consulting firm if part or all of your data mart project will be done by staff from outside your company

♦ Ensuring that any preparatory training has been satisfactorily completed

♦ Determining the cultural and organizational readiness for the end result of your data mart development effort (i.e., the ability of the users to perform analytical and data requests and then to really use the results as part of real-life business processes)

♦ Lining up support you expect to need from the organization(s) responsible for systems support and infrastructure functions (i.e., database administration, systems administration, network administration, the tape library)

The following sections discuss these issues and their importance to your data mart project's success.

Forming Your Development Team

Before you begin your data mart project, you need to know the following:

♦ The members your team during each of the various project phases

♦ The team members' capabilities

♦ The team members' levels of commitment to the data mart project

♦ Your contingency plans in case problems occur

The Team During Each Project Phase

There are two roles that are consistent across all phases, representing continuity throughout the entire project:

♦ *The project manager*. The individual who "owns" responsibility for the data mart's project success from the first day of the scope until the data mart has been successfully deployed. This individual is responsible for creating and managing all project plans, ensuring that all lines of communications (e.g., between the user community and the development team) are opened and used, facilitating problem and issue resolution, and performing all other "normal" project management functions.

♦ *Technical team leader and chief data mart architect*. The individual who "owns" the technical aspects of the data mart project, from the user desktop to the database to the infrastructure. This individual will direct the work of designers and developers throughout the project and is responsible for understanding all issues involving the way data mart components interact.

Additional team members will be needed during each phase of data mart development. The team composition will *not* be the same across all phases because of the different types of tasks performed during each portion of the project. Regardless, you need to make sure that all team members for each phase—including design and construction, which aren't scheduled to start until the third and eighth weeks of the project, respectively—have been identified and are available. Ensure that the following roles are filled during each of these phases:

♦ *Scope*. In addition to the project manager, who serves as the scope's team leader, and the technical lead (who basically stays in the background during the scope, performing real-time analysis of the technical and architectural implications of business requirements as they are discussed), a facilitator and scribe are needed to work alongside the user community's representatives. The chapter that deals with Week 1 of the project discusses these roles in more detail.

♦ *Design*. In this phase the rest of the data mart project's technical talent is added to the team. You will need individuals to perform the following tasks (these are discussed further in the chapter dealing with Week 3 of the project):

◊ Data modeling and database design for the data mart (one person)

◊ Analysis of data sources (usually, one person for *each* data source)

◊ Product evaluation and analysis (one person for the front-end tools and another person to handle middleware and database products)

◊ Business analysis and customer interfacing (one person)

◊ Process analysis and modeling (one person)

◊ Systems and infrastructure analysis and design (one person)

◊ Quality assurance and configuration control (one person)

♦ *Construction.* In most cases, the same team used during design will participate in the data mart construction process. Changes may occur if, for example, the design phase leads to a more complex environment than had otherwise been envisioned and additional people are added to assist with database development, source-to-target extraction and transformation, development of front-end user screens, quality assurance and testing, or other functions. Conversely, some roles could be combined and performed by a single team member if they prove during the design phase to be less complex than had been previously thought. In general, though, it's best to plan on the design team remaining intact throughout the construction phase.

♦ *Deployment.* Everyone needs to remain as part of the team during deployment week, even though development is, technically, completed. As complications occur (and they are likely to), you need to have the people in place to quickly fix them.

The Team's Capabilities

Building a team capable of rapidly developing and deploying a data mart is certainly more than an exercise in assigning names to various roles. You need to be absolutely confident that each role, in each phase, is filled by a qualified individual. Qualified people either have worked on, and performed satisfactorily on, a previous data mart project or are of such a high caliber in technical ability that you can be confident they can perform successfully. This philosophy doesn't exclude someone from your team who is recognized as an outstanding performer but who may not have previous data mart development experience.

Using Outside Consultants

Depending on available resources inside your company and your organization's philosophy regarding which functions are to be performed by staff employees and which should be contracted to outside firms, you may find that your data mart project will be staffed partially or in its entirety by outside consultants.

It's very important to understand that not everyone tagged as a "data mart consultant" or all consulting firms that claim expertise in this area are necessarily suitable for your project.

In general, there are two primary types of consulting firms that you are likely to encounter as you seek assistance with your project. The first is a project consulting organization; the other is engaged primarily in providing supplemental staffing. A project consulting firm is capable of putting in place an entire team that will work closely with your users and with your IT organization and will take full responsibility for your data mart's project success.

In contrast, a supplemental staffing consulting firm places one or more individuals onto a team that you (or someone else in your organization) heads, and the consulting organization has little or no responsibility for project success. Basically, it supplies technicians to temporarily fill slots that you have identified as necessary for your project but for whatever reason you can't fill from internal resources.

Both types of consulting organizations have value to a rapid data mart development project, but in different circumstances. If, for example, your data mart project will be staffed primarily by internal IT developers and analysts but there are a few slots you can't readily fill (e.g., the data mart's database designer and the QA/configuration control person), contracting with a supplemental staffing consulting firm to acquire the services of consultants to operate under the direction of your firm's project manager and technical team leader may be the best approach.

If, however, your organization lacks the expertise to rapidly develop a data mart in the manner described in this book—or if your in-house experts are all assigned to other data mart projects—your best choice may be to engage a project consulting firm for your data mart development. That firm would provide the entire team and be responsible from the first day of the project until deployment.

Regardless of which approach to consulting support is right for your project, you need to make sure that you have taken care of all matters regarding selection of a consulting firm and related contractual items as part of your project prerequisites.

Team Commitments

Whether outside consultants or in-house staff members—or both—are used, you need to be certain that appropriate team members are available to perform essential tasks throughout the project. Make sure that you have 100% guaranteed commitment as to resource availability and that there is universal understanding that diverting a team member, however briefly, is unacceptable because doing so would put the entire data mart project at risk.

Contingency Plans

In the real world, resources get pulled for higher priorities, tasks turn out to be far more complex than originally envisioned, contractual matters can disrupt availability of consulting support, and many other unplanned events can put your project at risk.

You need to have contingency plans in place before the project begins. If you think that you'll build your team primarily from internal resources but then an executive pulls those individuals a week before the project begins, is there a consulting firm that you can turn to? If your project's database designer resigns at the end of the design phase, who will take over that role during development? You may not have to enact your contingency plans, but be prepared!

Training

Before the project begins, make sure that all necessary training has been scheduled and completed. This training might include the following:

♦ Data warehousing and data mart basics for developers who will work on your project but have not previously worked on a data mart development effort

♦ Executive education about the expected business value when the data mart has been deployed

♦ Role-specific training in project management techniques, quality assurance and configuration control, and other project roles in the event that you need to use a novice in one of these roles

♦ Methodology training to ensure that all project team members will perform in a consistent manner

Determining Cultural and Organizational Readiness

Is your organization ready for a data mart? If you succeed in developing and deploying a data mart that collects and consolidates data from several different sources and then delivers the information requested by the user community, will the environment actually be used?

Not every organization is equally suited to assimilating information delivery and analytical processing into its business processes. In some organizations only the most basic data analysis has traditionally been done, using the results of regularly run reports pulled directly from operational systems.

In other organizations, most decision-making is accomplished in an intuitive manner, and almost no information-based decision-making exists.

If you are tasked to develop and deliver a data mart, be sure you understand the prevailing organizational culture with respect to what you will eventually deliver. If you sense trouble, raise issues early and try to deal with them proactively and aggressively. You may still be tasked with the rapid delivery of the data mart, but at least you won't be blindsided by noncooperation or resistance from the user community and/or the IT organization.

Negotiating for Expected IT Organization Support

You need to spend a significant amount of time meeting with the people in the core IT organization who are responsible for functions such as database administration, networking and communications, and systems administration (backups, configuration control, software distribution, etc.). Your data mart project will inevitably be dependent on support from people responsible for some or all of these functions, and these people will *not* be directly answerable to you or whoever is responsible for your project's success.

The degree of dependency you will have on other organizations will vary according to the policies and procedures that are in place. Learn what the policies are for relational database administration and how they might affect your project. Do all database schemas need to be approved by the chief database administrator (DBA)? Who are the individuals knowledgeable about the data sources you will likely need to deal with?

The main thing you want to accomplish with these discussions is awareness of your data mart project among the management of all those organizations in which dependencies are likely to exist. Data warehousing in general tends to be viewed by organizations responsible for IT infrastructure functions (database administration, systems administration, etc.) as a nuisance because of the data acquisition requirements from other sources (the "secondhand data phenomenon"). Build alliances—or at least neutralize potential problems—as early as possible.

T **I P** *Lining up data mart project support is a balancing act.* Discuss what you will likely need in terms of support, but be very careful about asking for commitments for support too early. You might, for instance, anticipate that your data mart will need to acquire data from a certain source application but during the scoping phase of the project determine that the source-to-target data acquisition for that source can wait until a subsequent version of the data mart. If you had obtained committed support for working with that source and then changed your mind, it would be difficult to get support later.

Methodology and Process Activities

Among the activities you will need to take care of in the areas of methodology and development processes are the following:

♦ Preselling the entire project to executive management

♦ Determining the data mart development methodology—including all deliverables—that you will use

♦ Determining and getting agreement on all project management reporting processes and plans

♦ Establishing that rapid development is *not* a 40-hours-per-week job

♦ Ensuring that all contractual matters will be handled in a timely manner

♦ Doing a pre-architecture to determine if rapid data mart development is really an option for you

The following sections discuss each of these items.

Get Executive Support Early

To help increase your chances for data mart project success, you need to enlist executive sponsorship from both the IT and business sides of your company. Further, this executive sponsorship needs to be as high in the organizational hierarchy as you can possibly get. Ideally, you want a chief operating officer (COO) or chief executive officer (CEO) to make it known that the project is key to the company's continued success and to ask everyone to support it. On the IT side, the chief information officer (CIO) needs to ensure that adequate administrative and infrastructure support will be supplied throughout the development effort.

In large corporations, of course, access to the CEO, COO, and CIO is sometimes difficult in terms of project sponsorship. Still, strive to get IT and business executives with as much authority as possible to stand behind your project.

Finalize Your Development Methodology

If your organization has a mandated development methodology, you need to spend some time synthesizing the principles and steps of the rapid data mart development approach presented in this book with the standard methodology by which you must develop the data mart. Before the project begins, you need to have this effort completed, with all appropriate walkthroughs and methodology waivers accomplished, to determine the way your team will proceed in each of the project's phases.

Determine Project Management Processes and Plans

Make sure that from the first day of the project, project management processes and plans are in place. If conflicts occur, what is the resolution process? If half of your business users suddenly can't participate in the second week of the project scope, what will happen? What status reporting procedures are required of the project manager?

Establish the Work Culture for a
Rapid Data Mart Development Effort

You and your development team need to acknowledge up front that a 90-day data mart development will *absolutely not* be a 40-hour-per-week job. It's not that you are trying to squeeze too much activity into too short a time frame. On the contrary, this book's approach is grounded in the principle that the duration of the development cycle, whether it's 90 days, 120 days, or more, should be set just right for the functionality that is to be delivered.

You can expect to discount the idea of a 40-hour work week because unanticipated problems and complications will inevitably occur at various points throughout the development. For example, you could find that the OLAP tools have bugs or uncover additional data quality problems that had been overlooked during source data analysis, requiring you to rewrite several of your transformation business rules. Perhaps the performance for key queries would fall short, and the database would need to be tuned.

Such problems are common with any type of application development, and data marts are no exception. The complicating factor, though, is that to adhere to a very rapid and aggressive development schedule, team members must make the extra effort to overcome those situations and get the project back on schedule as quickly as possible.

Some organizational cultures may not support this philosophy. Those that do not must be prepared for 90 days to stretch into 120 days or longer.

How About Your Consulting Support?

Will outside consultants conform to a work culture that requires more than 40 hours a week?

Why not? Consulting firms either charge you directly for the time spent on your project (commonly known as time and materials, or T&M), or commit to a fixed-time, fixed-price development model in which schedule slips are absolutely unacceptable. In a T&M situation, you need to carefully monitor the time consultants spend on the effort and ensure that unnecessary overtime isn't being charged to your project. In fixed-time, fixed-price arrangements, your financial risk (in terms of unanticipated consulting dollars) is minimized, but if all the consultants are consistently spending 80 or more hours per week on your data mart project, you need to learn the reason and the implications to the project (e.g., potential quality problems due to the overworked development and QA staff).

Acceptable overtime should be your guideline for both internal staff and outside consultants. It is important to accurately track hours spent on the project. If, for example, you succeed in delivering a data mart in 90 days but every team member worked at least 70 hours each week from the third week of the project until the end, you need to know the reason. It could be that the task complexity and duration were severely underestimated during the project planning process; the product selection process was flawed and significant workarounds were needed; or too much functionality was squeezed into too short a time frame. The next data mart development effort can benefit from the lessons learned during this one.

Complete All Contractual Matters

If your data mart will require syndicated data provided by an external source, if you will be retaining a consulting organization to assist with your project, or if there are any other tasks or activities for which contracts or agreements need to be in place, make sure that this has all been accomplished before the project begins to prevent any unnecessary delays.

Pre-Architect Your Data Mart

You should have some idea of what your data mart's environment—end to end, from source(s) to target—will look like. This pre-architecture should be developed in a manner that doesn't lock you into a particular solution or a set of products or specific technology; rather, it should provide a conceptual framework to help you determine whether or not you're being realistic about developing and deploying this data mart in a very rapid time frame. Answer the following questions:

- Does your organization have an existing data warehouse, stocked with ready-to-go high-quality data from which most or all of your data mart's contents can be obtained?

- Does a preliminary analysis of the contents and level of detail for your data mart indicate that you may have very large database (VLDB) issues to contend with?

- How large is your prospective user community? Where is it located, and are any communications and networking issues or complications anticipated?

- Have business requirements been expressed that indicate a "classical" batch-oriented restocking process will not be sufficient for your data mart, and instead source applications might need to operate in a "push" manner to support near-real-time refreshing of the data mart? (This may indicate that the data mart is more of an operational data store—ODS—and rapid development isn't possible.)

The key is to have a fairly clear idea of what you're likely to face before you begin your development effort. It's true that the requirements and business needs gathered during the scoping phase will dictate the length of your design phase, which in turn will determine the duration of construction. You can, however, come up with a fairly clear view of just how realistic rapid development will be by identifying and analyzing complicating factors or, on the other hand, determining that only one source—a high-quality data warehouse—may actually reduce your development time.

Summary

How long will your prerequisite tasks take? The answer depends on your organization's experience with a data mart project and your organizational culture with respect to support for activities like rapid data mart development.

In general, plan on two to three months to satisfactorily complete the necessary prerequisites. Particularly tough situations could easily take six to nine months, perhaps longer. Hint: If you can't complete your prerequisite activities in a timely manner because of lack of internal support, your chances of rapidly developing a data mart—in any relatively short duration—aren't good, so this is a way to test your organization's susceptibility to rapid data mart development before the project even begins.

Part Two

The Data Mart Scope Phase

What You'll Find in This Chapter

The Goals of the Data Mart Scope

Who Should Participate in the Data Mart Scope?
The Business Community
The Team Leadership

The First Week's Results: A Look at the Goals
The Mission Statement
Expected Business Benefits and Functionality
Creating the Functionality-Fact Matrix
Identifying Data Sources
Preliminary Technology Assessment
Risk Assessment
Consensus and Commitment

How to Achieve the First Week's Goals
The Kickoff Meeting
Building the Business Case through Facilitated Work Sessions
Creating the Functionality-Fact Matrix
More Facilitated Discussion

You Know You're in Trouble When

Scoping the Data Mart: The Mission Statement
and the Functionality-Fact Matrix

A Note to the Reader: By the end of Week 1, you will have a good idea about whether your data mart project will be successful. You will certainly know if your project is doomed to failure.

The first week's activities and targeted accomplishments are intentionally aggressive. Developing a data mart takes a high degree of commitment from all involved—the IT organization, outside consultants, the user community, and the executive sponsors—to be successful. Everything that occurs during the first week is absolutely necessary; there are no make-work activities. The pace may be a bit more hectic than your organization's members are used to, but it sets the tone for the rest of the project.

If "success in 90 days" is to be a reality, here's the starting point.

The Goals of the Data Mart Scope

The goals of the data mart scope are straightforward and include the following:

♦ Build and validate the business case for proceeding with subsequent data mart project phases (i.e., design, development, and deployment).

♦ Explore, evaluate, and decide upon the boundaries of your data mart: what business functionality will be supported, what facts—groups of data—are needed for the functionality, what data sources will be used to create the facts, who the users will be, and what business units will be served.

♦ Conduct preliminary explorations into the candidate technologies of the data mart, particularly front-end tools but also data mart middleware products (i.e., those that support the extraction, transformation, and movement of data) and the database management system (DBMS) upon which the data mart will be hosted.

By the conclusion of the scoping phase of activity, there must be general consensus from all stakeholders as to the reasons for constructing the data mart, what it will contain, and who will use it. Further, there must be widespread agreement on the following:

♦ The data mart can be successfully built in the allotted time, within the allotted budget.

♦ The design and development team assigned has the right base of skills to succeed in their assignment.

♦ Adequate support exists at the executive levels of the company, in both the user community and the information technology (IT) area, to see the project through.

♦ The business and technology risks discovered during the scope are manageable ones. The answers might not be immediately known but there is confidence that solutions will be found during subsequent phases of the data mart project.

These expected accomplishments may seem excessive for the short period of time allocated for the scope. However, a team that can successfully determine the properties that define the scope of the data mart (i.e., the data sources, the business functionality, etc., as listed above) as well as work through issues of organizational politics, identify and categorize risk, and quickly evaluate technology and products for suitability, has a significant likelihood of success as the data mart project moves into subsequent phases. Conversely, a team that fails to accomplish these tasks will be significantly *less* likely to succeed in building a data mart.

Who Should Participate in the Data Mart Scope?

The data mart scope's success is dependent in a large part on having the "right" people present. The difficulty, of course, lies in determining who those people are.

The Business Community

Everyone who could be considered a stakeholder in the data mart effort and its results is a member of the candidate population. This doesn't mean, for example, that every single user in a department of 50 analysts would be a member of the scope team, but it does mean the following:

♦ Every major business function that is expected to be supported by the data mart is represented.

♦ Every supporting function that will be incorporated into the sphere of the data mart is represented.

♦ Even though the data mart scope team must be a hands-on, working group to succeed, management (at the appropriate levels) must be involved.

Assume that a team is being created to work on a two-week scope for a budget-support data mart. Using the guidelines presented above, the scope team should include the following people:

♦ Business function representatives:

◊ One or two members of the group that prepares and distributes budgeting forms to all departments across the organization and also collects and consolidates the filled-in forms after they're completed

◊ One or two members of the department in which analysis and adjustment of the consolidated budget are done

◊ Five or six people who are responsible for receiving budget forms, gathering and entering budget numbers, and submitting the completed forms

♦ Supporting functions, which means the organizational members who go into various application databases and file systems across the enterprise, extract and prepare selected historical and forecast information that is needed to support the budgeting process, and make that information available prior to the distribution of budget forms.

♦ Management and executives whose job descriptions make them responsible for ensuring that the annual budgeting process is successfully completed in accordance with guidelines established by the corporate steering committee.

The inclusion of people in support functions, particularly data acquisition, might appear surprising given the business focus of the data mart scope and the deliberate downplaying of specific IT solutions at this stage of the effort. There is an important reason to include people from this category: they contribute a "raw data" perspective as part of the scope team's resources.

Typically these individuals have the clearest indication of the lowest levels (i.e., the degree of detail) of data available within the enterprise. Because a data mart is by nature a data-driven effort, this understanding complements the functional perspective represented by those in the first group of participants. The trick is to establish an appropriate balance between "data reality" and proposed business functions. On the one hand, the presence of certain data, or lack thereof, should not be a hindrance in creating the mission statement, building the business case, detailing the business functionality, and the other activities of the data mart scope.

At the same time, however, the project as a whole benefits from the perspectives of what exists today—and what doesn't. If a certain application that is a provider of historical expenditures is being retired, the person responsible for acquiring and preparing that data in today's environment is likely to be the one most familiar with potential issues regarding this source system transition. Since source system dependencies distinguish a data mart from a "regular application" (i.e., one in which data is created, not obtained from other sources), it's important not to overlook these individuals when you select members of the scope team.

Vision and "out-of-the-box thinking" are certainly key aspects to building data mart environments that will provide substantial business value in return. However, it is essential to be firmly grounded in reality when you are determining if your data mart can be built and deployed in 90 days or if desired functionality cannot be achieved in that time because of external factors such as severe data gaps (required data that isn't available in a timely manner), application migrations, and retirements.

The Team Leadership

Though the data mart scope team leadership will naturally vary from situation to situation, and by the overall methodology that is being used, several key roles must be present in every scope effort. These include the following:

- *The team leader.* This person is recognized by all members of the scope team, the executive sponsors of the project, and all people with whom the team will come into contact. The team leader is responsible for setting and communicating a realistic, achievable agenda; collecting interim deliverables and ensuring that the scope phase deliverables are completed and delivered to the appropriate recipients; resolving conflicts; and myriad other leadership roles.

- *The facilitator.* The facilitator leads daily discussions according to the agenda set by the team leader. This person ensures that all necessary points of view are heard, adequate participation occurs from all of those present, and discussion is kept to essential topics, such as what the data should do, and why.

- *The scribe.* This person uses flip charts, white boards, electronic printing white boards, or some other "room-scale" presentation medium to capture main points of discussion, issues, and questions.

The First Week's Results: A Look at the Goals

Though the data mart scoping phase will last for two weeks, it is essential that significant results—both tangible and intangible—be achieved by the end of the first week. These include the following:

- Agreement on the mission statement

- Agreement on the business case

- Creation of the functionality-fact matrix

- Identification of all data sources (though not all details will be known)

- Technology constraints and possibilities

♦ Risk assessment: tangible items

♦ Risk assessment: intangible items

♦ The level of support: consensus and commitment across the organization

The following sections address these items.

The Mission Statement

It's tempting to declare that the mission of a data mart project is to build a customer analysis (or credit risk, or some other subject) data mart. A data mart project that proceeds under such an ill-defined charter has a significant chance of failing because of the lack of a clear-cut business mission.

The first order of business during the scoping phase is to reach agreement on a *mission statement*, consisting of a paragraph or two, that is:

♦ Clearly stated with no ambiguity in the wording

♦ Business-focused (i.e., it refers to functionality and/or processes that are accomplished by the organization's users)

♦ A way to establish boundaries of the data mart (e.g., which organization will be supported by the mart)

At the same time, the data mart's mission statement should *not*: contain references to *specific* data sources or mention specific technologies or products.

Consider the following data mart mission statement:

> *To develop a Budgeting Support System (BSS) that will support the annual expense budgeting process of all North America Product Research Groups (PRGs). The BSS will collect and consolidate historical expenditures and revenue forecasts from relevant PRG activity management systems, and each BSS user will be able to access selected groups of data and specify how those data groups will be viewed.*

Let's analyze that mission statement:

♦ "Support the annual expense budgeting process." This is a clear statement of the business functionality for which the data mart is being developed.

- ◆ "North America Product Research Groups." From this phrase it is clear whose annual budgeting process is affected (i.e., this data mart will not be developed for the operations group or the sales organization).

- ◆ "Collect and consolidate historical expenditures and revenue forecasts." This section identifies the major categories of data that will be included in the data mart.

- ◆ "From relevant PRG activity management systems." Without mentioning specific data sources (though many, perhaps all, may already be known), this phrase clearly notes the distinguishing characteristic of a data mart or a data warehouse. It refers to the acquisition and usage of data from other applications and systems rather than the "creation" of data within the environment.

- ◆ "Each BSS user will be able to access selected groups of data and specify how those data groups will be viewed." Once constructed and deployed, the data mart will provide users with flexible query capabilities, not just batch runs of predefined reports (as is likely to occur in an existing mainframe-based system at the company, for example).

Once agreed upon, the mission statement will guide *all* subsequent discussion about the detailed functionality, the names and roles of those who will use the data mart, and the specific data elements that will be acquired from all the data sources.

The mission statement should be as follows:

- ◆ Prepared in advance by the team leader, using the data mart's project charter, background research, and other appropriate material as input

- ◆ Presented as part of the kickoff meeting (discussed later)

- ◆ Thoroughly discussed until consensus is reached among all participants

A common mistake is to assume that a one- or two-paragraph mission statement, such as the example, can be presented, discussed, and agreed to in a matter of minutes. As most people who have ever participated in a mission statement discussion know, however, seemingly innocuous wording often raises passions in a diverse audience. Organizational politics, cultural issues, even basic scoping and boundary issues (e.g., what organizations should be supported? What functions and processes should *not* be part of this effort?) can lead to prolonged, animated discussions from the outset. Therefore, as discussed later in this chapter in regards to the structure of the kickoff meeting, sufficient time needs to be allotted in the schedule for the presentation, discussion, and adoption of the mission statement. Adopting a mission statement without consensus because of time pressures would put the entire data mart project at risk.

Expected Business Benefits and Functionality

Although the mission statement is critical, creating it is only the beginning of the work that must be accomplished during the data mart scope. An entire business case now needs to be developed.

The *business case* is a consolidated picture of the functionality that will be supported by the data mart. If you look at the mission statement as a high-level, business-oriented description of the reasons time, money, and energy should be devoted to building a data mart, consider the business case to be the much more detailed version.

When creating the business case for data marts, people often make the mistake of focusing exclusively on data. A document that relies on statements such as the following is missing a very important element:

> *The BSS data mart must contain the previous two years' quarterly expenditures by category, by department, and by office; two years' historical head count by month, by department; and forecasted revenues by territory, by quarter.*

The statement does not explain *why* the mart should contain that information, nor does it show the business value that will be gained. It may turn out (as illustrated in the next section) that the data mart should contain the information listed above, but the surest way to promote indecisiveness, and even cause concern, among the data mart project's sponsors is focus exclusively on the data.

Where, then, should you begin when you are building the business case? The key is to focus on *functionality*, using concise, action-oriented statements that describe what must be done as part of the course of business activity. Examples of functionality statements would include the following:

- ◆ Establish targeted expenditures by top-level organization

- ◆ Fill in head-count projections for the year on the budget form

- ◆ Create a budget package for executive management

- ◆ Analyze first-draft submissions from all budget holders

It is important to remember that the statements of proposed data mart function-ality, as presented and discussed during the facilitated work sessions (discussed later in this chapter), must be in concert with the mission statement that was presented, discussed, and adopted. That is, every statement of functionality that is considered a candidate to be supported by the data mart must apply to the proposed user and organizational community as presented in the mission statement and be part of the overall sphere of functionality (in our example, "the annual budgeting process").

Some guidelines to use when you consider the statements of business functionality that will be adopted for further consideration within the context of the mission statement include the following:

♦ Activities that cannot be done at all today but should be

♦ Activities that are accomplished today when data is manually synthesized from reports, file extracts, and other sources, often requiring a great deal of time and energy

All business community members of the data mart must accurately and thoroughly present the functionality of their jobs as related to this initiative. At the same time, it is the job of the facilitator to keep the discussion on track, not letting proposed functionality stray outside the bounds of the mission statement and the team's charter.

The "Now or Future" Balancing Act

There needs to be an understanding from the outset of the data mart project of the philosophy of, and objectives for, process change and improvement in the context of the data mart itself. On one end of the spectrum, the charter may be that business functionality, and the processes that make up that functionality, will *not* change as a result of the implementation of the data mart. This means that, for example, if the members of the chief financial officer's (CFO's) staff currently kick off the annual budgeting process by holding a one-day meeting in which budget targets are set for the entire company, using a combination of historical revenue and expenditure data together with revenue forecasts, the same will occur following deployment of the data mart. The methods used to gather and analyze the historical and forecast data may be different (in fact, they had better be different if the data mart is successfully deployed!), but the process of the budget kickoff meeting will remain the same.

On the other end of the spectrum, there may be situations wherein the business processes are so "broken" that implementing a data mart in support of those processes would be a serious mistake. Rather, an effort to explore process improvement is not only desirable, but mandatory. Ideally, this need for process improvement has already been identified; the process improvement teams have already met and presented their results, and the mandate for the process has already been issued.

Sometimes, though, it is during the data mart scope that the first inklings of serious business process problems are raised. When severe problems are discovered during the data mart effort, your flow of activities should look something like that shown in Figure WK1.1.

In other words, *do not* waste time and money proceeding, because although you may develop and deploy some type data mart in a very expedient manner, the chances are very high that little, if any, enhanced business value will come out of this effort.

Creating the Functionality-Fact Matrix

So far, the majority of our discussion could be applied to application development projects of any type—not just data marts—for which a timely, no-nonsense path to implementation and deployment is desired. Because of the usage of and reliance on data from other sources, it is important to augment these standard best practices with those of particular importance to data mart environments. One such practice is the creation of the *functionality-fact matrix* (Figure WK1.2). This matrix features, on the vertical axis, a list of the major functionality components the data mart will be supporting. On the horizontal axis is a complete list of facts: business-oriented descriptions of groups of information. The shaded cells of the matrix are used to indicate which facts are needed to support which functionality.

The functionality-fact matrix will be a key method for identifying and recording tangible requirements that will be fed into the design phase. Coupled with the *fact-data source matrix* (discussed in the next chapter), it will provide detailed information from which your data mart design can be created. As discussed later in this chapter,

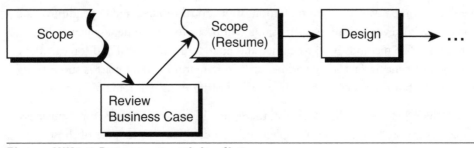

Figure WK1.1 Data mart activity flow.

Functionality \ Facts	Previous two years' quarterly expenditures by category, by department, and by office	Two years' historical head count by month, by department	Forecasted revenues by territory, by quarter	Previous three years' revenues by territory, by month
Establish targeted expenditures by top-level organization	▧	▧	▧	▧
Fill in head-count projections for year on the budget form		▧	▧	
Create budget package for executive management			▧	
Analyze first draft submissions from all budget holders	▧	▧	▧	▧

Figure WK1.2 The functionality-fact matrix.

sufficient time should be allotted during the first week—a minimum of a day and a half, longer if necessary—to ensure that a complete list of facts required to support the data mart functionality has been created.

Identifying the Data Sources

An important part of your first week's activities is to identify (not analyze) the data sources that will, or are candidates to, feed information into your data mart. Although intensive analysis of these data sources is certainly a necessary function in constructing the data mart, this immersion into details should occur during the design phase of your project. To promote efficiency and accuracy of this design phase work, though, it is important to have as thorough an understanding of the data sources as possible at a high level, including their respective elements, such as the following:

- Business functions

- Platforms

- Unique characteristics and quirks

- Usage today (or lack thereof) to provide data to functions that will be supported by the data mart

- Points of contact and system "owners"

An important goal of the scope is to define the boundaries under which the following data mart development activities will occur, so it is essential to know, as quickly as possible, which candidate data sources are to be considered "within scope" and which will be outside the scope of the effort.

Exploring the "How"

There is one caveat to the guidelines presented above with respect to the scope phase level of discussion about data sources (identify rather than analyze). It is inevitable that while discussing data sources, particularly those that are used in some fashion under the current business model (e.g., extracting subsets of data into a spreadsheet for subsequent analysis or using manual reports), the scope team members closest to that particular source application or system will make mention of the following, among other details:

- Difficulties in obtaining information

- Inaccuracies in data content

♦ Gaps in time ranges

♦ Changes in data structures over time and accompanying difficulties of dealing with them

A recommended way of capturing this information during the scope phase without getting immersed in details—to the detriment of the schedule and the work that needs to be done in a short period of time—is to have the facilitator and the scribe team create a chart called Data Source Issues and Questions. Before the discussion of data sources, the facilitator will present the following to the team:

> *Our discussion will focus on identifying the data sources, and there will be plenty of time during the design phase to look at all of the issues that you collectively deal with now as you acquire that data for your usage. We want to make everything operate much more efficiently and effectively once the data mart has been deployed. As we discuss each of these sources, anything that is mentioned about difficulties, data gaps, or other details will be recorded on the Data Source Issues and Questions list but only to make sure that we capture these items for use during the design phase. We don't want an extended discussion of any of these items at this time.*

The key is for the facilitator to achieve a balancing act with respect to data source discussion. This person doesn't want to repeatedly "shut down" team members as they call attention to areas of frustration to them today as they attempt to acquire data to perform necessary business functions, but the tight time frame of the scope prohibits exhaustive discussion at this time. By using facilitation skills to keep the discussion focused—yet quickly record issues and questions to ensure that they will be considered at the appropriate time, before moving the conversation forward—the facilitator will succeed with this balancing act.

Preliminary Technology Assessment

An interesting phenomenon about data warehousing projects (including data marts) is that people tend to revert back to the early 1970s—before structured methodologies and other disciplines were applied to application and system development—and to select hardware and packaged software *before* an understanding of the business problem has taken place. It is very common to see, for example, a project charter for a data mart in which the operating system, DBMS, front-end tools, and middleware have been selected before the first day of the scope!

The chances of selecting inappropriate platforms—hardware, system software, or packaged tools—increase dramatically the earlier in the development cycle that this occurs. At the same time, however, the principles and time frames of rapid development and deployment aren't conducive to prolonged, exhaustive evaluations of many different candidate DBMSs, business intelligence packages, or middleware tools.

It is recommended that during the scope, the team briefly explore the technology landscape under the same philosophy of establishing boundaries in which to pursue subsequent data mart design and development activities. The landscape could encompass the following:

♦ Identifying all corporate and organizational standards—both current and upcoming—with respect to servers, operating systems, DBMS products, network infrastructure, and services

♦ Surveying and cataloging hardware and software usage and experiences from any data mart activities elsewhere in the corporation that are similar to the effort you're beginning

♦ Appointing a technology point person from the team who, using the Internet, can quickly gather evaluations, surveys, analyst reports, and other material relative to both the standards and internal experiences

As discussed in the chapter for Week 2, one of the final activities of the scope phase will be a technology assessment report from the point person, who will use the results from the activities listed above. The report will be used during the design phase to guide the technology evaluation and selection effort.

Risk Assessment

By the end of the first week (at the latest) it will be obvious to everyone involved in the scope activity—not only the team members but also the executive sponsors—what degree of risk is associated with the development of the data mart. As discussed earlier in this chapter, there are two facets of risk that will be relevant to your effort:

♦ Tangible risks, such as needed data sources that are being retired with no planned replacement, or the realization that the scope of the data mart effort is significantly larger than the time, resources, and budget allotted

♦ Intangible risks, such as the lack of consensus and commitment among the team members as to the project direction (discussed next), organizational politics and conflicting priorities among executive management sponsors, or an awareness that the business process is so "broken" (discussed earlier in this chapter) that implementing a data mart in support of them is a foolhardy proposition

It is essential that time be allotted toward the end of the first week for an open, no-holds-barred discussion of the project risks at hand. By raising these risks to the forefront, you will significantly reduce the chances of leaving them festering, waiting to undermine the entire data mart effort later. This isn't to say that all identified risks will be defused; it's quite possible that some of these risks are so overwhelming that postponing or halting the data mart project is the best alternative. It's better to realize that in Week 1 of activity than in Week 11 or 12.

Consensus and Commitment

Related to the risk assessment (above) is the necessity that widespread consensus among the data mart team members and their respective organizational management be achieved to the proposed mission, business case, and follow-on plans for the data mart development. Further, it is important to get a widespread commitment to achieving the goals to which everyone agrees. That is, every organization that will benefit from the data mart construction must also be willing to do whatever is required, according to the project plans, to make the data mart a reality.

The level of commitment will vary from one organization to another. Some may be expected only to provide resources for quality assurance testing or for tools evaluation, for a short period of time. Other groups may be tasked to provide three resources, at a minimum 75% of each individual's time, for the duration of the data mart project. Commitment may be viewed as the instantiation of consensus; people must also contribute their effort to make the data mart a reality.

How to Achieve the First Week's Goals

Figure WK1.3 shows the calendar of activities that you should plan for during the first week of your data mart project.

The Kickoff Meeting

Several ground rules apply to the kickoff meeting for the data mart scope phase:

♦ Every team member must be present.

♦ The mission statement (discussed earlier in this chapter) must already be prepared, based on the background and preparatory work done to date.

	Monday	Tuesday	Wednesday	Thursday	Friday
Morning	Kickoff Meeting Introductions Objectives Agenda Methods Mission Statement	The Business Case Organize and List Functionality	Functionality-Fact Matrix	Functionality-Fact Matrix: Completed Status Check Data Sources	Technology Assessment
Afternoon	The Business Case	Functionality: Completed and Consensus Functionality-Fact Matrix	Functionality-Fact Matrix	Data Sources Risk Assessment	Review of Week's Work Prepare for Next Week

Figure WK1.3 The first week's calendar of activities.

◆ Everyone must understand the guidelines and rules that will be used to accomplish the massive amounts of work that need to be done in a very short period of time.

The kickoff meeting should begin with introductions of all members and their respective organizational roles, followed by an introductory presentation from the project's executive sponsor who will confirm the importance of this effort to the organization. This message should be couched in a discussion of what has led up to this group being formed and gathered and other background material as appropriate. It is recommended that the executive sponsor's presentation take approximately a half hour, which should be long enough to ensure that all team members know this is a serious effort.

Next, the project's leader will present the agenda for the entire scope (not just the first week), the methods that will be used (e.g., facilitated discussions), and the ground rules and guidelines that will be in effect for the duration. Following acknowledgment by the group that these rules and guidelines are understood and that all will abide by them, the mission statement (discussed earlier) should be presented, discussed, and adopted.

Expect to take a half day—the entire morning of the first day—to accomplish all of the above.

Building the Business Case through Facilitated Work Sessions

The majority of the first week's work will be done through facilitated work sessions. These will be general discussions, led by the facilitator and recorded by the scribe, in which all team members are expected to contribute.

The business case, which is the discussion of anticipated business benefits and functionality, is best built through this open discussion. Allot an entire day—the afternoon of the first day and the morning of the second day—to these facilitated discussions. By the end of the time allotted for the business case discussion, there will likely be an unstructured series of flip charts or electronic blackboard printouts that represent a pool of business benefits and functionality. A key facet is that this collection of material should be reviewed by the group, organized, prioritized, and validated. By the end of the business case discussion there should be a (mostly) structured list of expected data mart functionality and, for each item, the business benefit(s) that will be provided.

Creating the Functionality-Fact Matrix

The next step is to use the output from the facilitated business case discussions as input into the functionality-fact matrix (discussed earlier in this chapter). The facilitator and scribe should create a series of grids, with the organized collection of functionality serving as the vertical axis of the grid down the left side of each chart (refer back to Figure WK1.2).

Then, using the same facilitated discussion techniques discussed above, the team will identify the facts required to provide each piece of functionality. It is the role (and challenge) of the facilitator to steer the group's discussion on facts to keep them from veering into data source discussions or venting frustration about problems and issues. Allotting nearly two full days to the creation and *preliminary* validation of the functionality-fact matrix causes two things to occur:

♦ The business case functionality is again reviewed, and gaps and other potential issues are likely to be identified.

♦ The team is steered into thinking in terms of the relationship between functionality and facts—key to the data mart's use—which will be extremely beneficial and productive as the project moves forward.

More Facilitated Discussion

Following the creation of the functionality-fact matrix, the rest of the first week will be consumed by facilitated discussion about the items discussed earlier in this chapter: the data sources, the technology landscape, and project risk. There should also be discussions regarding a status check of the project to date and a review of the team's many accomplishments during such a short period of time, as a lead-in to the next week.

You Know You're in Trouble When...

♦ The mission statement is still being argued over at lunchtime of the second day, Clearly polarized factions disagree as to what the project's mission should be, and consensus is nowhere in sight.

♦ Attendance is perfect the first day, but three people are absent the second day, and five are absent the third day. A couple of them rejoin the team during the fourth day, but two others are now absent. Attendees complain that they don't know how much time they will be able to devote to the data mart scope during the second week.

♦ Word filters back to the team that the executive sponsor, despite the rousing introductory speech, was overheard expressing concern about the project and suggesting a halt for a while to see if it's really necessary to spend so much money.

We could list dozens, even hundreds, of instances in which it's apparent at the end of the first week that the data mart project is already in trouble. However, you will instinctively know by the end of the first week what your chances of success are. This isn't to say that there won't still be some design detail, or technological stumbling block, that adversely affects the project during week 5 or week 10 or whenever. But the up-front risks that will likely sink a project even if everything else is in order—specifically, the lack of consensus and commitment will be staring you head-on very early in the project.

So what do you do if this happens? The choices include halting the effort and regrouping and meeting one-on-one with the major dissenters for an off-the-record discussion of their concerns. Whatever you decide, do *not* proceed as if nothing is wrong, because failure is just around the corner.

Week 1 Spotlight on the Facilitator

If the first week of the data mart is a success, the most valuable player award will usually go to the facilitator.

Very often, members of the team gathered to determine the data mart's scope will arrive with their own agenda, particularly when the data mart will be used by people from different organizations. When attendees hear phrases like *prioritized functionality* and *delayed until the next release*, they are likely to adopt an "us versus them" mentality.

The facilitator can make a lasting contribution to the data mart project's eventual success at this point. The data mart-specific responsibilities of the facilitator include the following:

♦ *Real-time validation of functionality and facts.* As scope attendees present items for inclusion in the functionality-fact matrix (refer back to Figure WK1.2), the facilitator must perform what is akin to a "regression test"

Continues

Week 1 Spotlight on the Facilitator

(Continued)

after each one to make sure the team is staying on track with the agreed-to guidelines. For example, assume an attendee suggests that the data mart include functionality to compare the company's past two years of capital expenditures with those of the nearest two competitors as part of the budgeting process. Discussion then commences about the importance of having information about competitors' numbers. The facilitator reminds the group that the mission statement refers to expense budgeting, not capital expenditures. Therefore, all discussion of whether or not competitors' data is needed for capital budgeting is irrelevant. This realization quickly shuts down the discussion and moves the group ahead.

♦ *Controlling the data source discussion.* As discussed earlier in this chapter, not only should candidate sources to the data mart be identified, but some attributes of each (platforms, unique characteristics, and quirks) also need to be captured. Often, discussions about data sources degenerate into a gripe session. The facilitator needs to make sure that the pertinent aspects of each source are noted but that the team doesn't get too distracted. At the same time, any information that does surface needs to be discussed with the project's chief architect to make a risk determination (discussed next).

♦ *Presenting an open, complete risk assessment.* It's always a challenge for a facilitator to stand before a group at the end of the first week—a week in which a group of diverse individuals has gelled and made progress—and tell that group that the chance of successfully developing a data mart is not good. When this is the case, though, the facilitator must make sure that significant risk isn't just overlooked or understated. This person must facilitate a discussion about whether the data mart project should continue and if it does, what must be done to overcome the risk.

What You'll Find in This Chapter

The Second Week's Results: A Look at the Goals

Validating the First Week's Accomplishments

How to Achieve the Second Week's Goals

Deliverables from the Data Mart Scope

You Know You're in Trouble When

The Fact-Data
Source Matrix

A Note to the Reader: It's now Monday morning of Week 2. If the first week was productive, with a high degree of team "norming" (i.e., coming together philosophically), there will likely be substantial energy and enthusiasm as the second week begins. On the other hand, a first week that was so-so in terms of accomplishment and teamwork may have upset some people on the team. This may manifest itself in ill will, resentment, jealousy, and struggles for dominanace between the team members.

Therefore, the facilitator must ensure that the momentum and excitement gained during the first week is not lost as the second week of the data mart scope begins.

The Second Week's Results:
A Look at the Goals

At the highest level, there is a single goal to be achieved during the second week: complete the scope of the data mart and prepare to move ahead to the next phase of design activity. As mentioned in the previous chapter, *everything* identified as a goal of the scope phase activity needs to be successfully accomplished by week's end. More specifically, though, the following sections contain discussion about what you need to accomplish during Week 2.

Validating the First Week's Accomplishments

A key first objective each week is to "renew the vows" made at the end of the previous week. You want continued consensus about the objectives of the data mart project and commitment to achieving those objectives from all present and the organizations they represent.

It is the role of the facilitator to ensure that this revalidation occurs at the outset of the second week's activities in the context of a review of the previous week's accomplishments. Rather than dryly citing a list of last week's activities, the facilitator should encourage feedback from team members, emphasizing that *everything* is still open for discussion and review before they move forward. It makes no sense, for example, to create the fact-data source matrix and to align that matrix with the functionality-fact matrix (both of these activities are discussed later in this chapter) if a substantial portion of the functionality is incorrect, invalid, or otherwise nonapplicable to the business case.

The Fact-Data Source Matrix

Once the team members have revalidated consensus and commitment, they can start the real work. As mentioned in the previous chapter with respect to the functionality-fact matrix, a key deliverable of the second week is a companion matrix that relates the previously identified facts with the data source(s) used to build them.

It is during this activity that separate threads of the first week's work are woven together to help create a richer picture of the scope of the proposed data mart: what exactly is this system supposed to do once it's deployed, and how do we think it will occur? Recall that in addition to the time spent on the functionality-fact matrix during Week 1, there was some discussion about the identification of candidate data sources for the data mart. The fact-data source matrix is where these two activities are unified.

Figure WK2.1 illustrates a sample fact-data source matrix. Note that two of the columns refer to what appears to be the same data source: the Temporary Employees Assignments (TEA). In this example, there are two distinct TEA applications—one for the Eastern United States, the other for the Western United States—that need to be considered as separate data sources even though they are identical in terms of hardware, DBMS, data structures, and so on. Why? Simply because there is information in each without which there will be an incomplete picture of various facts (in the segment following, both quarterly expenditures and historical head count).

Data Sources

Facts	ERES—Enterprise Revenue and Expense System	TEA—Temporary Employees' Assignments (Eastern U.S.)	TEA—Temporary Employees' Assignments (Western U.S.)	PEA—Permanent Employees' Assignments
Previous two years' quarterly expenditures by category, by deptartment, and by office	▓	▓	▓	▓
Two years' historical headcount by month, by department		▓	▓	▓
Forecasted revenues by territory, by quarter				
Previous three years' revenues by territory, by month	▓			
...				

Figure WK2.1 The fact-data source matrix.

Suppose, however, that the Eastern U.S. TEA system provides a monthly rollup of detail-level data into the Western U.S. TEA system, and that the latter is considered the official "system of record" for all temporary employees nationwide. The fact-data source matrix might then look like that in Figure WK2.2.

The key is a thorough understanding of not only the candidate data sources to the data mart (as identified during Week 1), but also intersource flows of data that can affect the systemwide view of the data mart environment. If, in the above example, all required facts could be built from the Western U.S. TEA system, it's questionable whether the Eastern U.S. version of that application is needed as a data source. If, on the other hand, these two systems have diverged over the years in terms of functionality, data models, and content, it's possible that both are needed.

In the data mart scope phase, these questions and issues should at least be identified. Not all answers to the questions will be immediately known, but any uncertainties can be logged on the "Questions and Issues" list for further analysis and research.

Unifying the Functionality-Fact and Fact-Data Source Matrices

After the creation of, discussion about, and agreement with the fact-data source matrix, it is necessary to unify it with the functionality-fact matrix created the previous week. Essentially, the combination of these two matrices will give an accurate picture of the two distinct pieces discussed so far: the facts that are needed to support the proposed functionality and the data sources that are needed to create these facts. In addition, a third facet can be seen: the data sources that are needed to support the data mart functionality.

As the effort moves forward, two things will occur: First, a prioritization will occur later in the scoping phase (discussed later in this chapter) as to the functionality that will be considered within scope for the data mart. Second, during the design phase, intensive analysis work will proceed, with accompanying design and implementation details about how data will be acquired from the various sources and brought into the data mart. The analysis will focus on the elements, frequency, refresh/restocking model methods, the transformations that will take place, and quality assurance policies, among other aspects. (These are all discussed at length in subsequent chapters.)

By having the functionality-data source picture created from the unification of these two models, the data mart design team has guidelines for which data sources

| | Data Sources | | | |
Facts	ERES—Enterprise Revenue and Expense System	TEA—Temporary Employees' Assignments (Eastern U.S.)	TEA—Temporary Employees' Assignments (Western U.S.)	PEA—Permanent Employees' Assignments
Previous two years' quarterly expenditures by category, by department, and by office	▓		▓	▓
Two years' historical headcount by month, by department			▓	▓
Forecasted revenues by territory, by quarter				
Previous three years' revenues by territory, by month	▓			
...				

Figure WK2.2 Alternate fact-data source matrix.

from the candidate list *really* need to be analyzed and designed and which ones can be ignored during the upcoming development. If, for example, some functionality is deemed out of scope for data mart development (at least for now), and only the specific functionality items in this group use information from a given data source (i.e., no other functionality items use facts created from these sources), there is no immediate need to do any further work with that data source.

Figure WK2.3 illustrates a sample functionality-data source matrix, referring back to the matrices created and illustrated in Figures WK1.1 and WK2.1, respectively.

A Final Data Mart Project Risk Assessment

As Week 2 draws to a close, a substantial amount of tangible information about the scope of the data mart will be known. The work done in unifying the functionality-fact and fact-data source matrices, specifically, will provide teamwide understanding of the number of data sources that will need to be considered. In addition, members will understand how widespread their usage is in terms of the functionality supported and what facts the data mart will need to support in support of the functionality.

The team must once again consider the level of risk associated with the data mart project as a whole. The technique should be a facilitated discussion, as in the first week, and by the end of that session, the team will have an updated understanding of the project risk. If all has gone smoothly, members may have more questions and issues as a result from their intensive work, but their concerns should be considered manageable ones, not threats to the project. The key is an open, communicative environment in which all team members participate.

Technology Assessment Report

During Week 1 the team researched the technology landscape, examining constraints such as organizational standards and experiences of other organizations with similar projects. Those who did this work after the initial discussions and do, for example, Internet-based research and meet with other systems owners should present their findings to the data mart scope team as a whole in Week 2. They will answer project-related questions: Does OLAP Tool XYZ, Version 2.1, really fix all the bugs that were in Version 2.0? What's the status of the company-wide Desktop Upgrade Program (DUP) and how might that affect the deployment of front-end tools to the data mart to the candidate user population? Is it true that the IT organization will no longer support any departmental data marts that use a particular DBMS product?

	Facts			
Functionality	Previous two years' quarterly expenditures by category, by department, and by office	Two years' historical head count by month, by department	Forecasted revenues by territory, by quarter	Previous three years' revenues by territory, by month
Establish targeted expenditures by top-level organization	▪	▪	▪	▪
Fill in head-count projections for year on the budget form	▪	▪	▪	▪
Create budget package for executive management				
Analyze first draft submissions from all budget holders	▪		▪	▪

Figure WK2.3 The functionality-data source matrix.

Creating Design Phase Plans

The last objective of the scope phase is to prepare for the next phase, designing the data mart. To this end, a number of "end game" deliverables need to discussed and prepared as hand-offs to the design team. These include the following:

♦ A prioritized list of data mart functionality

♦ Project plans for the design phase

♦ Budgetary estimates, as required, for the subsequent phases of the project

Prioritized Functionality List

In a perfect world, the functionality proposed, discussed, and agreed to by the scope team will be carried forward in its entirety and be available by the time the data mart has been deployed. In many situations, however, a combination of factors—budgetary, resource constraints, time pressures, external dependencies, and others—combine to cause hard choices to be made about what can and cannot be delivered in the initial deployment of the data mart.

The scope team, representing the business point of view with respect to the project, will help determine priorities. Techniques that can be used to do so include the following:

♦ A sequentially numbered list, starting at one and counting through the entire list of functionality items until the end

♦ A set of three priority values identifying functionality that must be present, should if at all possible be present, or would be nice to have

However, priorities must be set in terms of identified business functionality, *not* data sources or even facts. One of the surest ways to raise the level of risk in a rapid data mart development project is to present the design team with a prioritized list of data sources rather than functionality that needs to be supported. If in-or-out decisions need to be made, it is more likely that high-priority functionality will not be available because, for example, a decision was made to go after a data source that supports the building of 15 different facts rather than one that would be used to support only two facts. Those two facts may be required to support the highest-priority functionality of the data mart, and the absence of that information essentially renders the data mart useless because of dependencies among the various business processes and functionality.

Project Plans

The work on the design phase project plan should have already begun, possibly before the scope phase itself was begun, but certainly during the first week as an increasing amount of information about the proposed data mart was discovered. The team leader, with staff, will have been working on and tuning the activities whenever possible.

At the end of the second week—the end of the data mart scope phase—the project plan should be presented to the team to give an idea of the activity over the next five weeks and the accomplishments that can be expected.

Budgetary Estimates

Many organizational environments have procedures that require expenditure requests to be presented for projects as a whole, even though a phased development methodology such as the one presented in this book makes it impossible to determine up front how much money will be needed. A compromise that has been adopted by most organizations is the use of budgetary estimates for expenditures on the outlying phases of a project.

By the end of the data mart scope phase, then, it is usually the responsibility of the team leadership to develop the following:

♦ A specific funding request for the design phase to follow

♦ Based on what has been learned during the scope phase, an estimate of the total funding required through development and deployment of the data mart

A budgetary estimate should be in place the design phase funding before the scope begins (otherwise, why do the scope?), so the key is to ensure that this is still accurate and to present a request for funding that should be automatically approved if the team is to move ahead immediately into the design phase the following week.

The policies regarding project funding will vary from one organization to another, so it's best to understand before you begin the scope phase.

How to Achieve the Second Week's Goals

Figure WK2.4 shows the calendar of activities that you should plan for during the second week of your data mart project as you finish up your scoping phase.

	Monday	Tuesday	Wednesday	Thursday	Friday
Morning	Review of Accomplishments Issues, Questions Begin Fact-Source Matrix	Fact-Source Matrix	Validate Functionality-Fact Matrix against Fact-Source Matrix	Validate Functionality-Fact Matrix against Fact-Source Matrix	Review of Scope Phase Activities Technology Assessment Report Issues, Questions
Afternoon	Fact-Source Matrix: Begin	Fact-Source Matrix	Validate Functionality-Fact Matrix against Fact-Source Matrix	Risk Assessment	Issues, Questions Prepare for Next Week/Design Phase

Figure WK2.4 The second week's calendar of activities.

More Facilitated Work Sessions

The techniques of the first week's activity, particularly the extensive use of facilitated work sessions, will carry through into the second week. Please refer to the discussion in the previous chapter for models, guidelines, and so on.

Techniques for Cross-Matrix Validation

It's likely that as team members discuss the unification of the two types of matrices, issues that hadn't previously surfaced with respect to functionality, facts, and data sources will become apparent. Looking at a three-level (or three-axis) model brings to light new things that aren't readily apparent when you look at pairs of items (functionality and facts, facts and data sources).

Though it may seem tedious, a way to wade through the mass of discrete information gathered is to sound out each functionality-fact-source trio to gain a further understanding of the inherent meaning and validate that it is correct. For example:

> *"To fill in head-count projections for the year on the budget form, we need two years' historical head count by month and department, as well as the forecasted revenues by territory and quarter. For that information to be available, it needs to be built from the two TEA systems and from PEA, and also from certain other sources."*

By walking through the information in this manner, the team not only gains an understanding of the intersection of functionality, facts, and data sources, but also begins to get a sense of the breadth and depth of the data mart itself.

Deliverables from the Data Mart Scope

Depending on the overall methodology or framework under which you're doing your data mart scope, the deliverables will vary from organization to organization. It's essential to understand what needs to be delivered (i.e., what's mandatory) and what is optional, as well as any guidelines about format, structure, approval process, and so on.

At a minimum, it is recommended that the following deliverables be produced from the data mart scope:

- ♦ A business case that will contain the mission statement, the list of proposed functionality, and the expected business benefits from the data mart

♦ All matrices created as part of the scope: functionality-fact, fact-data source, and functionality-data source

♦ A data mart project risk assessment, covering the tangible and intangible risks identified (in a "politically correct" manner)

♦ The project plan and cost information for the following phase and the project as a whole, as available

You Know You're in Trouble When

Your Week 2 risk assessment looks significantly more ominous than that of Week 1:

♦ Everyone was in agreement when functionality and facts were paired in creating the matrix, but when data sources were added to the picture, people started to question the functionality items themselves.

♦ On Wednesday of Week 2, a team member suggests looking at the mission statement again because it seems to have some problems. The team leader must immediately convene a meeting with the project sponsorship to put corrective actions in place, and must *not* permit the design phase to begin until such issues are resolved.

Week 2 Spotlight on the Chief Architect

During the data mart project's first week, the chief architect mostly has a quiet, behind-the-scenes role. As discussed in the previous chapter, the first week of the scope is very business focused, with only occasional discussion about technology matters. Though the business focus continues into Week 2, technical feasibility will now start to come into play. The chief architect needs to listen carefully to the group's discussion and determine the various architectural options for moving data from the source(s) to the data mart and the relative tradeoffs. This leader should also determine whether constructing a data mart for this particular business solution is even feasible.

Specifically, the chief architect needs to focus on these three areas during the second week:

♦ *The fact-data source matrix.* The first week's functionality-fact matrix is deliberately conceptual because team members need to focus on what should be rather than worry about the underlying mechanics of how the data mart will be populated and from what sources. However, discussion in the second week shifts to the way those facts will be created in terms of sources. Although the group will focus on the concepts and not worry too much about the mechanics, the chief architect must take each fact-data source relationship identified and quickly determine any potential issues that the team will face when the design phase commences. The information gained during the creation of this matrix will form the basis from which the architect will do much behind-the-scenes work—contacting appropriate IT members for additional information, perhaps even digging into the sources directly after each day's session has been completed.

♦ *Gap analysis.* The chief architect must conduct a real-time, high-level gap analysis based on the discussions that occur during the second week. Subjects of the analysis include applications that have been retired (or will be retired) that mean unavailability of data and user complaints about various levels of detail in two applications that perform similar functions. Much more gap analysis work will occur during the design phase, but the team needs an idea *now* about potential problems lying ahead.

♦ *The technology assessment.* One of the deliverables from the scope is an overall assessment of technical issues and challenges and the technical feasibility of successfully completing this project as planned. For example, if there is an enterprisewide desktop operating system upgrade occurring (e.g., from Windows 3.1.1 to Window 98) over a six-month period, everyone—including the project sponsor—needs to have a clear understanding of what that will mean to the project. If, for instance, an intranet-enabled data mart is being built, the impact may is minimal. However, classical front-end tools with significant client-resident functionality may be impacted by the upgrade. If it looks as if the environment could turn into a very large database (VLDB) situation—a requirement was expressed in terms of data volumes that indicate hundreds of gigabytes of storage may be needed—the chief architect needs to determine whether current platforms can support a VLDB and whether the expertise exists to bring in new platforms, among others.

Continues

Week 2 Spotlight on the Chief Architect
(Continued)

While the project manager gives the go-ahead recommendation from an overall project perspective, the chief architect must be able to determine if the next five weeks of activity will lead to a solid design, ready for the construction activity, or if an entire team of people will wind up wasting their time.

Part Three

The Data Mart Design Phase

What You'll Find in This Chapter

The Data Mart Design Process: An Overview
Your Design Phase Goals
The Parallel Streams of Activity
The Design Phase Team

Week 3 Activities
Functional Analysis
Business Processes and Flows
Data Mart Analysis and High-Level Design
Source Data Analysis
Product Evaluation
System and Infrastructure Analysis

How to Achieve the Third Week's Goals
Project Management During Week 3

You Know You're in Trouble When

Finalizing Data Mart Function
and Use Models

A Note to the Reader: The scoping phase is over by Week 3. The accomplishments and shortcomings of the scoping phase will directly affect your chances for success during the five weeks of the design phase. If your organizational culture perceives the scoping phase of a project as a questionable process, you are especially aware of the importance of accomplishing as much as possible, in as many different areas of your project as possible, during the first week of design. Moving directly from the scoping phase into design without an interruption and maintaining the momentum that you've achieved during the first two weeks of your project is ideal. If, however, you've had to pause to wait for approval to move ahead, it's essential that your team "spins up" to maximum productivity as quickly as possible to regain the momentum. Either way, Week 3 of your data mart project is a critical one for you, as you and your team transition from scoping activities into design tasks.

The Data Mart Design Process: An Overview

Throughout the data mart design process, you will be struggling to maintain a balance between two opposing forces:

- The need for speed

- The need to carefully look at the end-to-end implications of all technical decisions you make

The following sections discuss the goals you need to achieve by the completion of the five-week design phase, the fundamental premise you need to follow with respect to parallel streams of activity, and the composition of your data mart team during the design phase.

Your Design Phase Goals

You have a very straightforward and clear-cut objective to achieve by the end of the design phase: To have a detailed framework in place so that you can successfully complete the construction phase of your data mart project in the five weeks that will immediately follow the completion of design.

This framework will include the following:

- A decision about the data mart's user interaction model; that is, whether the data mart will be structured dimensionally to support multidimensional analysis or built according to another modeling strategy (e.g., denormalized relational tables) to support a small number of high-priority, standard reports

- A complete, detailed definition of your data mart's contents and data structures

- A complete, detailed road map of all source data elements that you will need to bring into your data mart and the processes (i.e., extraction, transformation, movement, and so on) that must occur for you to accomplish this source-to-target data acquisition

- A complete, detailed picture of the way the contents of the data mart will be used and by whom: not just what data will be accessed and how, but how the results of queries and reports will be used in business processes

- A complete assessment of the technical infrastructure on which the data mart will reside and identification of any support issues (and a plan to handle those issues)

- Identification of all off-the-shelf products and tools that will be used

- An updated data mart project risk assessment

- A detailed project plan for the construction phase activities

You are likely to have a few loose ends at the completion of the design phase—perhaps some source-to-target mapping issues, for example—and the key is to *not* let them derail your data mart development as the design phase transitions into construction. The more loose ends there are, the more risk there is to your project of having to cycle back, but you should have a clear idea of the state of your project as construction begins. If you have only a few noncritical issues remaining, plan on closing out design and moving into construction as those loose ends are tied up.

You want to get as close as possible to a complete construction framework by the end of the five weeks.

The Parallel Streams of Activity

A tremendous amount of work must occur during the five weeks of design. The key to accomplishing all the things that are necessary is to do as many activities in parallel as possible, operating in a "just-in-time" mode when it comes to the invocation of an activity that requires the output from another (or more than one other activity).

It's convenient to think of and manage parallel activities in streams, with each stream representing one part of your total data mart picture. These streams are as follows:

♦ Formal and final determination of the business functionality that will be delivered through the data mart

♦ Data analysis, modeling, and design

♦ Process analysis, modeling, and design

♦ Systems and infrastructure research

♦ Product evaluation and selection

Some of the streams are further decomposed into additional threads of parallel activity. For example, the analysis, modeling, and design of the database environment within the data mart will have parallel activities around source data analysis and target database design. Product evaluation and selection will occur in parallel for tools in the user desktop (i.e., OLAP or some other type of business intelligence tool), middleware, and database environment.

This chapter, and the others that discuss design phase activity, present a detailed picture of the tasks and accomplishments that must occur in each of these parallel streams, on a week-by-week basis.

The Design Phase Team

Your data mart team will change as the scoping phase transitions into design. From the outset of design, it is imperative that you add serious technical talent to the project team, covering the following activities:

- Data modeling and database design for the data mart (one person)

- Analysis of each data source (usually one person for each data source, depending on complexity)

- Product evaluation and analysis (one person for the front-end tools and another person to handle middleware and database products)

- Business analysis and customer interfacing (one person)

- Process analysis and modeling (one person)

- Systems and infrastructure analysis and design (one person)

- Quality assurance and configuration control (one person)

These team members are in addition to the project manager and the technical team leader/chief data mart architect, both of whom remain on the project from the scoping phase to design to provide continuity to the development effort.

Although a team of 10 to 12 people for a data mart effort may seem excessive, there really is sufficient work for each of these roles throughout design, and any attempts to scale back the size of the development team will result in one or both of the following:

- Less functionality being delivered than desired

- A longer development time period

Projects will, of course, vary from one to another, but it can be safely assumed that during your data mart development, there will be approximately 50 to 60 person-weeks worth of real work that needs to be performed.

Week 3 Activities

The activities in each of the parallel streams are different from their successor tasks in the following weeks of the design phase in one very important way: They have

TIP Don't even consider longer work hours as a labor-saving measure! You have some flexibility in how you accomplish that workload, but any attempts to institute, say, an official 50-hour work week as a means to have one or two fewer members on your team will almost always result in project failure. Any person on your team will likely face more actual work hours than are on the project plan as issues are uncovered and need to be resolved, design backtracking occurs, and other unforeseen circumstances surface.

In addition, trying to double an individual's workload with two different roles is rarely a good idea because something will have to give, and your project will suffer.

been established to have very few dependencies on deliverables from any other stream during the first week. Unlike, for example, Week 4, in which the source data analysis is very focused (and therefore dependent) upon data elements defined by the data mart element design activities of Week 3, the activities for Week 3 can be done mostly in isolation.

Some can be accomplished by a single team member, while others involve members of the user community or the IT support organization but still are "captained" by a single data mart team member.

These activities have been established in this manner to remove as much dependency risk as possible from the first week of the design, to enable Week 3 objectives to be met, and, therefore, to help build momentum to carry the team through the entire design phase.

Functional Analysis

The team member responsible for doing the business analysis and serving as the primary customer interface has two objectives for Week 3:

♦ Tie up any loose ends left over from the scoping phase

♦ Gather and finalize requirements for OLAP functionality (e.g., *drill-down* and *drill-up*) and reporting and querying needs (e.g., cross-tabular reports, "stoplighting")

Tying Up Loose Ends

As for Weeks 1 and 2, the primary deliverables related to data mart functionality from the scoping phase are the matrices in which the agreed-upon functionality is matched up against the data "facts" and the source(s) of each fact necessary to support each item.

Even though consensus has been reached and the data mart scope is now closed to additional features or requirements, a late addition may surface. More often than not, it will be a functionality component that has already been identified but deferred until a later development cycle for the data mart. After a weekend to consider this (and possible interaction with business management), a user comes back and requests that the functionality be moved to the current development cycle.

The business analyst will, as necessary during the first week, conduct a series of mini-mini-scopes in terms of the following:

♦ Fielding such requests

♦ Quickly convening any appropriate meetings to discuss these items

♦ Pushing back as much as possible in favor of delaying implementation until a later version of the data mart, emphasizing the impact on the project and the risk associated with adding functionality at this point

♦ If overruled and the functionality is to be added (e.g., as directed by upper management), *immediately* determining the impact on every other aspect of the data mart and working with the other team member(s) to avoid having this late addition derail the project

It is in this last item that an exception-driven interstream dependency *might* exist during Week 3 of the project, with the business analyst assisting wherever possible in making sure that the database design, process flows, source data analysis, and the other activities stay on course. Absent last-minute additions or changes to functionality, the business analyst can work with the business community with little or no impact on the activities of other data mart team members.

OLAP and Reporting/Querying Functionality

In addition to the gatekeeping activity described—which should be kept to a minimum—the business analyst must work with members of the data mart's eventual user community to add substance and detail to all the items of functionality defined during the scope. For example, Figure WK1.1 on page 62 identified functionality wherein users would be able to fill in head-count projections for the year on the budget form, using two types of facts: the past two years' historical head count by month and by department and the forecasted revenues by territory and by quarter. This particular piece of functionality, like most others that will be supported by the data mart, can be further decomposed.

The results of this further functional decomposition will, during Week 4, serve as input to the hands-on testing of front-end business intelligence tools to ensure that the tool that will eventually be selected can support all required functionality.

Work needs to be done with regards to determining the specific analytical processing that the data mart's users will perform. This includes the processes listed in the following sections.

Drill-Down and Drill-Up Analysis The paths users will take to see lower levels of consolidation or high levels of summarization for on-screen data are called *drill-down* and *drill-up* analyses, respectively. Figure WK3.1 illustrates an example of drill-down capability (drill-up would be the reverse path).

For every fact identified during the scope, a thorough analysis of the drilling paths must be conducted because this will directly affect the design of the data mart's database. For example, the forecasted revenues by territory and by quarter could be further decomposed into districts within each territory, business locations within each district, departments within business location, and so on. (For purposes of the examples in this section, assume that a territory consists of multiple districts, which in turn have multiple business locations, which have multiple departments.) Similarly, revenues for each quarter could be broken down by month, week, day, or even lower levels of consolidation.

But what makes sense? It is the responsibility of the business analyst to work with the user community and in the context of the data mart's mission to determine the level of consolidation at which business value can still be obtained and the additional consolidation level at which a point of diminishing returns has been reached. For example, suppose that for the coming budgeting cycle, district managers, who now have profit and loss (P&L) responsibility, will make their own budget requests. (In the past, it was the responsibility of territory managers to do budgeting at the territory level with informal inputs from district managers.) It will likely make sense, therefore, for the data mart to be able to manage facts at the district level instead of the higher territory level of consolidation. However, the ability to produce facts at the business location level is determined *not* to be of value for the budgeting process.

Q2 1997 Expenses (in $)

By Department	Permanent Headcount	Temporary Headcount	Office Supplies	Travel	Telephone	Other/Misc.	Total
1							
Total Expenses	*398,146*	*195,832*	*232,279*	*284,794*	*72,164*	*130,986*	*1,374,146*
Northeast Region	78,683	22,172	59,945	42,158	12,439	27,473	302,815
Southeast Region	88,661	51,121	19,877	77,655	8,875	21,334	267,523
Midwest Region	66,496	38,341	15,902	58,241	15,531	16,001	210,511
Northwest Region	77,578	44,731	17,889	67,948	12,203	18,667	239,017
Southwest Region	86,728	39,468	118,666	38,792	23,115	47,512	354,280
2							
Total Expenses	*398,146*	*195,832*	*232,279*	*284,794*	*72,164*	*130,986*	*1,374,146*
Northeast Region	78,683	22,172	59,945	42,158	12,439	27,473	302,815
Pennsylvania	56,000	8,130	26,344	22,366	7,171	14,986	161,341
New Jersey	22,683	14,042	33,601	19,792	5,268	12,487	141,474
Southeast Region	88,661	51,121	19,877	77,655	8,875	21,334	267,523
Midwest Region	66,496	38,341	15,902	58,241	15,531	16,001	210,511
Northwest Region	77,578	44,731	17,889	67,948	12,203	18,667	239,017
Southwest Region	86,728	39,468	118,666	38,792	23,115	47,512	354,280

Figure WK3.1 An example of drill-down capability.

Drill-Through The *drill-through*, sometimes referred to as *reach-through*, is the capability to access the underlying detail level of data that is consolidated to create the facts in a data mart. In a relational OLAP (ROLAP) environment, a drill-through path may exist from fact tables to other tables in which transactional data is stored, all within a single database. A new trend, though, is the creation of hybrid OLAP (HOLAP) environments in which a multidimensional database is used to store the summarized facts with cross-database links to relational tables that hold detailed data. Figure WK3.2 illustrates examples of both of these drill-through environments.

It's important that the business analyst *not* focus on specific technologies or cross-database access but rather on the business need for accessing detail-level data. A very straightforward manner for achieving this focus is in the context of exploring drill-down and drill-up paths. For example, following a path from territory to district to business location to department (the *organization path*) and from quarter to month to week to day (the *time path*) could conceivably continue to individual sales transactions. In the case of a data mart developed to support the budgeting cycle, access to individual sales transactions will likely be of no value, and including reach-through capability to data about those transactions, wherever it is stored, will probably be of no value. A data mart developed with a mission of supporting product sales and marketing decisions, however, may very well benefit from having drill-through access to detailed transaction-level data for all sales (for statistical analysis of revenue per transaction based on time of day and other factors, for example).

Cross-Tabular Reports Cross-tabular reports, or cross-tabs, are more within the domain of basic reporting and querying than OLAP functionality, but it is important to determine what types of cross-tabs will be needed. You could look at a cross-tab as the starting point for a drill-down analysis but without the drill-down capability.

So why look at cross-tab needs if they are basically a subset of drill-down capabilities? Simply because a particular data mart may have no need at all for drilling anywhere in any dimensions. As discussed later in the design phase, a decision could be made to switch from an OLAP front-end tool, with corresponding dimension-and-fact (dimensional) database design, to another tool that supports basic reporting and querying functionality with underlying denormalized database structures. At this stage, it is important that the business analyst validate that the facts identified during the scope are indeed aligned with user reporting and querying needs in the form of cross-tabs.

Q2 1997 Expenses (in $)

By Department	Permanent Headcount	Temporary Headcount	Office Supplies	Travel	Telephone	Other/Misc.	Total
Total Expenses	*398,146*	*195,832*	*232,279*	*284,794*	*72,164*	*130,986*	*1,374,146*
Northeast Region	**78,683**	**22,172**	**59,945**	**42,158**	**12,439**	**27,473**	**302,815**
Pennsylvania	56,000	8,130	26,344	22,366	7,171	14,986	161,341
Pittsburgh	28,888	3,232	8,590	15,722	840	12,088	69,360
Oakland	15,533	2,121	4,297	8,111	393	3,222	33,677
Downtown	13,355	1,111	4,293	7,611	447	8,866	35,683
Wilkes-Barre	2,112	544	88	5,000	4,433	777	12,954
Downtown	2,112	544	88	5,000	4,433	777	12,954
Philadelphia	25,000	4,354	17,666	1,644	1,898	2,121	52,683
Suburban	10,000	1,122	8,812	1,211	999	1,121	23,265
Center City	15,000	3,232	8,854	433	899	1,000	29,418
New Jersey	22,683	14,042	33,601	19,792	5,268	12,487	141,474
Monmouth County	18,637	2,036	30,258	2,604	2,615	8,965	95,373
Ocean County	1,000	2,340	1,580	656	887	664	8,707
Middlesex County	3,046	9,666	1,763	16,532	1,766	2,858	37,394
Southeast Region	**88,661**	**51,121**	**19,877**	**77,655**	**8,875**	**21,334**	**267,523**
Midwest Region	**66,496**	**38,341**	**15,902**	**58,241**	**15,531**	**16,001**	**210,511**
Northwest Region	**77,578**	**44,731**	**17,889**	**67,948**	**12,203**	**18,667**	**239,017**
Southwest Region	**86,728**	**39,468**	**118,666**	**38,792**	**23,115**	**47,512**	**354,280**

Figure WK3.2 An example of drill-through capability.

Slicing and Dicing It's one thing to identify that the data mart needs to be able to produce forecasted revenues by territory and by quarter for use in the budgeting cycle. It is critical, though, to determine the views that are needed by each user. For example, district managers should be able to see facts for their districts, but how about the other districts within the same territory or other territories? Is it a valid assumption that territory managers should be able to see slices of quarterly revenues for each of their districts? (Probably.)

Slicing and dicing analysis is also the starting point for the data mart's *security design*. It isn't only a matter of whether district managers would like to see facts for other districts; an equally fundamental question is whether they are allowed to do so?

For example, the business analyst, working with the user community, may determine that the following business rules should be in force: First, any district manager is allowed to see facts for other districts within the same territory, but *not* for districts in other territories. Second, any territory manager can see facts at the territory level, but *not* drilled down to the district level, for other territories. Based on these and other business rules, the *user-fact permissions model* shown in Figure WK3.3 can be created. During the data mart construction phase, these guidelines will be instantiated in the form of the database's security model.

Stoplighting Viewing data at the highest levels of summarization may give an inaccurate picture of what's really occurring within the overall enterprise. For example, a territory's actual expenditures for the current year to date may be right in line with the prior year's budget, although one of the four districts overran its budget by 75 percent. Why? Because another district is way under budget because of cutbacks and store closures (see Figure WK3.4).

It will probably then be of value to a number of data mart users, not only territory managers, to have an accurate picture of the state of activities at the district level. For example, the financial analysts who set the initial targets for the enterprise should have an idea that a district's current expenditures are higher than budgeted—perhaps to take advantage of revenue opportunities—so that the next year's territory target can be set accordingly, not just as a result of an automatic across-the-board adjustment. Similarly, reorganizations or districts in which cutbacks are occurring need to be factored into the territory's targets.

Trend Analysis and Statistical Processing Some data marts will be used for complex statistical processing such as trend analysis and classification (for example, newly formed districts with at least five business locations overrun their budget, on average,

Role	Fact	Permissions
District Manager	Expenses by Month by Category	Own District: Yes Other Districts in same Territory: Yes
		Districts in other Territories: Yes
	Revenues by Month	Own District: Yes Other Districts in same Territory: Yes
		Districts in other Territories: Yes
Territory Manager	Expenses by Month by Category by District	Own Territory: Yes Other Territories: No
	Revenues by Month by District	Own Territory: Yes Other Territories: No

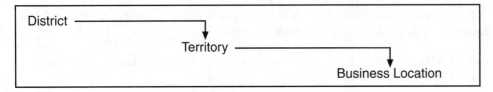

Figure WK3.3 An example of a user-fact permissions model.

during the first year by at least 10 percent). These requirements need to be identified by the business analyst, working with the users, to be included in the data mart.

"Passive" Data Mart Users

A commonly overlooked aspect of any data mart (or, more precisely, of any data warehousing environment) is that within the user community there will be "passive users." That is, all the functionality described previously will be used by some of the data mart's users; others, however, will likely be accessing only reports that are either automatically and regularly generated by the data mart environment or are created by others (the so-called "power users"). During Week 3, the business analyst must identify the passive users because during Week 4, the process modeler will work with these individuals to determine the flows of information among users of the data mart.

Territory	Total Expenses (Actual)	Total Expenses (Budgeted)
Eastern	$11,250,000	$11,400,000
Midwest	$10,000,000	$10,500,000
Western	$11,000,000	$11,500,000

Territory	District	Total Expenses (Actual)	Total Expenses (Budgeted)	
Eastern	1	$4,000,000	$2,300,000	Way Over
Eastern	2	$4,000,000	$4,200,000	
Eastern	3	$2,000,000	$1,900,000	
Eastern	4	$1,150,000	$3,500,000	Way Under

Figure WK3.4 Stoplighting used to highlight underlying inconsistencies.

It's quite possible that not all users of the data mart will be given the front-end OLAP or querying/reporting tool that is selected. Some users may interact with the data mart indirectly (e.g., receiving e-mailed reports that are run by others) or solely through their Web browsers to access reports that are posted on the company intranet.

Business Processes and Flows

A major risk to any data mart project team is to have insufficient knowledge of how interaction between applications and systems occurs in the organization's enterprise. For example, most data mart architecture diagrams will show one or more source applications with one-way lines drawn to the data mart, indicating the source-to-target flow of information. Upon further research, however, it may turn out that one of those sources has its own source-to-target bulk movement of data from another application elsewhere in the enterprise.

For example, as discussed earlier, the past two years' historical head count by month and by department was initially identified as a figure that could be created from three different sources: one that supported temporary employees in the eastern United States, another for temporary employees in the western United States, and a third that handled all permanent U.S. employees. However, it was later identified during the scope that the eastern U.S. temporary employee system provides a monthly rollup of detail level data into the western U.S. temporary employee system and that the latter is considered the official system of record for all temporary employees nationwide. Therefore, there would be two, not three, sources from which to build the head-count fact.

What are the implications on the data mart project? Questions such as the following need to be thoroughly understood:

♦ Exactly what does *monthly rollup* mean? Is it done the same day each month, and if so, what day?

♦ Is there ever any intramonth restatement or rollback of the intersystem data feed?

♦ How long does that feed take to occur?

♦ Are there any other systems impacted or involved? For example, does the eastern U.S. temporary employee system receive bulk rollups from regional offices?

The assignment of the process analyst during Week 1 is to take anything that could be considered a flow that was identified during the scope, such as interapplication exchanges of information (as described previously), dependencies and sequential ordering among business processes, or anything else along those lines, and find out everything about those flows, including timing, people and organizations involved, and any proposed changes.

Along with the functional decomposition discussed above, this process flow analysis will be input to subsequent design activities to help ensure that there are no unpleasant surprises during development.

Data Mart Content Analysis and High-Level Design

The team member responsible for database analysis and design of the data mart has one main assignment for Week 3: Develop a high-level conceptual database model that is as complete as possible by the end of the week.

Overview

Start the design phase with the premise that your database design will be multidimensional in nature, with facts and dimensions identified for use by the OLAP tool that will be selected by the end of Week 6. However, the information gained during the scoping phase may have already challenged that premise; the most common occurrence of this would be that the user community loudly and unanimously declares during the scope that they have no desire to do online analysis all they want is to be able to recreate the standard reports that they run against the extract files that are being taken away and replaced by the data mart.

The work performed by the business analyst during the week, described in the OLAP and Reporting/Querying Functionality section, will provide the additional information you will need to make this determination. If, for example, discussions with users about drill-down and drill-up paths get nowhere, you likely want to steer your data mart away from a dimensional orientation and OLAP functionality.

In this case, you may very likely (and quickly) find yourself evaluating reporting and querying tools instead of OLAP tools. The impact on your database design is that you may switch to a highly denormalized database design, with tables built to closely match the contents of the standard reports, instead of the more flexible (but more complex) fact and dimension data structures.

(Such a switch to reporting-driven denormalized data structures will almost always mandate the use of a relational database management system, whereas you could still select either an RDBMS or multidimensional database product to support OLAP functionality, subject to constraints such as data volumes.)

Attribute Analysis

Regardless of whether you stay with a multidimensional database design or switch to a denormalized design approach, the database designer's primary concern during the Week 3 is to take all the facts identified during the scope phase and do the following:

♦ Create a complete list of all attributes in each fact

♦ Determine the possible options for level of detail (granularity) for each of those facts

Aligning the Data Mart Mission with the Database Model

Recall that in Chapter 2 a variety of data mart content models were identified, bounded by the following:

♦ Geography

♦ Organization

TIP Database design structures (i.e., entities, attributes, relationships, dimension hierarchies, fact definitions, etc.) are not enough! The database designer should, as each structure is created, "populate" the structure with 50 to 75 pieces of sample data and then show the resulting output options, based on the level of detail that is being considered. For example, a fact wherein head count is tracked by department could result in various output options of head count by department, head count by higher-level department groups, head count by still-higher-level organization, and so on.

The best tool for this Week 3 data activity is a spreadsheet. (See Figure WK3.5.) You can sort data, create rows with subtotals, and hide other rows with lower levels of detail to show the various output options (and even mimic drill-down and drill-up options), and, in general, concentrate on the structure and content of the data mart's database in a single "tool."

♦ Function

♦ Competitors

The results of the work during the scope will tell you which of the models (or another model, such as dedication of the data mart to a specific business mission such as budgeting) will apply. You can use this information to guide the Week 3 database model creation. Figure WK3.6 illustrates how this can be accomplished.

Source Data Analysis

In many ways, source data analysis is the "fun" part of Week 3 activities. As mentioned earlier in this chapter, each source identified during the scope that is included in the version of the data mart currently being developed should have one individual assigned responsibility for everything relating to ensuring that data is extracted, transformed, and made available to the data mart—for initial load as well as on an ongoing basis, as required.

(An exception to the one-on-one relationship between analyst and source would be when there is a high degree of commonality for two or more sources—two identically structured temporary employment systems, for example. Occasionally, a

	A	B	C	D	E	F	G	H	I	J
1	Q2 1997 Expenses									
2	by Department	Permanent	Temporary	Office	Computer	All				
3		Headcount	Headcount	Supplies	Related	Group	Individuals	Other	Travel	Teleph
4	*Total Expenses*	$ 398,146	$ 195,832	$ 232,279	$ 10,000	$ 200,000	$ 10,000	$ 12,279	$ 284,794	$ 72
5	**Northeast Region**	**78,683**	**22,172**	**59,945**	**1,577**	**48,776**	**2,850**	**6,742**	**42,158**	**12**
6	Pennsylvania	56,000	8,130	26,344	234	20,000	1,000	5,110	22,366	7
15	New Jersey	22,683	14,042	33,601	1,343	28,776	1,850	1,632	19,792	5
16	Monmouth County	18,637	2,036	30,258	1,282	26,976	1,000	1,000	2,604	2
17	Freehold	9,761	1,717	28,282	1,282	25,000	1,000	1,000	1,717	1
18	Colt's Neck	8,876	319	1,976	-	1,976	-	-	887	
19	Ocean County	1,000	2,340	1,580	25	1,000	25	530	656	
20	Jackson	1,000	2,340	1,580	25	1,000	25	530	656	
21	Middlesex County	3,046	9,666	1,763	36	800	825	102	16,532	1
22	New Brunswick	2,309	8,766	776	26	700	25	25	6,654	
23	Somerset	737	900	987	10	100	800	77	9,878	
40										
41										
42										

Figure WK3.5 Using a spreadsheet as a Week 3 "data modeling tool."

Source	Slice for Data Mart
Revenues (worldwide)	Only U.S. Revenues
Head Count (worldwide)	Only U.S. Head Count
Expenses and Investments	Only Noncapital Expenses

Figure WK3.6 "Slicing" the data mart's database model.

team will combine two or more "very simple" data sources, but it's recommended that you do so only if an minimal amount of analysis and development work will have to occur with each one.)

Why is source data analysis fun during Week 3? Because team members assigned to this task spend an entire week doing nothing but digging through the data sources they are responsible for, looking for the following:

♦ Data structures that aren't consistent with printed documentation

♦ Data field contents that contain values that shouldn't be permissible (e.g., a code of "X" when the field is supposed to have either a "M" or "F")

♦ Data field contents that just don't make sense (e.g., total sales dollars for a particular customer order = $3,215,332,567)

♦ Data gaps (e.g., missing months when the data source has an aggregation table that is supposed to contain a rolling 24-month history of all activity for each customer)

♦ Invalid data relationships (e.g., "parent-child" data relationships across multiple tables or files that are invalid, such as a retail drugstore location incorrectly linked to the home office of a competing drugstore chain)

♦ Empty database tables or files that are supposed to contain data but don't

♦ Invalid record counts that indicate missing or additional data (e.g., the master customer table has 6,000 rows, but the supplemental customer table—which is supposed to have an equivalent number—has only 5,932)

Source data analysis isn't only about looking for errors; it involves understanding any oddities, such as inconsistencies in style.

The main tool each source analyst should employ is a means of directly querying the data source (or, more likely, a replica that has been copied to another platform or another area of a mainframe to avoid impacting production system performance). The analyst might use SQL for a relational database source; SAS, FOCUS, or some other type of fourth-generation query-oriented language; or any type of tool or language that can permit browsing and "poking around" to learn as much as possible about the data sources.

Though each source analyst will work mostly in isolation, anything interesting that is learned should be communicated to the team member performing the database design function if it could affect the design of the data mart's database. For example, there may be a requirement that analysts look at purchasing patterns (products purchased, average purchase amount, frequency of making purchases, etc.) for every customer who did not renew a purchasing contract with the organization during the previous three years. The source analyst may discover, however, that after 12 months, the mainframe legacy application that handles customer contracts and purchase history automatically purges all historical information about all customers who do *not* renew purchase contracts.

Obviously, it's important that this information be communicated as quickly as possible to the person responsible for doing the database design for consideration in related activities (as well as the project manager and the business analyst for similar consideration).

Special Source Data Analysis Situations

You need to be especially vigilant about two source data situations in your analytical functions during Week 3 and into subsequent design phase weeks: archived historical data and externally provided data.

Archived Historical Data If it is necessary to populate your data mart with historical data that is *not* currently stored in an application's database or file system but instead has been copied into some form of data archive (on tape, disk, optical storage, etc.) and purged from the application's data environment, then you need to make sure that you perform the analysis described earlier for each archived data set. Over time, structural changes may have been made to the application's data environment; fields may have been added, data structures changed, or permissible values in fields modified. With each change, there will have been modifications to the application code responsible for managing the data. If there has been very little volatility—only a minor change every six to nine months—you won't find too much variation between the archived data sets from the same source. If, however, the application's database structures have been unusually volatile, expect anything.

You need to treat each archived data set that will be loaded into the data mart during initial population as a separate data source. Accordingly, the number of these archived data sets will dictate how long your initial and subsequent data analysis will take. A seemingly simple data mart with only two sources identified during the scope becomes much more complex if each source's operational database is archived to tape and purged monthly. Suddenly, a requirement to initially stage, summarize, and load 24 months' worth of data means that you are, in reality, dealing with 48 different data sources.

Externally Provided Data Sometimes a data mart will be identified as needing externally provided data: credit rating scores and supporting data, supplied by one or more of the credit bureaus; competitive sales results for your company and your competitors, supplied by a market data research firm; economic forecasting data; or some other type of information not available from an application within your enterprise. Typically this type of information is available on a periodic basis and is transmitted to you from the provider on magnetic tape. Increasingly, though, the Internet will be used as the transmission medium, and updates will become more "behind the scenes" with less human intervention.

If your organization has already been using this information, you may have a series of archived versions of this data stored on tape or on disk, in flat file or SAS data set format. If so, then the discussion about dealing with archived historical data will apply here; be sure to carefully analyze each of these data sets that will become part of your data mart environment.

If, however, your organization has *not* previously used this information, you need to make sure that data is available as soon as possible for analysis. You need to request a data sample that is as close as possible in structure and content to what you will be receiving for inclusion in your data mart. Once this has been received, you will perform the analytical steps described in this chapter and in subsequent ones dealing with source data analysis.

Product Evaluation

Week 3 needs to be an intensive effort—actually, three intensive efforts—with regard to the products being considered for inclusion in the data mart. The following sections discuss what needs to be done by the team members assigned lead responsibility for each of these areas.

Front-End Tools

As discussed in Chapter 3, one of the data mart project prerequisites is to have a shortlist of candidate front-end tools. It is imperative that during Week 3 each one of the tools be installed on a test machine, and run through basic "check-out" procedures and evaluation.

During this third week, the team should put each product through the paces, looking for reasons to eliminate it from further consideration. Such reasons might include the following:

♦ Failure to successfully install the product on the test client machine (i.e., you can't get it to run)

♦ Failure to successfully establish connectivity between the front-end product and a database on a server

♦ Dynamic link library (DLL) clashes between the product and other client software that can't be resolved

Given the complex and sometimes unpredictable nature of corporate client/server environments, even industry-leading products could have problems working in your enterprise. Elimination might sound a bit harsh, but in a rapid data mart development effort, there is no time to waste on products that don't easily work in your environment.

Aside from looking for reasons to drop a product from further consideration, it is imperative to get a detailed look at each of your candidate products side by side. How do their drill-down capabilities compare in overall ease of use and specific features? What capabilities does one product have that either aren't included in the other products (or possibly don't work in other products)?

The key for Week 3 is to take an intensive, hands-on look at each product on your shortlist to get a feel for how the current version operates.

Data Mart Middleware

Week 3 of your data mart project is too soon to determine whether your middleware functions—extraction, quality assurance, transformation, movement, and loading—will be performed by a tool or through custom coding. It is recommended that, if possible, one or more tools be used; over the long run, tool-based middleware functions will usually be more maintainable than custom code.

At least two products should be evaluated. The functions that should be evaluated in a hands-on manner include the following:

♦ *The data mart's target database design.* Capabilities such as assistance with designing a star schema model and defining all of the metadata associated with a data mart's contents.

♦ *Source-to-target mapping.* The ability to import metadata about data mart sources, including (if applicable to your enterprise) sources from heterogeneous platforms, and to map source data elements to those in the data mart's target database.

♦ *Extraction.* The method for extracting data from each source—whether through reaching directly into a source database or flat file or writing custom code to first extract the data before proceeding with tool-based transformation— and the models of extraction that are supported, such as complete replacement and change oriented.

♦ *Quality assurance.* The use of monitoring scripts to watch for data integrity problems and the ability to do several stages of quality assurance: upon extraction from a data source and following transformation.

♦ *Movement.* The way data moves from one platform to another—through a tool's environment or separate file transfer programs.

♦ *Transformation.* In simple transformations, building a rule within a tool to change all "1" and "2" values to "M" and "F," respectively. In complex transformations, merging two or more sources into one, eliminating certain records, or using lookup tables dynamically built from the contents of one data source as input to transformation rules for another.

♦ *Loading.* The way data loaded into the data mart's database and the types of "fast load" capabilities that are available for very large data sets.

The objectives of the initial middleware product evaluation are the same as for front-end tools: To gain a thorough, comparative understanding from hands-on work with each and to look for show-stoppers that might eliminate a product from further consideration (e.g., serious bugs in a new release of a product).

Database

Interestingly, the data mart's database selection will likely be more problematic than either the front-end tool or the middleware product, for the following reasons:

♦ There is likely a corporate standard in place for departmental application database servers, meaning that you will automatically have to consider that product for your data mart.

♦ Your going-in premise will likely be that you will implement a relational OLAP (ROLAP) solution, but during the next few weeks, requirements and subsequent design work could steer you to a multidimensional database solution. This means that you will have, in addition to the always tough relational-versus-relational product comparison, an apples-to-oranges comparison of products from two different database models.

At this point, you don't have enough information to know if you will be facing architectural challenges in the database domain of your data mart. You may have a very large database (VLDB) environment, and the ways users will want to retrieve and use data may lead you to a very large number of dimensions that preclude using a particular product.

Therefore, you want to spend this week's efforts doing much the same thing as with the front-end and middleware products: installing the database, checking out configuration options and issues (for example, if you turn off logging during a database load, how much of a performance improvement do you get and what are the tradeoffs?), studying different tuning options, and working with test data to check out loading times.

It's also valuable to get an idea of some of the advanced features available in each product and how well they work: parallel database capabilities (and the different partitioning models available in each product), bit-mapped indexing, caching, replication, and others.

System and Infrastructure Analysis

Following the completion of the scope, you have a fairly complete picture of the systems and platforms that will make up your overall data mart environment. Sources have been identified, so now you need to research and analyze all platforms, operating systems (and versions), databases and file systems, application programming interfaces (APIs), and other aspects of each.

T I P Try to use data from one or more of your data mart's sources for your database evaluation, if acquiring that data isn't too time-consuming a process. By the middle of the third week, have a quick test run of each of the middleware products against one or more data sources to pull out data, and see if you can successfully accomplish an end-to-end extraction-through-loading of data into each candidate DBMS product's environment.

The networking environment needs to be analyzed so that you can determine what capabilities exist (and what bandwidth constraints there may be) for the data mart environment: both the *source-to-target portion* (i.e., the way data is moved from sources to the data mart) and the way users will access the data mart.

As a result of the scope, you have an idea of the members of the user community and where they are located. This general picture will be translated into local area network (LAN) and wide area network (WAN) infrastructure capabilities, as applicable.

If an intranet-enabled data mart is being considered, the analyst assigned to this role also needs to check out IP addressing, Web server configurations, security models, and supported browser environments.

The key during this week is to conduct a thorough yet controlled analysis of everything within the infrastructure upon which the success of the data mart will be dependent, yet over which you have little or no control. Rapid data mart development requires that you be able to plug into an existing infrastructure with minimal additional interfaces; anything more, and you will need to add significant time to your project, particularly to the construction phase.

How to Achieve the Third Week's Goals

Figure WK3.7 shows the calendar of activities that you should plan for during the second week of your data mart project as you finish up your scoping phase.

Project Management During Week 3

Good project management during Week 3 is especially critical because unlike the two weeks of the data mart's scope, in which the team was together most of the time, there are two complicating factors:

Activity Stream	Monday	Tuesday	Wednesday	Thursday	Friday
Business Functionality	User Meeting OLAP Functionality Model Review	User Functionality Session	User Functionality Session	User Functionality Session	Decisions about User Functionality Model(s)
Data Analysis (Data Mart Contents)	Attribute Analysis	Attribute Analysis	Coordination Meeting	Attribute Analysis Begin Report	Complete Attribute Analysis Report
Source Analysis	Source Data Analysis	Source Data Analysis	Coordination Meeting	Targeted Source Data Analysis	Targeted Source Data Analysis
Process Flows	Cross-System Flows	Cross-System Flows	Cross-System Flows	Write Cross-System Flow Report	Complete Cross-System Flow Report
Front-End Product Evaluation	Installation	End-to-end Checkout/ Evaluation	End-to-end Checkout/ Evaluation	Focused Testing with Sample Data	Focused Testing with Sample Data
Middleware Evaluation	Installation	Transformation Rules	Transformation Rules	Extraction	Extraction
DBMS Evaluation	Installation	Load Sample Data	Support Tool Evaluation	Support Tool Evaluation	Support Tool Evaluation
Systems/ Infrastructure Analysis	Review/ Analysis	Review/ Analysis	Review/ Analysis	Review/ Analysis	Review/ Analysis

Figure WK3.7 The third week's calendar of activities.

♦ The number of parallel activities described in this chapter, each being captained by a different team member

♦ The addition of a number of new team members at the start of the design phase who weren't involved in the scope (discussed earlier in this chapter)

The project manager's chief responsibility during Week 3 is to ensure that all the threads of activity described in this chapter progress to the point where all objectives and deliverables are achieved. By the beginning of Week 4, the point at which activities in each are now dependent on satisfactory completion of others, the project manager must ensure that schedule slips don't start to appear because of those dependencies.

The project manager needs to do the following:

♦ Facilitate cooperation and productive work among the data mart's team members, the user community, and others with whom interaction needs to occur (e.g., IT managers)

♦ Ensure that scope creep is managed and that any additional requirements identified by users (discussed earlier in this chapter) are carefully screened and if added to the data mart's overall proposed functionality, have a minmal impact on schedule and budget

♦ Constantly function in an early warning capacity, spending sufficient time with each team member, ensuring that morale stays high, and so on

You Know You're in Trouble When

Watch out for the following symptoms of big design-phase problems to come:

♦ The business analyst reports that not only are a large number of requests for additional features coming in from users, but much of the data mart functionality identified and agreed to during the scope is being challenged.

♦ Only one or two of the products being evaluated have been successfully installed; the rest continually "bomb out" and can't be used.

♦ The source data analyst is unable to gain access to any of the data sources.

♦ The team member responsible for the data mart's database design doesn't come close to finishing the list of all attributes that the data mart will contain.

TIP Pay particular attention to how results from the data mart scope are used. As mentioned earlier in this chapter, Week 3's activities are structured in such a way as to minimize dependencies among the parallel threads. Even so, the project manager needs to sense the potential for problems the following week as the interweaving among these activity streams begins. One way to do that is to see how well each team uses the results of the project scope (functionality-fact matrix, identified data sources, etc.) as input to its Week 3 work.

♦ The infrastructure and systems analyst is spectacularly unsuccessful in scheduling necessary meetings with networking and database administration managers.

♦ There is disagreement that is not resolved by the end of the week about information flows among the various source applications. No one can be found who can authoritatively describe the details of the eastern U.S. temporary employee system's contents being loaded into the western U.S. temporary employee system.

Basically, failure to make significant progress in any of the parallel streams of design activity is cause for worry that serious problems will occur in the weeks ahead.

Week 3 Spotlight on the Business Analyst

Even though the entire team is working at a quick pace during Week 3, the key individual is the data mart business analyst. The intensive, week-long work with the users yields two significant benefits with regards to the project being able to move forward through the design phase: validation and closure of the functionality to be provided by the data mart and a much more detailed, "data martish" look at those requirements.

The data mart business analyst must be able to straddle both the business and technology worlds. An analyst who, for example, is highly qualified to work with the users to validate and close requirements but couldn't translate requirements for drill-down paths, or the varying views of data required by different users, will be of little value to moving the data mart project forward in pace with rapid development.

It's important that the person assigned to this role have adequate familiarity with the different types of business intelligence that could be provided by the data mart, to ensure that users are guided effectively and

Continues

Week 3 Spotlight on the Business Analyst
(Continued)

efficiently as they make a first pass at the "look and feel" of the environment that will shortly be deployed to them. There is a major difference between the "tell me what happened" business intelligence function of basic querying and reporting and the predictive "tell me what *might* happen" capabilities that can be gained from data mining. A data mart could be built to support either model or both.

The business analyst needs to guide users in this decision by focusing on real-world situations as to how data would be accessed and used and what the business consequences would (or could) be from doing so. A business analyst who is solely a technology-focused front-end tools expert with little or no business skill and experience will, at best, have to give examples to the users in terms of vague generalities rather than in real-world terms that will help them make effective choices in their data mart's functionality.

What You'll Find in This Chapter

Week 4 Activities

    Finalizing the Data Mart Model

    Source Data Analysis

    Data Mart Database Design

    Front-End Tool Evaluation

    Database Product Evaluation

    Middleware Product Evaluation

    System and Infrastructure Analysis

    Information Flows Among Users

How to Achieve the Fourth Week's Goals

    Project Management During Week 4

You Know You're in Trouble When

Analyzing the Data
Environment

A Note to the Reader: Week 4 is crucial in the data mart development, for one main reason: at this point you will be able to see how well the critical path on your project plan will work. Specifically, each of the activities in this week is dependent on the outcome of one or more others from the previous week's work, a trend that will continue throughout design. By the end of this week, how close you are to your project plan will tell you whether or not your design phase will be completed on time.

Expect at least one late night and some weekend work for the entire team. You will also be able to determine, by the end of the week, how well the data mart team has jelled and how efficiently the ever-increasing number of interperson dependencies will work in the upcoming weeks.

Week 4 Activities

In Week 4, design activities take a marked turn toward hands-on work. Some of the activities described in the Week 3 chapter involved some hands-on tasks, but most of those were very preparatory in nature.

This week, though, you start making decisions about design issues. Remember, at the conclusion of Week 4, 40% of the design phase will have been completed, and this means making substantial progress toward converging your Week 3 basic research and analysis with the now-solidified functionality requirements.

Each of the following sections describes the activities that will be performed by team members this week, along with the inputs from previous tasks that are needed to successfully accomplish the week's work. Unlike in Week 3, most of the Week 4 activities will continue for another week or two; therefore, each section also includes a discussion about the amount of progress the team needs to make by the end of the week.

Finalizing the Data Mart Model

At the beginning of Week 4, you need to decide once and for all whether the data mart will be dimensionally oriented to support user OLAP functions (drill-down, multidimensional analysis, etc.). In the chapter dealing with Week 3, it was mentioned that the business analyst's work with the users will provide the input needed to make this decision. Based on what you decide, you may need to do some quick shuffling of data mart project tasks, including the following:

♦ Halting evaluation of OLAP front-end tools and adding one or two more querying/reporting tools to those being considered

♦ Halting evaluation of the multidimensional database product

♦ "Spawning" a thread of analysis activity to work with users on the formats and contents of standard reports that will be regularly generated from the data mart

♦ Switching the focus of the data mart database design from a dimensional orientation toward entity-based design, closely aligned with the report formats that are being defined

Fortunately, most of the design phase activities can continue on their same paths even if your database model changes; source data analysis still needs to be done, systems and infrastructure research and architecture still must occur, and so on.

Source Data Analysis

During Week 3, the team members performing source data analysis were mostly "digging around" their respective data sources. These activities were somewhat unstructured to facilitate discovery of potential problems and issues without the constraints of preconceived notions about data contents and their quality. In Week 4, substantial progress must be made in understanding the source data.

Inputs

All source analysts start with their logs of Week 3 findings, such as the following:

♦ What is in each data source (both structure and content)

♦ What is missing (data gaps)

♦ What data elements have rows or records with invalid values (or at least a value that doesn't match the documented permissible ranges or lists of values)

♦ What the cross-table data integrity problems are (e.g., values don't match)

Because each analyst was working in a free-format manner, though, it is highly unlikely that for all but the smallest data sources a comprehensive study was completed during the week. At best, a general survey has been completed.

To better focus Week 4 activities, the completed list of data mart elements prepared by the target database analyst is used to guide what elements will be analyzed in detail (Figure WK4.1).

Tasks

Not only does each data element that will be included in the data mart need to be analyzed (or reanalyzed) in detail, but a complete first draft of all source-to-target mappings needs to be created.

To most effectively and efficiently create the source-to-target mappings, the team must divide specific tasks into three groupings: *basic analysis tasks*; *advanced analysis tasks*, and *transformation analysis tasks*. Recall that it is recommended that each data source be assigned to one team member, meaning that sets of tasks will be occurring in parallel. Also, if there will be more than one data source, not all data

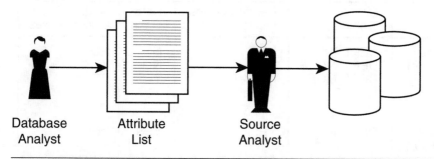

Database   Attribute   Source
Analyst   List   Analyst

Figure WK4.1 Inputs for Week 4 source data analysis.

mart elements will be applicable to each source; therefore, source analysts need to figure out whether they need to spend any time on each data element.

For basic analysis tasks, complete each of the following steps for each data element identified for inclusion in the data mart:

1. Determine if the data mart element will be supplied from the source. If it will not, skip it and go on to the next element; otherwise, continue with the following steps.

2. Note what the data mart analyst has determined so far for that element: what has been determined about the data mart's content model (e.g., only data applying to certain organizations, functions, or geographies), applicable time frames (e.g., only data from the past 18 months), and so on.

3 Review the analysis work (if any) done during the previous week for that element and what was learned.

4 Armed with the information from steps 2 and 3 and using whatever data access tool is available for that source (as discussed in the previous chapter), conduct a thorough study of everything you can possibly find out about that element: whether or not the values needed (i.e., those applying to the organization or function or geography of interest) are included in that source, range of values and list of value discrepancies and data gaps, and so on. Figure WK4.2 illustrates sample output from this step.

Advanced analysis tasks need to be accomplished for any situations that will have a many-to-one mapping between data sources and the data mart. Recall that during the second week of the scope, one of the major activities was the creation of

Source	Data Element	Needed Values Included	Data Gaps	Value Discrepancies
Expenses (worldwide)	DEPT_ID DEPT_NAME DEPT_MGR	YES YES NO	NO NO YES	NO YES *****
Revenues (worldwide)	DEPT_ID	YES	YES	YES

Figure WK4.2 Sample output from detailed data element analysis.

T **I P** Combine elements when appropriate. Though the steps for basic analysis tasks are written to be accomplished for each data element of interest, there will likely be some data elements that are so closely related that it makes sense to combine them and perform the steps for each in conjunction with one another. This is usually the case with elements that could be considered as "amplifying data" for basic concepts such as products, customers, or organizations. For example, you might want to combine your analysis for product family codes and product family names; likewise, elements relating to customers (names, addresses, cities and states, etc.) could be handled together.

Note that for most of these combined-element situations, you are likely analyzing data related to what will eventually be the dimensions of your database model.

the fact-data source matrix (illustrated in Figures WK2.1 and WK2.2). This matrix will be a guide whether or not the following steps need to be accomplished for each element. When a row in the matrix has more than one cell shaded—indicating that more than one data source will provide inputs to a fact—all source data analysts need to do the following tasks:

1. Since the fact-data source matrix shows the relationships between data sources and groups of elements, you need to decompose each fact-data source relationship to the element level and determine whether there is a many-to-one relationship for that element (as shown in Figure WK4.3). If not, you can skip the following steps; otherwise, proceed.

2. Determine if each of the sources for that element will supply a different "slice" of data to the data mart (i.e., the many-to-one relationship is non-overlapping). An example would be when each element about temporary employees in the eastern United States *always* comes from one application's database, and the equivalent elements about temporary employees in the western United States *always* coming from the other application.

3. Analyze the encoding of each of data source for the element to see if there are any potential problems, such as four-digit unique departmental IDs in one application and six-character alphanumeric fields in another, or overlapping values (e.g., the same four-digit number for different departments in each

Data Sources

	ERES—Enterprise Revenue and Expense System	TEA—Temporary Employees' Assignments (Eastern U.S.)	TEA—Temporary Employees' Assignments (Western U.S.)	PEA—Permanent Employees' Assignments
Facts				
Previous two years' quarterly expenditures by category, by department, and by office	▓	▓	▓	▓
Two years' historical head count by month, by department		▓	▓	▓
Forecasted revenues by territory, by quarter				
Previous three years' revenues by territory, by month	▓			
...				

Fact	Element	Many-to-One?
Two years' historical head count by month, by department	MONTH	NO
	YEAR	NO
	NUM_EMPS	YES

Figure WK4.3 Decomposing the fact-data source relationship.

source). If there are no encoding problems, note that fact; otherwise, document the problem.

With transformation analysis tasks, be aware that you will not come close to completing work in the area of source-to-target mapping and transformation during the fourth week, but you should use the preceding information to get to the point where you have a fairly detailed first draft of what will have to occur. To ensure adequate progress during Week 4, this group of tasks needs to begin by midday Thursday:

1. For each element, determine whether there will be an exact match between the contents in the source(s) and the data mart—basically, a straightforward copying operation. This means no summarization or transformation of any type will occur.

2. If there will *not* be a simple copying operation from data source to data mart, make a best guess as to the type of transformation that will need to occur: summarization, convergence of content from multiple sources (see Figure WK4.4), change in encoded values (e.g., through a look-up table).

Progress by Week's End

By the end of Week 4, you should have no big surprises of the project show-stopper variety waiting for you with regards to your data mart's sources. You won't know all the answers, but you will have, for all data elements, enough information so that

T I P All the steps described in this section are absolutely necessary for any data source. If, however, the data mart's contents will be provided in their entirety (or primarily) from an existing data warehouse, you can likely move through the sometimes tedious analysis steps more quickly than when data sources will be used directly to supply the data mart. This assumes, of course, that these steps were already done when the data warehouse was created and that there is high confidence that the data warehouse's content is "clean." You do, however, need to make a pass through every warehouse-resident data element to make sure of this, so *never* skip the source analysis effort just because a data warehouse exists. Just increase the pace as you see fit.

Fact	Data Element	Source(s)	Source(s)
Head count by Department by Month	NUM_EMPS	Temporary Eastern Employees	SUM(HC)
		Temporary Western Employees	SUM(HC)
		All_PERM_EMPS	SUM(EMPS)

Figure WK4.4 Multiple sources supplying a single data mart element.

you can dedicate the following week's activities in this stream of activities to closing up a small, manageable number of issues rather than scrambling to catch up as data mart design is completed.

Data Mart Database Design

The following sections describe the database design activities you need to accomplish during Week 4.

Inputs

During Week 3, the data mart team's business analyst worked with the users to define how data will be used in terms of cross-tab report formats and drilling paths (both up and down). This information, coupled with the initial attribute-oriented data analysis work done the previous week, serves as input for the database design work done this week.

Tasks

During Week 4, the database designer should concentrate on analyzing dimensions and levels that are likely to be part of your data mart's data model. The goal is by the end of the week to have a good idea of the framework of your data mart in terms of the pathways into the mart's contents and the way pieces of data will correlate. A recommended set of steps follows:

1. Identify all the dimensions that your model is likely to require. During the scope, you identified all the facts required to support the data mart's functionality (for example, two years' historical head count by month, by department). It's a fairly straightforward process to create a consolidated list of dimensions

from the facts (time and organization in the example). Other dimensions likely to be part of your data model are geography, product, and customer.

2. Identify all the possible levels for each of your dimensions. It's critical to analyze each dimension identified in the previous step with regards to the levels of detail possible in each. For example, time might be represented by the following hierarchy:

   ♦ Year

   ♦ Quarter

   ♦ Month

   ♦ Day

   Likewise, an organization may contain the following levels:

   ♦ Business group

   ♦ Territory

   ♦ Region

   ♦ Business location

   ♦ Department

   The complete set of levels you identify will play a critical role in the steps that follow.

3. Determine whether a dimension can be categorized as "rapidly changing" or "slow changing."

   ♦ Some dimensions will be fairly constant throughout the life of the data mart in terms of the framework provided by their contents or at least be affected by change infrequently. For example, the "organization" may be affected only by reorganization activity (something that seldom occurs within the company) or by the addition of new business locations (an infrequent occurrence). However, a "sales organization" dimension may change frequently (new salespeople added and taking over existing accounts from other salespeople).

   The reason you need to identify the frequency of change in each dimension is that your physical design will be affected by this facet of your data model.

Rapidly changing dimensions will likely require reorganization of the data mart contents as change occurs, subject to the business rules you determine for each hierarchy. For example, if new salespeople are added and assume responsibility for sets of customer accounts, there may be a business rule that they will still be measured against the sales history of those customers. A data mart designed to track and analyze sales performance needs to be able to support the reassignment of past revenue based on hierarchy changes.

4. Perform combinatorial analysis on the dimensions that relate to one another. The next thing you need to do is take the basic dimension and level information you've determined and catalog various combinations that will be significant to the data mart. For example, forecasted revenues by territory by quarter are bounded by two dimensions: organization and time. If you use those two dimensions and the levels you identified in Step 2, the following combinations are possible:

- Business group by year

- Business group by quarter

- Business group by month

- Business group by day

- Territory by year

- Territory by quarter

- Territory by month

- Territory by day

- Region by year

- Region by quarter

- Region by month

- Region by day

- Business location by year

- Business location by quarter

- Business location by month

♦ Business location by day

♦ Department by year

♦ Department by quarter

♦ Department by month

♦ Department by day

The principles of combinatorial analysis would tell you that more dimensions bounding a given fact and more levels for each dimension yield a very large number of combinations. Use your discretion for, say, a fact bounded by six dimensions, each having between 7 and 10 levels: don't catalog every possible combination, but rather the ones that make the most sense in likely business use. Even in the above example, you would likely eliminate all the ...by day combinations because the mission of the data mart—budget support—doesn't require information about daily expenditures (as determined during the scope phase).

5. Assign a weighted business value to each of the combinations identified in Step 4.

The purpose of identifying the cross-dimension, cross-level combinations is to provide a detailed framework for the purpose of what-if analysis and subsequent assignment of a weighted measure of perceived business value if data is available at each specific combination. For example, a scoring system with 10 having the highest value and 0 the lowest might yield the information about the levels necessary to bound the fact "forecasted revenues by territory, by quarter" shown in Table WK4.1.

Using the business community's consensus about the need for data at various combinations of levels, as represented in Table WK4.1, you will have a fairly clear conceptual picture of the dimensions and levels of detail you'll need as you progress further in your database design.

Progress by Week's End

By the end of Week 4, you have a detailed understanding of hierarchies and levels that is grounded in the business value to be delivered by the data mart. Coupled with the detailed attribute analysis of the previous week, that understanding gives you a fairly detailed picture of what your data mart's contents should be.

Table WK4.1 Cross-Level Business Value Matrix

Level Combinations	Business Value
Business group by year	10
Business group by quarter	10
Business group by month	5
Business group by day	0
Territory by year	10
Territory by quarter	10
Territory by month	7
Territory by day	0
Region by year	10
Region by quarter	10
Region by month	10
Region by day	0
Business location by year	10
Business location by quarter	10
Business location by month	10
Business location by day	0
Department by year	0
Department by quarter	0
Department by month	0
Department by day	0

Front-End Tool Evaluation

The following sections describe the activities you must perform with regards to evaluating front-end tools.

Inputs

During Week 3, the following were accomplished:

T I P Use the drill-down and drill-up analysis for validation. During Week 3, the business analyst worked with users to identify (among other pieces of data mart functionality) the drill-down and drill-up paths that need to be supported in the data mart. The weighted business values of the various cross-dimension combinations of levels can and should be validated against the word-oriented drill path requirements.

T I P Look at other data marts and data warehouses when you analyze dimensions and levels. Even if your mission is to create a tactical, "quick-strike" data mart, it is a good idea to look at other data marts and data warehouses in the enterprise with respect to the levels of detail represented for dimensions that will be part of your data mart. A geographically bounded data mart for western region sales analysis and another dedicated to eastern region sales analysis should likely have the same levels of detail within their respective corresponding dimensions, for example.

♦ Installation and configuration of each of the tools being considered (and, possibly, the elimination of those that couldn't be successfully installed)

♦ Identification of OLAP and reporting/querying functions by the business analyst, working with the users

♦ Creation of a list of data elements that will be in the data mart, along with sample data, by the database analyst

All these deliverables will be used during the Week 4 evaluation of the front-end tools.

Tasks

The first activity that needs to be completed as soon as possible in Week 4 is the creation of a small sample database that will be used for the week's hands-on activity. Ideally, this should be small scale that it can be created and populated with test data in one day (i.e., Monday of Week 4). A typical test database will have three or

> ## What About Nondimensional Data Mart Databases?
>
> Analysis of dimension hierarchies and their respective levels is necessary only if you've decided that you will implement your data mart using dimensional modeling techniques, either with a multidimensional database engine or through fact and dimension tables organized as a star schema in a relational DBMS—right?
>
> Wrong. Even if you decide that your data mart will support standardized reporting and therefore be designed exclusively through use of denormalized relational database tables, it's still critical to analyze dimensions and the respective levels. The reports generated from the data mart can still occur at various levels, regardless of the underlying physical implementation (e.g., report-time joining of dimension and fact tables versus prestoring dimensional information within the structure of your denormalized tables, which are, basically, fact tables). You need to be able to determine the level of granularity of the various data elements in combination with one another. What is the lowest level of detail you'll need? What specific aggregations of data need to be prestored for performance reasons, and which ones can you create at report time by grouping and summarizing lower level data together?
>
> Your physical database design will be impacted by dimensions and their respective levels of detail, regardless of the underlying physical implementation, so don't skip this process.

four fact tables, each bounded by two or three dimensions, and with 75 to 100 rows of sample data in each fact table. Nothing too elegant, nothing too complex: Just enough so that queries can be executed and reports run throughout the week as the team digs into the functionality and usability of each tool.

Next, starting with the business analyst's detailed list of OLAP and reporting/querying functionality, the team will see whether each tool can support the required functionality. These tests should be run side-by-side on each tool to most efficiently make comparisons between the products and be run by the users, assisted by the data mart team members.

You must evaluate many aspects of each tool under consideration. To apply some order to this process over the three-week period in which this will occur, it is recommended that Week 4's activities focus on *business capabilities* (i.e., whether or

Why Not Create a Star Schema Model Now?

An admittedly controversial point is why the piecemeal approach to the data mart's database design discussed so far—attributes first, then dimension and level analysis—should be used. Why not just go straight to star schema modeling?

Although star schema modeling from the outset of the design phase is a possibility, the database designer will very likely get quickly bogged down in implementation-specific, physical design issues: Star schema or snowflake schema? Natural keys or surrogate keys? Should a unique identifier be part of each row in a fact table in addition to the foreign keys that relate back to the dimension tables?

It's recommended that you concentrate on concepts and the business aspects of your database environment first; the more you learn, the smoother your eventual database design will be.

not a tool can satisfy the identified business requirements) and *usability* (how easy it is to perform each function). During Week 5, following this initial study, effort can switch toward product infrastructure and systems issues.

Progress by Week's End

By the end of Week 4, you need to be at the following state with regards to your front-end tools:

♦ All functionality identified by the business analyst and the users will have been tested in each product

♦ Ease of use—admittedly a subjective evaluation criterion, but an important one—will be evaluated for each functionality item, in each tool, and discussed in the group

♦ Any problem that has surfaced during the week has been checked out with the vendor with respect to a resolution

By this time you will have two weeks of intensive, hands-on work with each product. If any product doesn't seem to be capable of doing the job, or the startup problems (installation, connectivity, etc.) are too troublesome, and no solutions are imminent, you will likely want to eliminate that tool from further consideration.

Database Product Evaluation

The following sections describe the product evaluation tasks you need to perform during Week 4.

Inputs

During Week 3, the team member responsible for evaluating DBMS products performed a variety of preliminary tasks, including some hands-on checking out of each product after installation. In addition, the database analyst had created a list of attributes that will be in the data mart.

Tasks

This week the database product evaluator will begin by doing the following:

♦ Creating first-draft versions of the database structure in each of the products, based on recommendations provided by the database analyst

♦ Creating flat files with sample data, extracted from one or more of the eventual data mart's sources

♦ Loading the data from the flat files into each database

Ideally, the above tasks should be completed by midweek, leading the way for two or three days of thorough hands-on analysis of each database product's performance. Failure to complete the tasks indicates that you may have problems ahead in your database environment.

Specifically, you want to take a first look at how each RDBMS performs when a large number of tables are joined, as will likely occur in your data mart. A number of queries need to be run to establish likely performance patterns within each of the products. With regards to the multidimensional database product under consideration, you want to take a careful look at initial load and calculation times and recalculation times when the database is refreshed.

Progress by Week's End

This week's work sets the stage for formal database product evaluation during the following two weeks. As with front-end tools, any product that appears to have insurmountable problems in terms of installation and configuration, or abysmally poor performance, should likely be removed from further consideration.

Middleware Product Evaluation

The following sections describe how you should evaluate middleware products during Week 4.

Inputs

During the previous week, the middleware product analyst conducted preliminary evaluation of each tool under consideration. In addition, the source data analyst(s) and data mart database analyst completed preliminary work in the source and target environments, respectively. Finally, the business analyst's work in identifying drill-down and drill-through requirements provides a fairly accurate model of the lowest levels of summarization or detail that need to be present in the data mart.

Tasks

As with the database product evaluation, the team member assigned to middleware product evaluation needs to add more substance to the initial, cursory work done during Week 3. Starting with the basic information about source data analysis— known data gaps, cross-source data value inconsistencies, business rules, and so on—source-to-target mappings and transformations will be created in each tool. Any "cannot do" situations (or situations that require custom code to be written and interfaced with the tool) need to be noted.

Features to be evaluated include the following:

♦ The way summarization is performed

♦ The way contents from multiple sources are converged to provide input to a single data mart target element

♦ Whether transformation look-up tables can be created (including dynamically) and the way they are used

♦ Other product capabilities that the work done during Week 3 has indicated will likely be needed

Progress by Week's End

As with the other threads of product evaluation, the goal is to provide a bridge between Week 3's basic research and the decision-making that will occur during Weeks 5 and 6. Eliminating a product by the end of the week is a possibility.

Systems and Infrastructure Analysis

It's important not to overlook systems and infrastructure analysis tasks during Week 4. The following sections describe what you need to do.

Inputs

The systems and infrastructure analyst will use several inputs in the required Week 4 work:

♦ Work done in this area the prior week (i.e., the basic research)

♦ The results of the process analyst's study of interapplication data flows

♦ Any issues that have surfaced with regards to problems with any of the products currently under evaluation, such as poor performance, concerns about scalability, and connectivity or configuration incompatibilities

Tasks

During Week 4, systems and infrastructure work will concentrate on two areas. First, and most important, is supporting the ongoing product evaluation efforts. The systems/infrastructure team member will act as point person to analyze any reported problems and come up with a solution (if there is one). Whenever possible, this individual will be the one performing the trouble-shooting; if necessary, though, the analyst will be the conduit to lining up support from the IT organization.

The other area is the work done by the process analyst, with preliminary work done with regard to populating the data mart (i.e., all the source-to-target movement of data). Although it's desirable to have the middleware tool handle extraction, movement, and loading, it's always possible that scripts or utilities will be needed if the tool won't suffice. A high-level, end-to-end architecture of all data movement, together with possible implementation alternatives (languages, platforms on which functions will be performed, etc.), needs to be prepared.

Progress by Week's End

The systems and infrastructure stream of tasks is notoriously unpredictable. On some data mart projects it involves little or no activity other than a few trouble-shooting tasks. This is particularly the case for low-tech data marts: restocking the data mart directly from monthly source database backup tapes with SQL

INSERT statements rather than using a middleware tool, for example. It is also often true when a data mart's content is being provided from a high-quality data warehouse.

Other times, however, system problems seem nonstop, and the systems/infrastructure analyst is constantly on the project's critical path, multiplexed among several problem areas. Therefore, it is the responsibility of both the data mart project manager and the systems/infrastructure analyst to carefully and continuously monitor the "state of the data mart project" in this area and to respond aggressively to problems, if necessary. This area of activity is usually more reactive than are the other parts of the data mart project, but they are just as important.

Information Flows Among Users

During Week 3, the process modeler concentrated on system- and application-level flows of information. This week, activity switches to the flows of information among users.

Inputs

As discussed in the previous chapter, the business analyst's week-long work with the users has identified a community of passive data mart users who won't be directly slicing and dicing data or performing complex OLAP functions or creating their own report templates. Instead, these passive users will rely on activity by other users or the system itself for the business intelligence they will receive once the data mart has been deployed (Figure WK4.5).

Tasks

The process modeler needs to spend significant time this week working with each of the passive users who has been identified or at least one knowledgeable member from each organization who can, with certainty, represent the business intelligence needs of his or her colleagues. The process modeler needs to determine the flows of information among the user community as they apply to the passive users. Specifically, the following questions need to be answered:

♦ Is a passive user's need for data mart-generated information *static* or *dynamic*? Regularly accessed, unvarying reports are examples of static information; specific, unpredictable requests made of others (i.e., the "power users" of the data mart) are considered dynamic information.

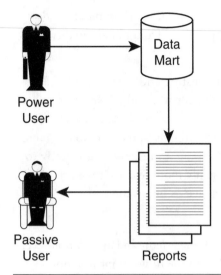

Figure WK4.5 Classes of data mart users.

♦ For each of the information requests, what is the proposed interaction between the users and the data mart? Will the data mart automatically generate a report? Under what circumstances is a request made from the passive user to the person who will create a form or execute a query?

♦ What is the exact mechanism through which the passive user will access information? Is it *push oriented* (i.e., e-mailed to the person) or *pull oriented* (i.e., posted on the company intranet and accessed only when the user wants or needs it)?

Progress by Week's End

The goal of the process modeler's work is to provide enough input to the front-end tool evaluation team so that during Weeks 5 and 6, tools can be evaluated for their capability to serve the needs of the passive users as well. Regularly scheduled report runs, report distribution, and all other aspects of passive user support can be reviewed for each tool.

How to Achieve the Fourth Week's Goals

Figure WK4.6 illustrates the day-by-day progress for each of the team members during Week 4 of the project. Again, it's important to realize that compared with

Week 3, there are many interdependencies among tasks in each of the activity streams. And given the tight schedule the team is operating under, it's important to stick as close as possible to the times allotted on your project plan.

Project Management During Week 4

A new set of challenges faces the project manager during Week 4. In addition to the increased interaction among team members already mentioned, the dependencies on people external to the data mart project—specifically IT personnel—become very noticeable.

The project manager needs to do a day-by-day assessment of progress and do whatever is necessary to overcome roadblocks encountered by any team members. It is imperative that this manager wander around, spending time with each team member. There should be a minimum of formal meetings this week. Instead, the project manager should have many quick interactions with each team member throughout the week, both to get verbal feedback and to home in on any nonverbal cues that problems are brewing.

Finally, judging by the progress during this week, the project manager needs to take a fresh look at the project plan late on Friday and determine if the design phase schedule is still realistic and achievable.

You Know You're in Trouble When

The two areas in which significant problems are likely to surface this week are product evaluation and source data analysis. For example:

- ◆ Users are totally unimpressed with all the front-end tools after spending a week working with them.

- ◆ Users spend a lot of their hands-on time musing about functionality that has never been requested up to this point (e.g., access to different sets of data). All attempts to get the users back on track are met with resistance.

- ◆ "Show-stoppers" are reached in every product in at least one of the categories (front-end tools, middleware, and/or databases). All attempts to resolve configuration issues or other problems come to naught.

- ◆ A source data analyst finds serious problems that data transformation cannot address, such as serious data gaps, duplicate IDs, or large numbers of anomalies

Activity Stream	Monday	Tuesday	Wednesday	Thursday	Friday
Data Analysis	Review user functionality models	Group and organize Attributes	"What-if" alternative models	"What-if" alternative models	Select data model type: dimensional; denormalized; other
Data Modeling	Dimensions: identify	Levels of dimensions	"What-if" dimensions and levels	"What-if" dimensions and levels	
Source Analysis	Focused data analysis	Focused data analysis	Focused data analysis	Preliminary Transformation Analysis	Preliminary Transformation Analysis
Front-End Product Evaluation	Create sample databases	Business capabilities evaluation	Business capabilities evaluation	Business capabilities evaluation	Business capabilities evaluation
Middleware Evaluation	Extraction	Extraction	Transformation	Transformation	Transformation
DBMS Evaluation	Create "first-draft" database structure	Create flat files with sample data	Finish loading	Test database access and performance	Test database access and performance
		Load data from flat files into database	Test database access and performance		
Systems/ Infrastructure Analysis	Review process analysis flows	Research cross-system flows and dependencies	Research cross-system flows and dependencies	Research cross-system flows and dependencies	Research cross-system flows and dependencies
		Support testing	Support testing	Support testing	Support testing

Figure WK4.6 The fourth week's calendar of activities.

with respect to business rules. For example, unique identifiers are supposed to exist for all departments across the enterprise, and a department can belong to only one business location. It turns out, though, that department IDs are *not* unique across business locations, meaning that what appears to be a many-to-many relationship between departments and business locations is actually a meaningless jumble of budget information that will take a long time to untangle.

Week 4 Spotlight on the Source Data Analyst

From the beginning moments of design, hands-on source data analysis is a top priority, and your source data analyst absolutely cannot just go through the motions. This person must dig into the data and as the contents of the data mart become defined, narrow the area of activity to those elements that are of the highest priority because of the imminent need for their inclusion in the data mart.

The source data analyst needs to work with both the structural and content aspects of each data source, such as:

Structural:

Database table and column definitions, constraints, and other Data Definition Language (DDL) statements.

The structures of source data files (e.g., VSAM or ISAM files on an IBM mainframe.

RMS files on a VAX/VMS system; etc.), as described in source program listings.

COBOL copy book definitions (if used) definitions that may be stored in a centralized data dictionary or repository.

Content:

Using simple SQL SELECT statements to analyze data source samples, obtain row counts within a table (e.g., using SELECT COUNT(*) FROM...), determining if values of columns are within the appropriate ranges of values, etc.

Continues

Week 4 Spotlight on the Source Data Analyst
(Continued)

Using complex SQL statements, such as nested SELECT statements with IN, NOT IN, EXISTS, and other clauses to do referential integrity analysis (i.e., ensuring that appropriate cross-table row-to-row relationships exist within the source and, when they don't, identifying those rows of data that need to be addressed as part of the extraction and transformation process).

Using fourth-generation language (4GL) code, such as FOCUS or SAS, to analyze the contents of non-RDBMS sources (e.g., flat files) or to supplement the SQL analysis of relational data sources.

Notice that the tasks listed above, and dozens of other similar tasks, require that a source data analyst be multifaceted in his or her repertoire. SQL experience and knowledge is, in almost all situations, a mandatory requirement but it also needs to be supplemented by knowledge of data access tools for nonrelational sources. When preparing a data mart project team through proactive just-in-time training, it's a good idea to take a quick look at the tools that are likely to be needed for source data analysis. If members of the project team don't already possess those skills, *adequate* training needs to be scheduled as quickly as possible.

What You'll Find in This Chapter

Evaluating Front-End
Tools

A Note to the Reader: There are now three weeks ahead in the design phase, and you still need to finalize your tool selection, complete the data mart's database design, and finalize all extraction and transformation routines.

During Week 5, your most significant task is to take all the front-end tool evaluation work done during the previous two weeks, combine it with the database design work done so far, and embark on an intensive two-week final selection process. Team members will work together to provide a broader, integration-oriented perspective of the various areas of the data mart as follows:

♦ *The business analyst and process modeler will continue to work with the data mart's users on front-end tool evaluation.*

♦ *The process modeler will work with the systems and infrastructure analyst on the data mart's security model.*

♦ *The source data analyst(s) and the database designer will work together to develop an end-to-end conceptual model of data movement from source(s) to the data mart's database.*

♦ *The team members assigned to database and middleware product evaluation will work together, determining how various combinations of products operate.*

This is all in preparation for Week 6, when everyone on the team will join together to embark on end-to-end, comprehensive testing and product selection.

Week 5 Activities

The activities pursued by the project team during Week 5 are partly continuations of those that occurred during the previous weeks (product evaluation, for example) and partly new sets of tasks that must be completed during the design phase (an example of the latter is the data mart's security model). The sections below describe the activities and tasks that must occur during Week 5.

Front-End Tool Evaluation

This section assumes that your project is continuing along the OLAP/multidimensional path. If you decided during Week 4 that your data mart will be switched to a basic reporting/querying mission, using denormalized database tables, you will want to modify your evaluation criteria for the products you're considering. You still want to evaluate look-and-feel usability, comparative features, and performance, but you don't need to be concerned about the dimensional criteria listed below.

Input

The front-end tool evaluation team—users, the business analyst, and the process modeler—will build on their "poking around" work from the week before. The database product evaluator has also created draft structures within each of the products under consideration; these should be frozen for use by the tool evaluation team during Week 5.

Tasks

There are many different ways you can proceed with front-end tool evaluation during Week 5 (and during Week 6, as well). The list presented in this section can be used as a guide. (This list—Dr. E.F. Codd's *Twelve Rules for Evaluating OLAP Products*—is adapted from the one presented in www.arborsoft.com/essbase/wht_ppr/coddc3.html.)

Among the areas you need to evaluate are the following:

♦ *Each product's multidimensional conceptual view.* A closer look, in the context of the data mart's business mission, needs to be taken at how information is viewed in a multidimensional manner. Any product features not explored in the

TIP For more information about OLAP product evaluation and selection, see *OLAP Solutions: Building Multidimensional Information Systems*, by Erik Thomsen (John Wiley & Sons, Inc., 1997).

previous week need to be carefully researched to give users as complete an understanding as possible of what the product will be able to do for them if they select it.

♦ *Transparency*. Some analytical environments use a spreadsheet program such as Microsoft Excel as the primary user interface. Data is brought back into Excel and manipulated accordingly through the spreadsheet's functions (including pivot tables). If this is being considered for your environment, carefully review the interfaces between the underlying OLAP engine and the spreadsheet program to ensure that the interfaces are transparent to users.

♦ *Consistent reporting performance*. As the underlying database grows or becomes more complex (e.g., additional dimensions are included), users' response time and the overall systems performance should not considerably degrade. In other words, the tool and its supporting environment must be scalable.

♦ *Architecture*. Dr. Codd's rules state, "It is therefore mandatory that the OLAP products be capable of operating in a client/server environment." It's important to realize, though, that *client/server* should *not* be deemed to mean a classical two-tier environment. It's quite possible that your data mart will be built around Internet technologies— it will be Web enabled—with a browser-based, thin client front end. The important point for your Week 5 evaluation is to carefully study all the architectural options you have for each tool, along with the respective tradeoffs.

♦ *Generic dimensionality*. All dimensions are created equal. You need to make sure that if you create a model with five dimensions—organization, time, geography, customer, and product—you can do reporting functions based on any of them.

♦ *Dynamic sparse matrix handling*. You want to see what each product does with respect to storage efficiency; even if you have an underlying relational database, the relational OLAP (ROLAP) product will likely perform some degree of caching of models it creates from the underlying data. How those models are stored, how much disk storage is needed, and other physical implementation factors need to be thoroughly understood.

◆ *Multiuser support.* You want to make sure that users aren't "put on hold" because someone else is accessing data mart contents.

◆ *Unrestricted cross-dimensional operations.* Coincidentally, the example given in the referenced Web site is a budgeting one, with five dimensions: accounts (sales, overhead, etc.); corporate (a geographical/organization hierarchy); fiscal year (decomposed into quarters, then into months); products; and scenario (budgeted, actual, variance). A cross-dimensional operation would be needed in the case of overhead allocation, according to the business rule that overhead equals the percentage of total sales represented by the sales of each individual local office multiplied by total corporate overhead. Note that this calculation involves data from the organization and accounts dimensions. You want to see if your tools under consideration have any restrictions in this area.

◆ *Intuitive data manipulation.* You want to determine how intuitive it is to navigate through a tool's capabilities. Can you do this without having to continually access pull-down menus or to reset a navigation path?

◆ *Flexible reporting.* Having a robust, efficient dimensional model of your business's data in your data mart is one thing. Being able to gain business intelligence through very flexible reporting and querying is another. Your users have to explore the outer bounds of each tool's reporting capabilities, including features and options they may rarely use, to see how the tools stack up against one another.

◆ *The number of dimensions and aggregation levels.* The referenced Web site refers to a 19-dimensional actuarial model as an argument that a tool should support an unlimited number of dimensions. What is more important to you is whether your anticipated number of dimensions, and the levels of each, can be supported within each product.

Note: The "accessibility" evaluation criterion from Dr. Codd's rules—guidelines that deal with schema mapping rules—is not included in the list because it's more of an architectural issue for large data warehouse environments.

In addition to the areas on the list, report distribution and/or posting support for passive users (discussed in the previous two chapters) need to be evaluated.

Progress by Week's End

By the end of Week 5, there should be a clear-cut front-runner in the tool evaluation derby. There is still one more week of work left before product selection occurs, but you want to ensure that during Week 6 the majority of your efforts can be concentrated on one of the products with minimal interaction with the other.

Narrowing the field is an important milestone to reach in the project because during Week 6, end-to-end implementation-specific (physical) design of the data mart, from sources to the data mart to the user interaction, needs to begin. Given that front-end tools vary from one another in many ways (scripting languages, screen painting, parameter passing, connectivity models, etc.), you don't want to have to design all of these characteristics for more than one tool.

Database and Middleware Product Evaluation

During Weeks 3 and 4, preliminary work with each DBMS product occurred; you checked out tuning and performance enhancement options, utilities (backup, restore, etc.), and other capabilities. Additionally, there is now a draft design of the data mart's database, prepared by the database modeler.

In the area of middleware products, a very clear picture should now be available of the relative capabilities of those products under consideration.

Finally, the source analysis work from the previous two weeks presents an accurate picture of the state of each of the data mart's sources: the quality of the data, the characteristics, and the attributes (i.e., data types and sizes, the way fields are encoded, etc.).

Tasks

In Week 5, initial end-to-end integration design of the source-to-target will occur. The team members assigned to the database and middleware product evaluation will work together, along with the source analysts (who will also work with the database designer, as discussed later). The group will spend the week performing a series of tests, starting with a fairly simple attempt to establish end-to-end connectivity for data movement. Each successive test builds on the success of the prior one to the point where the team will know exactly what is possible in the real-world data mart environment for each product configuration under consideration. A sample day-by-day schedule for these tests that you can use as a framework for your data mart project is as follows:

♦ *Monday*. Starting with any of the data sources (if more than one), perform an end-to-end (i.e., source-to-data mart) movement of at least 50 data elements, loaded into at least three target tables in the data mart (Figure WK5.1). Do this with each of the possible configurations for the middleware tools and DBMS products under consideration (i.e., if two middleware products and two DBMSs are still in contention, four different configurations need to be tested). The team's objective at this point is to establish that end-to-end connectivity can be done with all the product configurations under consideration; only minimal attention needs to be paid to the semantics of the data movement (i.e., worrying about whether or not summarization is done correctly and at the right level, whether or not exception handling is set up). The objective is that by the end of the day, there will be a clear understanding of which end-to-end configurations work in terms of the connectivity and which ones don't.

♦ *Tuesday*. If there is more than one source to the data mart, Monday's activity needs to be repeated for each data source. Again, the goal is to verify end-to-end connectivity, but now on a systemwide basis rather than just a test data source.

If, however, there is only one source to the data mart, the steps described for Wednesday will be moved up to Tuesday, and the rest of the week's activities will be accelerated by one day. Friday is a flexible day, so the following week's evaluation activity can be accelerated into this week (which could happen anyway if Thursday's testing goes well).

♦ *Wednesday*. Once connectivity is established, the team's goal for the first data source tested is to perform a realistic end-to-end initial load test for the data mart. This will be done as follows:

◇ *Wednesday morning*. The draft design of the data mart's database will be used as the starting point, and the team will quickly develop a complete source-to-target design to populate the data mart in half a day (Wednesday morning). If the data mart's database will be modeled dimensionally, an ideal target database for this test will be two to three fact tables with at least three dimensions for each. The data volume moved from the source should be at least 10 megabytes.

◇ *Wednesday afternoon*. The middleware evaluator and the source data analyst (the one responsible for the source being tested) will, successively for each of the middleware tools, create the mappings, transformations, scripts, callouts, and whatever else is necessary to instantiate the morning's design work. In parallel, the database product developer will create a database schema in each DBMS product based on the target environment.

- *Thursday.* The team will spend the day doing end-to-end testing of the configuration developed Wednesday, alternating among the middleware-DBMS configurations. In addition to verifying that connectivity is maintained and that each configuration works with the additional breadth of data in this round of testing compared with Monday's, the team now will also start looking at performance. The time it takes for each configuration's end-to-end, extraction-through-loading processing will be logged and compared with that for the others. Any problem areas must be analyzed to learn what issues might exist.

- *Friday.* If everything went well on Thursday, the end-to-end testing will be expanded to include larger volumes of data, more data mart tables, and the other data sources, allowing a head start on Week 6's evaluation work. If, however, problems have occurred and Thursday's work wasn't completed, Friday becomes a catch-up day to ensure all the configurations are tested.

Progress by Week's End

The goal of the team working on the database and middleware product evaluation for Week 5 is to set the stage for Week 6, in which much more intensive testing of

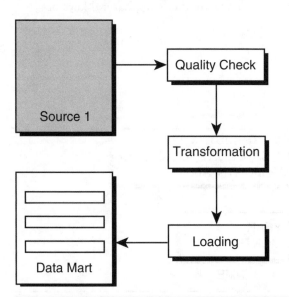

Figure WK5.1 The first end-to-end test for data extraction and loading.

the products will occur. If you think of Week 6 as the dress rehearsal for database and middleware development and Weeks 3 and 4 as the auditioning process, Week 5 has been that in-between stage wherein the team members are learning their lines and adjusting the script based on how each daily rehearsal looks.

Data Mart Database Design

In Week 4, the database analyst created a first-draft database design: either a dimensional model or one based on denormalized tables closely aligned with standard reporting needs, depending on which path the project has followed.

Tasks

During Week 5, the database designer has two primary tasks. The first is to solidify the conceptual database model to the point where it is about 95 percent complete and only a few minor items and open issues remain. For a dimensional model, the database designer needs to do the following (shown in Figure WK5.2):

♦ Finalize the attributes and key fields of every fact table that will be in the model

♦ Finalize the dimensions that will be associated with each fact table

♦ Determine the levels that will be supported for each dimension

♦ Determine how tables will be related to one another (e.g., natural keys or surrogate keys)

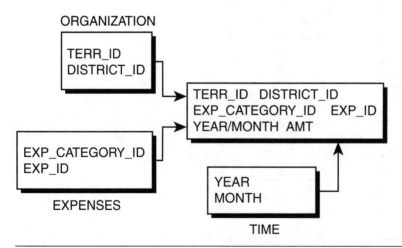

Figure WK5.2 A segment of the data mart's database design (Week 6 version).

If a denormalized relational model will be used, the design of each table needs to be finalized based on the reports that are generated and the query patterns by which users will access the database.

In addition to working on the conceptual database model, the database designer will work with the team performing the database and middleware product evaluations (discussed earlier in this chapter) on an as-needed basis, assisting with definition of the target databases and the loading rules.

Progress by Week's End

The key to success in Week 6 is continued, with steady progress on the data mart's database design.

Systems and Infrastructure: Security Modeling

At this point, the team member responsible for systems and infrastructure analysis has a clear understanding of the capabilities available within the enterprise upon which the data mart will be built. Policies and procedures for hooking up a new application to the enterprise have been discussed with the appropriate IT personnel.

Tasks

This week, the systems/infrastructure analyst teams up with the process modeler to develop the data mart's security architecture. This function is absolutely critical to determining what data will be accessible by various users, and under what circumstances. An entire week should be set aside for these two individuals to work on the security architecture to ensure that by week's end, there is 100 percent clarity as to the complexity of what needs to be implemented in terms of data mart security.

These two team members are assigned to this function because two types of security models need to be created: business rule driven and technology driven (see Figure WK5.3). Together, these two models will make up the data mart's security architecture.

The Data Mart's Business Rule-Driven Security Model Business rule-driven security takes several different forms. At the simplest level is the *data access permissions model*, which is a complete picture of who is permitted to access which pieces of information within the data mart (Figure WK5.4). Note that the data access permissions model also must include data values, when appropriate. For example, it's not sufficient to model that district managers have access to "district head-count estimated growth by business location"; it needs to be noted that the regional district managers have access to information only for their own districts.

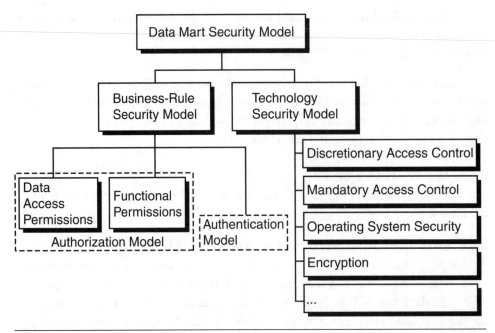

Figure WK5.3 The framework for the data mart security architecture.

The *functional permissions model* explains who is allowed to modify the structure and contents of the data mart, who is permitted to delete contents, who can make a copy of (i.e., replicate) the data mart's tables, and so on. Though many data marts permit only read-only access to its users, some permit users to input data as part of the business mission being supported.

For example, a data mart supporting the budget process may very well be constructed not only to present data to users for their analysis and use, but also (as shown in Figure WK5.5) to collect inputs (e.g., first-line managers' budget requests or district managers' approval or disapproval of their subordinates' requests). In these circumstances, a create-read-update-delete (CRUD) permissions model needs to be defined just as it would be for a transaction processing application.

Together, the data access and functional permissions models make up the data mart authorization model. Authorization, though, is the lowest and simplest level of the overall enterprise security model. Other security and permissions rules that must be considered include the following:

Role	Fact	Permissions
District Manager	Expenses by Month by Category	Own District: Yes Other Districts in Same Territory: Yes Districts in Other Territories: Yes
	Revenues by Month	Own District: Yes Other Districts in Same Territory: Yes Districts in Other Territories: Yes
Territory Manager	Expenses by Month by Category by District	Own Territory: Yes Other Territories: No
	Revenues by Month by District	Own Territory: Yes Other Territories: No

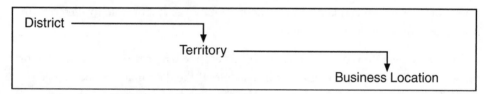

Figure WK5.4 The data access permissions model in the data mart.

- *Authentication.* In a general sense, authentication requires users, applications, or other components of the enterprise to prove that they are who they are supposed to be.

- *Nonrepudiation of delivery.* Users who receive something from another user or directly from the data mart (such as an automatically generated report through e-mail) cannot deny (repudiate) that the delivery has occurred.

- *Nonrepudiation of transmission.* Users who send something to another user (reports that they created, for example) cannot deny that the transmission occurred.

- *Network security services.* If data transmissions need to be encrypted, the transmission points at which such encryption will occur need to be identified

Role	Expenses	Revenues	Working Budget Models
General User	R	R	C R U D
Data Mart Support	R U D	R U D	C R U D

C – CREATE
R – READ
U – UPDATE
D – DELETE

Figure WK5.5 The functional permissions model and read-write data marts.

(e.g., from the data mart to a local area network [LAN]-based user; from the data mart to a remote user over a wide area network [WAN]; or perhaps both.)

The Data Mart's Technology-Driven Security Model While the process modeler focuses on the business rules with respect to data mart security—the *what* aspect of security—the systems/infrastructure analyst is responsible for determining *how* those rules will be implemented.

The implementation decisions made will determine whether or not rapid development of the data mart will continue on schedule. If the data mart can be plugged into infrastructure security services that already exist in the enterprise, there should be little, if any, complexity to implement the appropriate level of protection, and the construction phase can immediately follow the completion of design in Week 8. If, however, it is determined that security services are needed that do not currently exist, the rapid pace of development needs to be immediately halted and a security architecture and design phase commenced before construction begins (Figure WK5.6).

In almost all situations, authorization (both the data access permissions model and the functional permissions model, as described previously) can be implemented through the permissions inherent in the DBMS product you'll be using. Formally known as *discretionary access control*, the SQL grant-revoke statements, or the equivalent in other database products, will be used to specify which users can access various data (or portions of data, such as regional or organizational slices of certain facts), who can modify the data mart's structure, and who has delete permission.

Don't Neglect Security, but Don't Overdo It

Security is absolutely critical to your data mart. As much as hackers intending corporate espionage would like to slip into your corporate network and browse, collecting little tidbits of data here and there, they would be overjoyed to gain access to a data mart in which you've created a tidy, organized package of your corporate business intelligence. Therefore, it's essential that you do an earnest study with regard to the data mart's security requirements.

At the same time, you need to carefully consider what security services are necessary and what others add very little to the protection of your data mart's contents. For example, *traffic padding* is a network security service that is sometimes used in highly sensitive military and national security applications.

The premise behind traffic padding is that not only should the contents of certain transmissions be protected, but the actual volumes of data being transmitted are just as sensitive. If intelligence officials of one country can build an accurate picture of volumes of data being sent from radar sites back to their country of origin at certain times, then by matching those volumes against troop movements, missile test launches, or other military affairs, they can gain insight into the activity a particular radar site is monitoring and take precautionary measures.

With traffic padding, though, transmissions during times of inactivity are padded with garbage data on a regular basis to mask when actual, meaningful messages are being sent. In effect, they try to render any monitoring of the line ineffective if all a hostile country can do is determine volumes of data being sent but not break encryption codes and interpret the contents.

Could traffic padding services be built into network-based transmissions from data sources into the data mart? The answer is yes. Would there be any value in doing so? Almost certainly, no.

The important thing to understand, then, is that although authorization and authentication services should almost certainly be part of your data mart environment, don't go overboard and specify an environment that is oversecure. Not only will the data mart cost much more to build (security is expensive), but there is usually an inverse relationship between ease of use and degree of security. You want to achieve the right balance of cost-effectiveness, usability, and information protection.

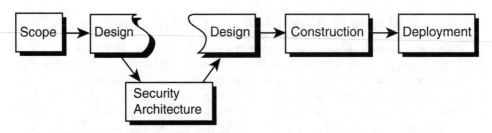

Figure WK5.6 Inserting a security architecture phase into the data mart development effort.

If the enterprise network infrastructure already has a robust authentication service, the data mart should be architected to use the authentication services that already exist. The systems/infrastructure analyst will need to work with the network administration and security administration organizations to determine compatibility or incompatibility issues, design the end-to-end flows of user IDs and passwords, and determine how they're used.

If, however, advanced security services (nonrepudiation, for example) are deemed necessary because of a particularly sensitive mission of the data mart, then even if existing services can be plugged into, a separate security architecture phase should occur.

Progress by Week's End

By the end of Week 5, you need to have an agreed-to end-to-end security architecture for the data mart and determine how it relates to the rest of the enterprise. Both the security business rules and the way those rules will be implemented will be determined.

How to Achieve the Fifth Week's Goals

Figure WK5.7 shows the activities that will occur and the teams that will perform them during Week 5 of the data mart project.

Project Management During Week 5

In addition to the usual project management functions, such as monitoring project schedules and progress and facilitating issues resolution as necessary, the project manager needs to be closely involved with the product evaluation activities during

Activity Stream	Monday	Tuesday	Wednesday	Thursday	Friday
Front-End Product Evaluation	Status check of tools still in contention	Comprehensive testing	Comprehensive testing	Preliminary decision Comprehensive testing	Final testing
Middleware and DBMS Evaluation	End-to-end movement (first attempt)	Repeat end-to-end movement for each	Source to target design Create mappings Create database schema	End-to-end testing	End-to-end testing for larger volumes of data
Data Mart Database Design	Finalize attributes	Finalize dimensions	Finalize levels	Complete design review and walk-through	Adjust design
Systems/ Infrastructure Analysis: Security Modeling	Permissions model	Permissions model	Permissions model	Advanced security	Advanced security

Figure WK5.7 The fifth week's calendar of activities.

Week 5. The middleware and database product evaluation threads of activity converge now. Next week, the front-end tool evaluation starts, and the majority of the team members will be working together, everyone committed to selecting the products that will be used.

Therefore, the project manager needs to make sure that the combined middleware-database evaluation activity goes smoothly and that progress remains on track during Week 5. Similarly, by the end of the week, there should be no surprises in the front-end tool area; end-to-end testing needs to occur.

While paying close attention to the product testing, though, the project manager also needs to be preparing for the construction phase that is rapidly approaching. Development hardware and software must be in place, the production hardware and software need to be on order, and all logistics such as work locations must be determined. The project manager needs to make sure that construction is not delayed because of logistical issues.

You Know You're in Trouble When

Serious problems are most likely to occur in the product evaluation activities during Week 5. If either of the following conditions exists at the end of the week, the project is at risk:

♦ None of the middleware-database product combinations work. Despite late nights, frequent calls to vendors, and frequent reinstallation of all products, the team cannot establish even the most basic end-to-end connectivity.

♦ As the team members take a closer look at each of the front-end tools still under consideration, they become increasingly disenchanted with their options. Last week, the products were acceptable; this week, enthusiasm for the tools has all but disappeared.

Week 5 Spotlight on the Front-End Tool Specialist

It's challenging enough to captain a team evaluating several OLAP or querying/reporting tools at the same time. The team's front-end tool specialist needs to deal with configuration issues, pushy vendor sales representatives (all of whom have sales quotas at the top of their respective lists of priorities), users from various organizations, and a host of other issues.

Perhaps the biggest challenge the tool evaluator has, though, is to steer the users through the evaluation process in a manner that is authoritative about tool functionality yet places the selection process squarely on the shoulders of the users. For example:

♦ The tool evaluator may have had extensive experience on four or five data mart projects over the past two years, using a particular OLAP tool (one that is under consideration for this project). Its drill-down capabilities are, the evaluator feels, unparalleled in ease of use. However, one of the other products being evaluated has undergone intensive revamping and the current version has received rave reviews during the past few months. It is imperative that the front-end tool specialist remain objective in discussions with the users about comparative features of the tool.

♦ One of the querying/reporting tools being considered is, essentially, a PC-based version of a long-running mainframe fourth-generation language (4GL) product. Its user interface is erratic and doesn't even approach the ease of use of the other products being evaluated. However, the user community's power users all have extensive experience with the mainframe 4GL product. The users show a preference for the desktop version of the product with which they are all familiar; it's not the place of the tool evaluator to disrupt the selection process by continually disparaging the interface and capabilities of that product, emphasizing its shortcomings as compared with other tools.

As the team approaches a decision about a product, the front-end tool specialist needs to spend as much time as possible learning every little nuance about that product. Even if the specialist is familiar with an earlier version, time needs to be spent reading manuals, checking out websites for product support and user groups, and just playing with the product.

What You'll Find in This Chapter

Week 6 Activities
Preliminary Product Selection
Integrated End-to-End Product Testing
Implementation-Specific Design

How to Achieve the Sixth Week's Goals
Project Management During Week 6
You Know You're in Trouble When

Finalizing Product
Selection

A Note to the Reader: If fate has smiled on your data mart development team, you are now entering Week 6 with the wind at your back. Specifically, you have the following behind you:

- *Product evaluation and testing have gone smoothly, from the initial activities to multiproduct integration testing.*

- *User functionality has been translated into data mart terms, and you have sufficient knowledge about how users will need to access and manipulate the data mart's contents.*

- *Enough is known about the contents of each data source so that you have a high degree of confidence that the data mart can be successfully populated with meaningful contents.*

The flip side, of course, is that perhaps you have hit bump after bump, problem after problem throughout the first weeks of design. For example:

- *Several severe data source issues around gaps or quality have been identified and can likely be overcome, but the exact method of resolution has yet to be determined.*

- *The products under evaluation work well enough on their own (in isolation), but the integration testing and evaluation have been problematic.*

♦ *One or more of the parallel streams of activity have proceeded more slowly than expected, resulting in delayed progress in other activities that depend on the results of the first.*

Week 6 might be viewed as the point at which you decide whether to forge ahead at the current pace of activity, targeting the completion of design at the end of Week 7, or perhaps slow design activity down to allow any "laggard" activity streams to catch up with the others.

In the latter case, change your focus from the expected Week 7 design phase completion to getting the design effort back on track. An all-hands meeting to take stock of the project, covering all activities accomplished to date and all associated issues and problems, should be held early in Week 6 (Monday afternoon at the latest). Then—only then—should you take a fresh look at and revise the project schedule. Should your project be on target, proceed with Weeks 6 and 7, be prepared, however, to dump your schedules for Weeks 6 and 7 should it be necessary to get your project back on track. Once there you can pick up with a revised project schedule.

Week 6 Activities

Week 6 will see two teams working in parallel. One team will continue and finalize the product selection for the data mart. This team will consist of the following:

♦ All the product evaluation leads

♦ The business analyst

♦ The infrastructure analyst

♦ The quality assurance/configuration control team member

♦ The process analyst

The other team will begin implementation-specific design activity so that it can complete this design early the following week in time for a midweek design review. This team will consist of the following:

♦ The database designer

♦ All of the source data analysts

♦ The middleware product evaluation lead (who works the same amount of time for both teams)

The sections that follow describe in detail the activities performed by these teams and their expected accomplishments.

Preliminary Product Selection

Week 6 begins with a Monday morning preliminary selection of the front-end tool, middleware product(s), and database management system that will be used in the data mart. This selection will be based on what was learned during the previous week with regard to the various product combinations that were tested and evaluated.

The data mart development team must now make choices. The pool of candidate products in each category has been slowly (and carefully) whittled down throughout the previous weeks. Initial candidates were chosen by factors such as market presence, perceptions of a product's fit to the needs of the data mart's business mission, and similar ideas. Over time, concrete data points have been added to your body of knowledge about each product, individually and in concert with others.

Now, using that body of knowledge, you need to choose the products with which you want to proceed with development. Chances are that Week 5's integration testing has given you a fairly clear indication of the product combinations most suitable for your specific data mart. They are the most suitable because the necessary business value will be obtained from the data mart if these tools are used, and you have a high degree of confidence that construction will proceed smoothly when you use these products.

Following your decision, you will proceed with several days of integrated, end-to-end product testing for your entire product suite, as discussed next.

Integrated End-to-End Product Testing

Three days—Tuesday through Thursday—should be set aside for your integrated testing of your entire data mart product suite. A similar but more focused set of steps performed during Week 5 needs to be accomplished with your product set.

A Quick-Paced, Three-Day Schedule

A sample set of day-by-day activities is listed below.

♦ *Tuesday.* Select at least two data sources (assuming your data mart will be populated from more than one source), preferably on different platforms (e.g., one

T **IP** Remember your objective! It's important to understand that your objective during these three days is product testing, not product evaluation (as was done during the previous weeks). During your earlier product-versus-product comparisons, you spent significant time "what-iffing," testing the bounds of each product in each category, and seeing what each was capable of just in case you needed such functionality. This week, stay focused! You know what the products are supposed to be capable of, and you've already checked them in controlled environments. Now, make sure they work in a real-world environment.

using DB2 on an MVS mainframe, the other Oracle running on a Unix server). Between 50 and 75 data elements from the sources should be identified for usage in the testing.

Next, create at least 10 tables within your data mart's database that will be populated from those sources. A good mix for your testing would be four tables populated solely from one data source, four tables populated from the other, and two tables that require data merged from the two sources. (Even if your data mart won't have tables built from data merged from multiple sources, you should simulate a multisource convergence into a single table to ensure that it can be accomplished if necessary as your data mart evolves.)

Once the data sources and the respective target destinations for those elements have been identified, the extraction, quality assurance, transformation, movement, and loading procedures need to be created as quickly as possible. If more than one tool will be used to accomplish these tasks, it's recommended that you proceed in the order listed above (extraction tool first, loading tool or utility last).

At the same time, the business analyst and the team member responsible for the front-end tool should create a limited set of front-end functionality using as many of the selected data elements as possible. Front-end functionality involves queries, reports, user screens, pivot tables, or other capabilities that are specific to the tool. Even though your focus is testing, try to make the queries and reports that you create as realistic as possible in the context of the data mart's mission.

◆ *Wednesday.* Assuming that Tuesday's task list has been successfully completed, Wednesday's activities should be to proceed as expeditiously as possible with the following:

◊ Extracting significant volumes of data from each of the sources

◊ Performing the specified quality assurance checks and transformation routines

◊ Performing whatever cross-platform data movement is required (e.g., from a data source on a mainframe to a target NT server)

◊ Loading the data mart's database contents

◊ Ensuring that all the reports, queries, and other data usage scripts run properly

Expect the above steps to take an entire day.

◆ *Thursday.* The database activity you've tested so far has been with regard to the initial population of the data mart. Because your data mart will have to be periodically refreshed with new contents (more on that later in this chapter), Thursday's set of activities should be dedicated to ensuring that restocking can be accomplished when the data mart is deployed and operational.

Make sure that with the products you've selected (preliminarily) you can do the following:

◊ Add new rows of data to existing data mart database tables

◊ Add new rows and, at the same time, delete others

◊ Perform a complete replacement of any table's existing contents

◊ Perform in-place updates by changing the value of a particular column of data within a particular row (e.g., change the value of TOTAL_MARCH_OFFICE_EXPENSES for the packaging department from $145,234 to $167,896) because of a change to the corresponding value in the data source

If everything goes according to schedule, Thursday's close of business will find you with absolute confidence that your Monday morning product selection was a good one.

Finalizing Product Selection

On Friday, product selection is closed for good for your data mart project. Everything that happens from here on out for the duration of the project—not only design and construction, but all the support activities (training, documentation, contract management, vendor relationships, preparation for help desk support, etc.)—will be done in the context of the products you have chosen and on which you are basing the eventual success of your data mart effort. From now on, no more conceptual or general thinking and planning.

T I P Be explicit! It's important to formally announce the results of the product selection process, along with the rationale behind the choices you made. In addition, you should make the results of all testing and evaluation activity (not only that of Week 6, but also that of the previous weeks) available in a public forum (e.g., posted on the company's intranet in a project bulletin board). This way, you reduce the likelihood of any construction-phase disruptions as a result of someone's challenging the product selection process. It does happen; be prepared!

Implementation-Specific Design

In parallel with the final phase of integrated testing, the data mart team needs to begin implementation-specific design activity. There is, of course, a slight chance that the final integrated product testing could be a flop and the entire design effort could wind up back on the drawing board. If that occurs, Week 6's detailed design activity may have to be scrapped.

More likely, though, Friday will arrive with confirmation of your product selection occurring in parallel with a head start on implementation-specific design based on the features particular to those products and the way they interact with one another (again, be "cautiously daring" throughout your data mart effort). Therefore, the following sections describe the design activities that need to occur during Week 6. Again, there is a fundamental shift this week in the way team members proceed with their respective design assignments. Although it's important to keep the conceptual properties of the data mart in mind, it's now time to think of contents and functionality in the context of the products that will be implemented and deployed.

T I P Work together in a design center. Implementation-specific design activities and decisions are highly dependent not only on the specific products—database, middleware, and front end—but also the interaction of those products. Therefore, it's strongly recommended that the design team perform all its tasks during Weeks 6 and 7 in a design center setting. Members should work side by side, constantly considering the cross-product implications of every choice each team member makes.

Database Design

During Week 5, the database design progressed to the point where it was about 95% complete, at least in a conceptual sense. Facts and dimensions, and the respective levels of each dimension, have now been identified, and some early decisions were made about how keys would be handled within the data model.

During Weeks 6 and 7 the following activities must occur:

♦ The data model must be finalized; any remaining issues or questions need to be resolved as quickly as possible.

♦ The data model must be "physicalized," or adjusted to any product-specific peculiarities of the DBMS preliminarily selected. For example, decisions need to be made about the database's indices: how many, on what column(s), and of what type.

♦ Based on knowledge about data volumes and the capabilities of the DBMS product you'll use, any decisions about database parallel processing need to be made. For example, if you'll be implementing parallel processing within your database, you need to determine which way the partitions will be organized:

◊ By a range of values (if so, on what column, and what ranges within each partition?)

◊ By round-robin techniques (for example, if your database will have four partitions, data will be loaded into those partitions in the following order: 1,2,3,4,1,2,3,4,1,2,...)

◊ By a hashing algorithm (assigning rows of data to a partition in a quasi-random manner that isn't determined by either load order or content of a particular field)

◊ By another algorithm supported by the particular DBMS

Extraction

One of the most often overlooked design issues with respect to data mart development is in the area of data extraction. Attention in the source-to-target area is usually focused on data transformation processes that need to occur, but a more basic question needs to be addressed: How exactly will you get data out of each source so that it will be available for transformation and the other processes that need to occur on the way to the data mart?

Extraction needs to be addressed in two domains:

♦ For purposes of initial loading of the data mart

♦ On an ongoing basis each time the data mart needs to be restocked

During Week 6, focus on the initial loading models; during Week 7, you can build on what you decide about initial loading as you design the restocking/refreshing processes.

Consider the following items as you design your extraction processes:

♦ *The importance of moving data off-platform, away from the source.* Perhaps one of your data mart's sources is a finely tuned, mission-critical transaction processing application. In this case, your first objective with respect to acquiring data for your data mart is to get that data away from the application's environment as expeditiously as possible before performing any of the downstream processes (quality assurance, transformation, etc., as discussed shortly).

The degree to which you need to move data off-platform will vary from source to source, which is why it was so critical to perform the system and infrastructure analysis work of Week 3 to gain a thorough understanding of those respective source environments. For example, a mainframe-based application running on a hardware platform with plenty of unused capacity will likely enable you to perform some functions (e.g., QA) on that hardware platform with negligible impact

For More Information About Database Design

The subject of dimensional database design is a very complex one, particularly as you move beyond the fairly easy-to-understand concepts of facts and dimensions into the physical design issues and product-specific constraints that will dramatically affect your data mart's storage requirements and performance. For example, you will need to make decisions about whether your model should be organized as a *simple star*—a single fact table surrounded by and connected to one table for each applicable dimension—or perhaps as a *snowflake schema*—a model in which a sequence of normalized tables instead of a single denormalized dimension table is used for each level of a dimension.

Many other issues await you. For example, how should the time dimension be represented: should you use a DATE data type if the lowest level of detail on that dimension you'll have is MONTH, and if so, what do you do about the value in the "day" portion of the DATE field (always set it to "1," for example)? Suppose your lowest level of detail on the time dimension is WEEK, but you also need information at the MONTH level; how do you represent that, and what should you do about the fact that weeks cross month boundaries?

Data mart database design is far too complex a subject to discuss at length in this book, particularly the physical, implementation-specific issues that vary from product to product. It's recommended that you use the contents of this book's design chapters (Weeks 3 through 7) as a framework for understanding the basic concepts (e.g., the importance of analyzing the possible levels of each dimensional hierarchy) and as a sequence of analytical activities to get you to the point where you have a fairly complete conceptual data model. When you need to translate that model into a design, though, you are better served by studying this process in detail through other sources. Rather than present you with superficial discussion about such design techniques, this book points you toward sources that will give you sufficient detail about the many issues and options you'll face. Specifically, you may wish to consult *Practical Techniques for Building Dimensional Data Warehouses* by Ralph Kimball (John Wiley & Sons, Inc., 1996), as well as the database design guidelines available from each DBMS vendor for its products. Likewise, a wealth of information is available on the Internet through various data warehousing-related sites, bulletin boards, and list servers.

on the application's performance. However, you may not want to stage your extracted data within that application's database (e.g., in a temporary table) as you perform that quality assurance (QA) because you could run into database performance issues (e.g., additional overhead on the lock manager, which in turn causes undesirable slowdown of the application's throughput).

Having a data source hosted on a PC server with severely strained capacity and performance, however, would likely lead you to conclude that as soon as data is extracted from the source, it should be moved onto another platform before any further processing occurs.

♦ *Leverage of existing processes.* Don't overlook already existing data extraction processes that you may be able to leverage. For example, it may be possible to obtain your data mart's contents from backup tapes made from the operational database (which, basically, are extraction processes in their own right). You could handle the extraction of both initial data and subsequent restocking portions from tape, avoiding any additional impact on the source environment.

Also look at any data extraction processes that exist for the purpose of creating extract files for simple decision support or statistical processing. It's common for organizations to already be "pulling out" a few key data elements and placing the extracted contents into a PC database, a server-based ASCII file, a SAS data set, or some other data storage place. Although you will likely need contents different from those currently being handled, you may be able to leverage the setup and connection code that already exists.

♦ *Translation.* Don't overlook the need for character set conversions (e.g., source data in EBCDIC on an IBM mainframe that needs to be translated into ASCII, or even PC-based ASCII data that needs to be converted into a multibyte international character set). Utilities abound to perform these basic translation functions, but don't forget to consider the processing impact on the time windows you have available for extraction (discussed next).

♦ *Frequency.* How frequently does extraction need to occur, and what triggers that process: Time? A business event?

♦ *Data volumes and corresponding windows.* You have a higher degree of risk if you need to extract very large volumes of data (hundreds of megabytes, perhaps gigabytes) from a source than if you need only smaller amounts (e.g., a few megabytes). Although the extraction processes and steps shouldn't be affected by data volumes (at least conceptually), you need to take a long look at the window(s) you have in which you can perform the extraction. Extracting small amounts of data over the weekend from a non-mission-critical database isn't too much of a challenge; extracting large volumes from a 7 x 24 mission-critical application is.

♦ *Recovery.* If problems occur during the extraction process, does it need to be restarted or is some interim-point recovery possible? What types of checkpoints need to be created to ensure data integrity if extraction is restarted?

♦ *Extraction model.* Will you be pulling out the entire contents of a source's data environment? Perhaps you need slices that don't vary from one extraction cycle to the next (e.g., every month, you will extract the *entire* contents of certain columns for a selected database table). Or it's possible that your extraction rules will be based on incremental change: only new rows of data added since the last extraction cycle should be extracted.

If you're going to extract only new or changed data from the source, you also need to decide exactly how you will determine what subset of the source's content you need. Can you determine your extraction targets by time stamps in the database log, or do you need to do content-based determination from the data itself?

♦ *Change management.* If a source's structure changes, what is the impact on the extraction process? There may be no impact, particularly if you handle extraction by dumping the contents of a database backup tape onto a separate platform for further processing. On the other hand, if you're pulling selected data on each extraction cycle, you need to have a clear idea of how changes to source data structures will be interfaced with the extraction process to prevent the next cycle from failing.

Data Quality Assurance

Now is the time to make a key determination with respect to your data quality assurance processes. You could combine QA functions with data transformation (discussed next), checking each piece of data for correctness and as part of transformation, fixing any problems you identify (if possible).

Alternatively, you may consider having a separate QA cycle immediately following extraction but before transformation begins. (You could also combine QA with the extraction processes discussed above; as each piece of data is extracted from its source, it is quality-checked at that point. This method may be desirable in low-volume, non-mission-critical sources, but adding QA to the extraction process will likely adversely affect your goal of off-platform movement of data away from the source's environment.)

Whether or not you decide to combine QA with another middleware function, you need to make sure your design includes processes, as applicable to your specific data mart environment, for the following:

- *In-place QA.* Many QA functions are extremely basic, and you can handle them by applying a static rule without including any other pieces of data. For example, if a DEPARTMENT_ID column is supposed to have a five-digit numeric value that begins with 1, 2, or 3 and always ends in a 5, it's simple to check each DEPARTMENT_ID to see if it conforms to the rules.

- *Intrasource, dependency-based QA.* Slightly more complex than in-place QA are rules that can still be determined from within a single data source but require several pieces of data to be dynamically compared to determine the correctness (or lack thereof) of one or both. For example, a master DEPART-MENT_DATA table may contain a complete list of all departments within the organization and attributes about each; it's likely that rows of data in the DEPARTMENT_DAILY_EXPENDITURES table need to be cross-referenced against DEPARTMENT_DATA to ensure that no invalid department IDs slip into the data mart. Although it's possible to create a static rule to do this function, if departments are frequently added or deleted within the company, every change would require a change to the static QA rule. A better option is to use the contents of the source data environment themselves as part of the QA rule.

- *Cross-source dependencies.* Still more complex than either of the above scenarios are dependencies in which the dynamic QA of one source's contents requires information from another source. An example is a master customer management application that is determined to be the system of record for all of an enterprise's customer relationships, and the correctness of customer data pulled from the sales processing application must be validated against that single, official customer management and tracking application.

- *Feedback loops.* What do you do when you find data quality problems? If possible, you correct them before sending data downstream toward the data mart. But shouldn't you provide some type of notification to the source environment from which the problematic data was extracted? If this is desired, the exact mechanisms of the feedback loop need to be designed. A simple mechanism is to create a report that you send to the person responsible for that application for corrective actions, as necessary. A significantly more complex solution is to generate an electronic, semantically understood set of corrections that are passed back directly to the source application for automatic processing (or possibly semiautomatic, user-assisted processing). Perhaps an application programming interface (API) exists against which this set of corrections can be written, but given the state of most computer applications, that's unlikely. Therefore, a customized interface would need to be created from the data mart middleware back to the source. (Doing this would be very time-consuming and should be deferred past your current rapid data mart development effort towards a subsequent release.)

♦ *Go/no-go decisions.* Your QA design needs to consider business rules with respect to points at which you might need to make a no-go decision because of severe, uncorrectable data quality problems. For example, one of the problems you're likely to encounter in building a budget process support data mart is invalid department IDs against which revenues or expenses can't be correctly allocated. You may choose to implement the following business rule as part of the QA process:

> If the total amount of indeterminable revenue is less than $150,000, write out those records to an error file but proceed with the population of the data mart. If that amount exceeds $150,000, halt the entire source-to-data mart process until the data errors can be corrected in the sources.

Transformation

Transformation functions are probably the most understandable of the data mart middleware functions you need to design. A great deal of early 1990s explanation of the rationale for data warehousing was based on the business case for a single unified view of enterprise data. One of the stumbling blocks always mentioned was having different encoding of data across various sources. Likewise, the tradeoffs of lightly summarized versus highly summarized have been well documented.

The starting point for your transformation design is your data mart's database model. Even though this is still an in-progress work, enough work has been done to date in identifying attributes and determining the appropriate levels of detail on each dimension that transformation work can safely begin. And, as discussed earlier in this chapter, having design work performed in a design center setting will

TIP For discussion about the basics of data transformation and granularity issues, you may wish to consult *Building the Data Warehouse, 2nd Edition,* by W. H. Inmon (John Wiley & Sons, Inc. 1996).

facilitate regular communications and dialog between the database designer and the middleware analyst's transformation-related activities.

As discussed in the section dealing with QA, your transformation design may or may not include data quality checking. You need to take an end-to-end look at the flow of data from all sources into the data mart to determine where it's best to conduct the necessary QA.

You will likely need to design the following types of transformation rules:

♦ *Simple transformations.* Like simple QA checking, these are static and rule based: "1" and "2" are changed to "M" and "F," respectively, or "000" is added to the end of all region IDs from one source to make them consistent with the expanded REGION_ID field of another source.

♦ *Simple groupings and summarization.* If you have decided that the lowest level of organization data within the data mart will be at the business location data, and all expense data is maintained in two sources at the department level, it should be a straightforward process to roll the department data up to the business location level.

♦ *Single-source dynamic transformations.* These will function almost identically to single-source dynamic QA processes. For example, you can do a lookup within the TERRITORY_MASTER table to obtain new values for columns that have now superseded obsolete, but unchanged, values in another table from which data is being extracted for use in the data mart. Your design needs to consider the mechanism by which this can be accomplished: In-place lookup of the correct value versus a multipass cross-table comparison is a common design choice with which you'll be faced.

♦ *Cross-source transformations.* Transformations that are dependent on contents from multiple sources tend to be architecturally complex. You may need to consider a staging area of some type into which interim extracted data can be placed until everything necessary for the transformation processing is ready (see Figure WK6.1).

♦ *Recovery processes.* If problems occur during data transformation, what recovery processes should be implemented? Does transformation need to be restarted, or can it resume from some interim point (e.g., a checkpointed location)?

TIP Strongly consider post-transformation quality assurance. Very often, one QA phase is not sufficient for your data mart's source-to-target flow of data. If significant multisource merging is occurring, you should have a separate post-transformation QA phase to ensure that your own data mart processes haven't introduced errors into the data (e.g., by transformation script errors).

Movement

Cross-platform movement of data is another overlooked middleware function. Usually, overly simplistic data mart architecture diagrams neglect the movement of data, and during construction you find yourself faced with a surprise or two. For example, it's likely that following transformation, the data mart's contents will need to be transferred to the hardware box on which the data mart's database resides for

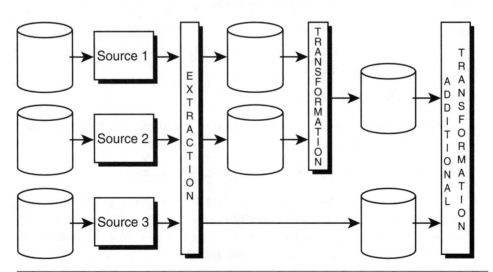

Figure WK6.1 Cross-source transformations and staging areas.

the loading process (discussed next) to occur. Could transformation processing occur on that same box? Possibly, but it will likely not because of the impact on the data mart's operational performance.

You need to take a look at, and design, all cross-platform flows of data and the mechanism by which they will occur. Some of those flows may occur through a tape-based medium of exchange, others via standard File Transfer Protocol (FTP) operations, and perhaps others through movement services integrated with a middleware transformation tool.

As with the other functions discussed so far, design for recovery and determine what will have to occur if a movement operation is interrupted before completion.

Loading

In Week 7, significant design work will occur with respect to the model(s) by which the data mart's contents are restocked. Restocking operations will very likely require some type of deletion within the data mart. Entire tables may be dropped and replaced, or selected rows may be deleted as part of a rolling time frame model. In-place updates to data mart contents could also occur.

Therefore, one of the Week 6 activities is to preliminarily design update models to the data mart's database as part of load operations. You can't get too detailed yet because the exact nature of the restocking model hasn't been determined, but you can get a head start in terms of preliminary research.

You can also make some preliminary design choices about the different loading options available to you, based on the previous weeks' research and testing, by answering the following questions:

◆ Will you employ a parallel loading utility?

◆ Can data be loaded exactly as it is, direct from transformation, or do surrogate keys need to be generated?

◆ For small load volumes, will you use SQL INSERT statements?

◆ Will you turn database logging off for loading models in which tables are dropped and then reloaded in their entirety? If so, what will your recovery model be if a loading process is halted for a data integrity error that hadn't been caught, or perhaps because of system problems?

How to Achieve the Sixth Week's Goals

Figure WK6.2 shows a schedule of Week 6 activities.

Project Management During Week 6

In addition to normal project management functions during Week 6—keeping everything running smoothly and on schedule—an interesting challenge may confront the project manager as product-specific design begins. It's not uncommon for one of the team's designers to complain that the product doesn't do some function with regard to the design choices that designer is making.

It's important that the project manager intercede in these situations as quickly as possible because the entire team is supposed to be well past the point of figuring out what a product can and can't do. It's impossible, of course, for every feature of a product to be checked out over the course of a few weeks' worth of research, but by now there should be high confidence that the product will meet the business needs.

There may be undiscovered features, workarounds, or product add-ons that will solve the "can't do" problem. It is the role of the project manager to make sure that these are determined as quickly as possible to prevent any disruption to the design process.

You Know You're in Trouble When

Most of the serious problems you will encounter during Week 6 will be in the realm of the final integrated product testing. You would naturally assume that because your testing activities this week are significantly more focused than in the past weeks and you are now dealing with products with which you have a high confidence of interoperability—in fact, you've already demonstrated this interoperability—the three days' worth of final testing will proceed smoothly.

If, however, you suddenly have connectivity and interoperability problems that take a long time to solve, or perhaps Week 6 ends and these problems are still unresolved, your entire effort is in jeopardy. The good news is that if the products worked together at one time, they can work together again. You need to look at anything that has changed (configuration options, platform migration, etc.) to try

Activity Stream	Monday	Tuesday	Wednesday	Thursday	Friday
Preliminary Product Selection	Review selections (all-group meeting)				
Integrated End-to-End Product Testing		Two data sources: test extraction Create target tables Create middleware Subset of functionality	Test Tuesday's work	Add complications to testing	
Finalize Product Selection					Make final selections (all-group meeting)
Implementation-Specific Design	Database design Middleware design QA Design	Database design Middleware design QA Design	Database design Middleware design QA Design	Database design Middleware design QA Design	Database design Middleware design QA Design

Figure WK6.2 The sixth week's calendar of activities.

to get back to the baseline that worked at one time. Call in all available support, though, because the longer the interoperability problems drag on the greater the project risk.

Week 6 Spotlight on the Middleware Tool Specialist

Though every team member has a key role to play during Week 6 (as is true throughout the entire data mart development effort), the star of this week is the person responsible for middleware evaluation and, eventually, development. This individual must play a dual role through this entire week, likely making for some long hours.

On the one hand, the middleware specialist needs to be involved in the end-to-end integrated product testing. Moving data from the sources to the data mart in the controlled environment requires extraction, transformation, cross-platform movement, and loading functions, all of which are within the realm of responsibility of the middleware specialist.

At the same time, a significant amount of design effort needs to occur in those same in addition to the mechanisms by which data quality will be assured.

It's important that this person's activities are carefully balanced between these two critical sets of activities. It is the responsibility of the project manager to take a realistic look at the workload, the timing, and the duration of all associated tasks and to call in additional help if necessary.

What You'll Find in This Chapter

Completing the Design
Refreshing the Data Mart's Contents
Management and Operations
Metadata Management
The Design Review
The Aftermath of the Design Review
How to Achieve the Seventh Week's Goals
Project Management During Week 7
You Know You're in Trouble When

Conducting the
Design Review

A Note to the Reader: In Week 7 the data mart design—at least the design of the data mart's database, the way it will be populated, and the way users will access its contents—is almost finished.

But what about the ways the data mart will be kept up to date and periodically restocked? Portions of the previous chapter have alluded to this all-important aspect; now is the time to decide what the restocking model will be.

And how about the management and ongoing operations of the data mart—what needs to be defined at this point in the design phase? And what about metadata? It's too late to start worrying about these areas after you have deployed the data mart; you need to design these capabilities now.

Before you move ahead with the construction phase, it's also important to conduct an end-to-end comprehensive design review. Finding design holes or potential issues now is much less problematic than doing so in, say, Week 12 of the project in the middle of testing.

The chapter covers the design activities and the review process that are often overlooked in the rush toward construction activity. Rapid development? Certainly. Careless development? No!

Completing the Design

The following sections discuss the additional design phase activities that need to occur during Week 7. Your objective should be to complete these activities by no later than Thursday. As discussed later in this chapter, Friday should be set aside for an all-day, end-to-end comprehensive design review.

Refreshing the Data Mart's Contents

Initial data mart population is a one-shot event. Even though it may be fairly complex, there is one aspect that makes the target database side of the flow fairly straightforward: you start with a clean slate, because there are no existing contents to worry about.

The refreshing (or restocking) process, however, needs to absolutely take the data mart's contents into consideration. Therefore, you need to pay careful attention to the appropriate business rules when you are designing the refreshing processes.

In general, data mart restocking can be categorized into are four models:

◆ Complete replacement

◆ Appending

◆ Rolling append

◆ In-place updates

The sections that follow discuss each of these models with respect to what you need to consider for your data mart design activities during Week 7. Note that your data mart isn't limited to operating under only one of these models; some of your tables may be completely replaced and others will be appended with new contents, for example, with a few in-place updates also occurring. Therefore, it's important that you thoroughly understand the business rules and requirements guidelines that apply to your data mart.

Complete Replacement

Complete replacement (shown in Figure WK7.1) is the most straightforward data mart restocking model. Basically, it's the same design you use for initial population prefaced by DROP operations to make sure your data mart's database is empty. If you determine that a significant portion of your data mart's contents will

	DeptID	ExpenseCategory	Amt
Source Data	NE12	PERS5	3333.55
	NE12	PERS6	2222.11
	NE12	OFFC85	1111.22
	NE14	PERS5	2211.78
Data Mart Before Restocking	NE11	PERS5	8888.66
	NE12	PERS5	1212.12
	NE12	PERS6	4545.67
	NE14	PERS5	5730.92
Data Mart After Restocking	NE12	PERS5	3333.55
	NE12	PERS6	2222.11
	NE12	OFFC85	1111.22
	NE14	PERS5	2211.78

Figure WK7.1 Complete replacement during data mart restocking.

change at each refresh cycle, you probably want to consider a complete replacement model.

Appending

The append model (shown in Figure WK7.2) is useful when existing data mart contents will not be modified or removed when a refresh cycle occurs and proportionally small amounts of new data will be acquired from one or more data sources.

In many situations, appending is fairly straightforward, almost as much as complete replacement is. You need to be careful, though, that you don't overlook hidden complexities that could affect your data mart's contents. For example, suppose that your budget support data mart will be restocked every month with expenditures for each business location. At first glance, a simple append operation seems to be the most appropriate, and it may very well be.

But suppose reorganizations cause various business locations to be periodically reassigned to new regions. What happens to expense data based on existing business location-to-region relationships? You need to have a clear understanding of the business rules that apply to reorganizations and budgeting. For example, are a business location's historical expenditures "carried" to a new region, which would mean that changes need to be made to existing data mart contents?

	DeptID	ExpenseCategory	Amt
Source Data	NE12	PERS5	3333.55
	NE12	PERS6	2222.11
	NE12	OFFC85	1111.22
	NE14	PERS5	2211.78
Data Mart Before Restocking	NE11	PERS5	8888.66
	NE11	PERS6	1212.12
	NE12	OFFC98	4545.67
	NE14	PERS4	5730.92
Data Mart After Restocking	NE11	PERS5	8888.66
	NE11	PERS6	1212.12
	NE12	OFFC98	4545.67
	NE14	PERS4	5730.92
	NE12	PERS5	3333.55
	NE12	PERS6	2222.11
	NE12	OFFC85	1111.22
	NE14	PERS5	2211.78

Figure WK7.2 Appending new inputs to the data mart.

Rolling Append

Some time-dimensioned data is useful for analysis for only a finite period of time—say, the past two years. Therefore, data older than two years could, if desired, be removed from the data mart each time a restocking process occurs.

The most common way to remove this data is to use a *rolling append* model, which appends new data while removing obsolete data. Figure WK7.3 illustrates the rolling append model.

In-Place Updates

In-place updates of data mart contents (shown in Figure WK7.4) may be appropriate for your data mart in certain circumstances, such as when a small number of attributes of a small number of existing rows of data need to be changed. As with data warehousing in general, in-place updates aren't commonly used in data marts, though if you determine in a situation that it seems to make sense to refresh a portion of the data mart's contents this way, you should strongly consider in-place updates.

	DeptID	ExpenseCategory	Period	Amt
Source Data	NE12	PERS5	11/97	3333.55
	NE12	PERS6	11/97	2222.11
	NE12	OFFC85	11/97	1111.22
	NE14	PERS5	11/97	2211.78
Data Mart Before Restocking	NE12	PERS5	11/96	1111.22
	NE12	PERS6	11/96	3333.22
	NE12	OFFC85	11/96	4444.86
	NE14	PERS5	11/96	5555.66
	NE12	PERS5	12/96	9999.88
	NE12	PERS6	12/96	8855.21
	NE12	OFFC85	12/96	2233.44
	NE14	PERS5	12/96	4312.09
	.			
	.			
	.			
	NE12	PERS5	10/97	1092.83
	NE12	PERS6	10/97	3982.76
	NE12	OFFC85	10/97	4948.76
	NE14	PERS5	10/97	9902.87
Data Mart After Restocking	NE12	PERS5	12/96	9999.88
	NE12	PERS6	12/96	8855.21
	NE12	OFFC85	12/96	2233.44
	NE14	PERS5	12/96	4312.09
	.			
	.			
	.			
	NE12	PERS5	10/97	1092.83
	NE12	PERS6	10/97	3982.76
	NE12	OFFC85	10/97	4948.76
	NE14	PERS5	10/97	9902.87
	NE12	PERS5	11/97	3333.55
	NE12	PERS6	11/97	2222.11
	NE12	OFFC85	11/97	1111.22
	NE14	PERS5	11/97	2211.78

Figure WK7.3 The rolling append restocking model.

	DeptID	ExpenseCategory	Amt
Source Data	NE12	PERS6	3333.55
Data Mart Before Restocking	NE11 NE12 NE12 NE14	PERS5 PERS5 PERS6 PERS5	8888.66 1212.12 4545.67 5730.92
Data Mart After Restocking	NE12 NE12 *NE12* NE14	PERS5 PERS5 *PERS6* PERS5	8888.66 1212.12 *3333.55* 5730.92

Figure WK7.4 In-place updates in the data mart.

Management and Operations

Though data mart administration can be boring, it is imperative that your design activities take management and operations into consideration.

In addition to the ongoing refreshing of the data mart's contents (discussed above), consider the following:

♦ Usage monitoring

♦ Security management

♦ User community management

♦ Support services and assistance

♦ Database backup

♦ Scheduling

The following sections briefly discuss the facets of each of these areas and some of the issues you need to consider.

Monitoring Data Mart Usage

The following questions, and many more like them, will come your way after the data mart has been deployed:

♦ How's the data mart performing?

♦ Are we making good use of the data mart?

♦ Why does it take so long to run certain queries when others give us answers back in mere seconds?

T I P Several of the topics covered in this chapter are included in *Managing the Data Warehouse* by W. H. Inmon, J. D. Welch, and Katherine L. Glassey (John Wiley & Sons, Inc., 1997). You may wish to consult this source for more detailed information.

Unfortunately, one of the most overlooked features of any rapidly deployed, tactical system (not only data marts, but transaction processing applications as well) is the ability to monitor usage.

It's likely that the urgency of the business mission that has led you to pursue a rapid development data mart strategy will preclude (at least for a while) the creation and deployment of monitoring facilities. That's all right; if your data mart is well received and successfully used, you can (and should) add those capabilities shortly after the data mart's initial operational capability (IOC) is achieved.

However, you should design the monitoring capabilities you'll eventually need now, at least at a high level. Early design activity of monitoring capabilities is primarily a political strategy. By having these design plans available, you can demonstrate that even though your rapid data mart development may be aggressive and daring in comparison with your company's traditional, slower development methods, you have an eye for ongoing operations and aren't just focused on development. When you're asked questions about usage, display the design plans for data mart monitoring capabilities.

Consider the following in your design:

♦ Who is using the data mart, how frequently, when, and for what purposes?

♦ What data is most commonly accessed, and what data is least frequently accessed (including data that is never accessed)?

- When does usage peak, when is usage slight, and why?

- How does response time vary over different periods, and why?

- How does the size of results sets (e.g., how many rows of data are returned as the result of a query) vary?

- When may multiple servers be part of the data mart environment, and what is the workload distribution across them?

- What network traffic is specifically due to data mart activity?

- How many "runaway" queries are occurring (and who is responsible for them)?

- What are the database's physical characteristics (e.g., table space management)?

TIP If your data mart will eventually have a hybrid OLAP (HOLAP) environment consisting of both multidimensionally stored summaries and relationally stored detailed data, you want to have an idea of how the respective data environments are being used in relationship to one another. Look at drill-through activity and determine whether (and if so, how frequently) dynamically created aggregates are reused.

Fortunately, you can purchase and install a number of monitoring tools in your environment to perform most or all of the above administration functions, so you won't have to worry about custom development for these functions.

Data Mart Security Management

Recall that the chapter dealing with Week 5 discussed the data mart's security design issues. Designing and implementing security measures isn't enough; you need to make sure that you have an effective security administration program in place to ensure that security breaches are prevented or, if they do occur, can be handled appropriately.

The majority of your data mart's security aspects can be leveraged on top of the security capabilities of your enterprise's infrastructure. For example, authentication (proving that users and applications requesting access to the data mart are who they claim to be) should be a consistent function across the entire enterprise, not just for the data mart, and the data mart should tap into whatever monitoring facilities exist with regard to authentication management.

As part of managing the data mart's user community (discussed next), your security design should also specify how new users will be granted permissions to various pieces of data, the circumstances under which data access permissions should be revoked, and ways to detect attempted security violations.

Managing the User Community

Your data mart's initial user community will change. New users will be added, existing users will move to new jobs or resign from the company, and users will change roles, requiring a shift in what they can and can't do within the data mart's environment.

You need to design procedures for managing the user community throughout the life of the data mart. Leverage as much as you can of your enterprise's overall user management procedures (part of the systems administration function, usually) to keep your data mart's user models consistent with those of other systems. (Hint: Leverage the analysis work done by the data mart team member responsible for systems and infrastructure research during the first few weeks of design.)

Data Mart Support Services and Assistance

Initially, data mart support will almost always be provided by traditional help desk services: one or two people who have been "supertrained" in the operations and characteristics of the data mart will be assigned to assist users.

Ideally, though, support services should be provided in as much of an automated manner as possible through context-sensitive help, browser-based problem submission and resolution processes, and computer-assisted training and education courses in data mart usage. Design these capabilities now; after the data mart has become an accepted and valued member of the organization's IT assets, it should be no trouble at all getting funding to proceed with developing these support capabilities, and you'll be prepared.

Database Backup

How frequently should the data mart's contents be backed up? One school of thought is that because a data mart (or, for that matter, a data warehouse) can always be reconstructed from its original data sources, it's a foolhardy proposition to back up the database, particularly if it's very large (several hundred gigabytes or more). Those opposed to this approach point out that reconstruction from a standing start would be an extremely problematic, if not impossible, task given all the undocumented nuances and tweaking throughout the system's life cycle.

You need to decide whether or not database backup needs to be done for your data mart and, if so, the details of how backup will be performed. A relatively small database can be backed up in its entirety whenever necessary; in a data mart that has no user updates between restocking events, a logical choice would be immediately after each refresh cycle has been completed. Larger databases could be backed up through incremental backup facilities of the DBMS. You could periodically back up the entire database (say, every three months) and between those times, do incremental backups at each refresh cycle (for example, on the first day of every month).

TIP Be careful if you're updating your data mart.

Don't forget that your business rules may very well cause update transactions to occur in the data mart as a result of user actions. For example, interim results of what-if modeling may be stored for subsequent use, or a data mart that is operationally oriented instead of retrieval oriented (a good example of which would be a budget support data mart) may have update transactions as a natural part of how the data mart is used. If your data mart will support update transactions, it is especially important to do a careful database backup design.

Also, remember that whatever gets backed up may have to be restored. Make sure your design includes database restore functions, and make sure that you do a careful analysis of the business requirements for time-to-restore windows.

Scheduling

Ideally, data mart restocking, backup operations, reports from monitoring processes, and other administrative functions should be done on a scheduled (i.e., automation-supported) basis rather than being "kicked off" by manual processes. Your design for the data mart's scheduling services may include the following:

♦ Time-based activities (e.g., restocking of part or all of the data mart on the first day of every month)

♦ Event-based activities (e.g., after operations are restored following a database crash, a series of recovery scripts, including restoring the database, should be automatically started and managed)

♦ Standard report production and distribution (such as those from the data mart monitoring service)

Metadata Management

Metadata, or data about data, can be an important part of your data mart environment if you have enough commitment and foresight to think past the short-term implementation challenges toward long-term benefits.

The idea of metadata has gone through several up-and-down cycles since the late 1970s when data dictionaries, the predecessors to repositories, were seen as key components to managing a production database environment from development through operation. Data dictionaries would contain the metadata about a database and the applications with which it interacted. The idea faded, but when CASE (computer-aided software engineering) was popular in the early and mid 1980s, metadata was once again seen as a key success factor, this time in intertool exchange of information (e.g., a data flow diagram tool coordinating its data flows with the entities and attributes of a data modeling tool). As CASE fell out of favor near the end of the 1980s, so too did the idea of metadata (again).

When data warehousing became popular in the early 1990s, the concept of metadata was revived. There was a key distinction in the data warehousing orientation of metadata as contrasted with the earlier interest that faded away. Both the data dictionary/database and the CASE approaches to metadata were predominantly system oriented and were promoted as techniques and models to assist systems developers and administrators. Although data warehousing oriented metadata also has a system-oriented flavor (e.g., source-to-target mapping and transformation support), there is also a user-oriented aspect.

Even a relatively modest tactical data mart may contain hundreds of data elements, many of which have similar-sounding names. Novice users may quickly find themselves lost as they try to navigate through the data mart's contents and quickly turn into ex-users. Even experienced users who may have previously used data elements extracted from the data mart's sources or constructed their own queries piecemeal by querying multiple sources and combining the results in a spreadsheet are now faced with an unfamiliar naming scheme for their "favorite" data elements, new business rules, and other changes.

The data mart's metadata represents a means of providing a consolidated, consistent map to information such as the following:

♦ The data mart's contents

♦ The origin of the contents (i.e., what sources)

♦ The transformations that occurred along the way

♦ The business rules associated with each data element (e.g., range or list of values, time frame covered)

♦ Natural associations between various elements (e.g., how facts can be used according to the various dimensions and their respective levels)

♦ Associated information (e.g., corresponding detailed data that can be found in the organization's data warehouse or sites on the Internet where supplemental information can be obtained)

On the "system side" of the data mart's metadata, there should also be information about items such as the following:

♦ Restocking procedures and schedules

◊ The details of all necessary connectivity and interoperability

♦ Physical database structures and layouts

♦ Links to electronically stored data models

♦ Information about version control

♦ The details of the relationship between the data mart and a data warehouse from which it is stocked (if applicable)

If your objective is to quickly deploy a tactical data mart, your metadata management capabilities may initially be fairly sparse. At least plan on including information about all source-to-data mart mappings and transformation; doing so has benefit to both the user community and the systems staff responsible for data mart administration. Over time, though, strongly consider adding additional metadata management capabilities, particularly if your data mart will evolve and be extended to support additional functionality.

In Week 7, just as the data mart's design is about to wrap up, pick only an item or two and design the support capabilities you think can be implemented by the time the data mart is deployed, or as quickly as possible thereafter. (Again, source-to-data mart mappings and transformation are almost always the best idea for a starting point.) Fortunately, most middleware tools (those that handle some or all of the necessary extraction, transformation, quality checking, and the other source-to-target functions) do a fairly good job of creating and managing metadata, so if you're using a tool for these functions instead of custom code, you have a head start on deploying metadata-oriented functionality along with the data mart's business-driven capabilities.

The Design Review

On Friday of Week 7, it's time to converge all the design activity to date and conduct a comprehensive design review to determine if the team is ready to commence with construction the following Monday.

Though the topics covered in data mart design reviews will vary depending on the particular attributes of each, the following discussion presents a framework you can use and adapt to your particular needs.

Everyone involved in the data mart effort—the design team, the project manager, the project's executive sponsor, and the users who have participated throughout the design phase—should be present at the design review. This way, both business and technology perspectives can be considered throughout all discussions. Elements include the following:

◆ *Database design walk-through.* The entire database design—dimensions and levels, facts and their attributes, and physical choices—should be thoroughly reviewed. Pay particular attention to the choices made about granularity to ensure that nothing has been overlooked in terms of required level of detail.

◆ *Functionality review.* The designs for reports and queries, drill-down and drill-up capabilities, pivoting, and other capabilities that will be supported by the data mart need to be discussed.

◆ *Initial data mart population review.* Discuss the methods of data extraction, transformation, quality assurance, movement, and loading. If archived, off-line data will be loaded into the data mart, make sure to cover the design issues particular to each variation of the source (structural changes, etc.).

♦ *Data mart restocking review.* The same processes listed above (extraction, transformation, etc.) need to be reviewed with respect to the data mart's restocking.

♦ *Systems and infrastructure dependencies.* All scripts, utilities, and other "outside the data mart" dependencies must be reviewed.

♦ *Security architecture.* The entire security model, from both business and technical perspectives, is covered.

♦ *Expected performance.* Based on user requirements and what has been learned about the infrastructure for the data mart, give a careful end-to-end look at queries or reports deemed as critical to make sure that performance will be satisfactory.

♦ *Administration and operations review.* All the work performed this week, especially that dealing with backup and restore operations, needs to be reviewed carefully.

♦ *Integration and interoperability.* Even if your objective is to develop a tactical data mart without consideration for any down-the-road integration, at least take a cursory look at the design review about corollary data marts or data warehouse components with which integration may eventually be desirable.

♦ *Metadata review.* Discuss the current plans for metadata, particularly the user perspective (e.g., how users will be able to access metadata to help them navigate through the data mart and its functionality).

The Aftermath of the Design Review

If all has gone well, Friday afternoon will arrive with widespread agreement that there are no gaping holes in the design, and data mart construction can proceed on schedule.

Of course, an oversight or two may be uncovered during the design review. If the mishaps are minor ones, perhaps they can be corrected during the first few days of Week 8, construction can commence only a day or two late, and the missing time can be made up. If, however, the oversights are significant ones, the design phase is *not* concluded; it's time to cycle back, fix the problems, and proceed once again to a design review.

How to Achieve the Seventh Week's Goals

Figure WK7.5 illustrates the schedule of activities during Week 7, leading up to Friday's design review.

Project Management During Week Seven

If design has gone well, the project manager should be preparing for the construction phase, ensuring the following:

♦ The construction phase team is ready to go (including any newcomers who will join the team during Week 8).

♦ All development hardware and software is set and in place.

♦ Plans are under way for user training.

♦ Support services have been scheduled.

♦ Early work for deployment (Week 13) has begun.

You Know You're in Trouble When

You could face two serious problems during the week leading up to the design review. First, you could have to postpone the design review because the team was far from ready—*very* far. At Week 6, you determined whether you were one week away from being able to successfully conduct a design review, so sudden trouble at this late stage is not a good sign.

Or you could proceed to the design review on schedule only to have it become a complete flop. It shouldn't happen, especially if the data mart team has worked cooperatively and openly throughout the first seven weeks of the project, but if it does, you're in trouble!

Week 7 Spotlight on the Systems and Infrastructure Specialist

The team member responsible for systems and infrastructure work on the data mart project is, in many ways, the unsung hero of the project.

Continues

Activity Stream	Monday	Tuesday	Wednesday	Thursday	Friday
Additional Design Activities	Restocking design	Restocking design	Restocking design	Restocking design	
	Management and Operations design	Management and Operations design	Management and Operations design	Management and Operations design	
	Metadata management	Metadata management	Metadata management	Metadata management	
Design Review					**All-day, all-team all-area design review**

Figure WK7.5 The seventh week's calendar of activities.

Week 7 Spotlight on the Systems and Infrastructure Specialist *(Continued)*

To date, this person has played more of a supporting role than a front-line role. Make no mistake about it; it's been a critical role, but the purpose of having a single person assigned exclusively to infrastructure and systems work is to make sure that everyone else's work can make a smooth transition from the conceptual to the physical as the project moves forward.

Now, in Week 7, it's time for this team member to take center stage, becoming involved in some of the activities that will become important after the data mart has been deployed: usage monitoring, metadata management, database backup and restore operations, and so on.

At the design review, the systems and infrastructure specialist needs to play yet another key role: "reality gatekeeper." Every point of discussion, from initial population of the data mart's database to expected performance for reports and queries, should be carefully reviewed by this team member to make sure that the design ideas put forth can actually be implemented.

Part Four

The Data Mart Construction Phase

What You'll Find in This Chapter

The Data Mart Construction Phase

> Two Phased Releases
>
> Integration Testing
>
> The Construction Phase Team

Populating the Database

Beginning Front-End Database

Quality Assurance

How to Achieve the Eighth Week's Goals

> Project Management Activities During Week 8

You Know You're in Trouble When

Populating the
Target Database

A Note to the Reader: At long last, the data mart construction phase begins!

Along the way you've probably run into some impatience on the part of your development team and your user community, even though it's less than two months since the start of the project. "Why couldn't we have had some basic capabilities a few weeks ago?" some users might be grumbling. The developers, on the other hand, may have done their own grumbling about the amount of analysis and design they've had to perform.

It's at this point, though, that you and everyone else associated with the data mart will start to see the payoff from the path you've taken. A strong business orientation during the first two weeks of the project (the scope) led to a very focused five-week design phase, which now gives way to an even more focused construction effort.

The key word to remember is construction. *Just as you wouldn't build a home or standalone garage that varies widely from the approved design and underlying architecture, your team's activities during the next four weeks should likewise be constrained within the bounds of the data mart design that has just gone through a review process and is now accepted by all as the way to proceed.*

Now, it's normal for the team members to channel their natural curiosity into the products with which they're constructing the data mart. They have gained enough knowledge about the front-end tool, the middleware product(s), and the DBMS to know that there are usually several different ways of implementing desired functionality. They should also have gained enough knowledge in product evaluation during the design phase to evaluate which techniques are better under various circumstances. Even if that's the case, every developer will face choices during the next four weeks. Developers need to keep their mission in mind: check out different ways of implementing pieces of functionality as necessary, but the objective now is construction of the data mart, not product evaluation or testing.

As long as everyone on the team keeps this in mind, construction will likely proceed smoothly because of the strong foundation you have built over the previous seven weeks.

The Data Mart Construction Phase

The following sections provide a brief overview of the events and activities that will occur during the data mart construction phase (Weeks 8 through 12). Plan on four weeks of rapid-paced development activity—database creation and population, the generation of user screens, and the building of middleware scripts and business rules—followed by one week filled with end-to-end, comprehensive testing.

Two Phased Releases

Your four weeks of construction activity should be organized to provide you with two fully functional releases of the data mart (Figure WK8.1). The first phase (Weeks 8 and 9) should be dominated by the creation and initial population—ideally, *complete* initial population—of the data mart's database. In parallel, though, basic user functionality should be built so that the release at the end of Week 9 can actually be used in a limited capacity by one or two users. The details of these two threads of activity during Week 8, plus the necessary quality assurance procedures of each, are discussed later in this chapter.

Weeks 10 and 11 will build on the limited user functionality, with the majority of the development team's efforts devoted to completing the remainder of the screens, prestored queries, report formats, and other components that together will make up the capabilities for which the data mart is being built.

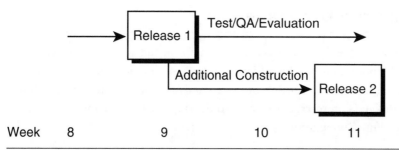

Figure WK8.1 Two releases during the construction phase.

Integration Testing

By the time Week 11 concludes, a *code freeze* should be instituted to permit one week of intense testing of the entire data mart and near-immediate response by the developers to problems that are discovered. The details of the data mart's integration testing are discussed in the chapter dealing with Week 12 activities.

The Construction Phase Team

Ideally, the construction phase team should be the same people who successfully completed the design phase activities. Some of the individuals will switch roles—the front-end product evaluator will now be the primary developer of user functionality, for example, assisted by the business analyst and the process modeler—but if it's at all possible, try to maintain the continuity of the team that has been functioning so effectively thus far.

A sample construction phase team might include people to perform the following roles:

- Database creation, development, loading, and administration (one person)

- Interfaces and support for the data sources (usually one person for each data source, depending on complexity)

- Development of user screens, reports, queries, scripts, and macros (three or four team members)

- Middleware functionality—extraction, transformation, quality assurance, and assistance with loading (one person)

- Systems and infrastructure support (one person)

- Quality assurance and configuration control (one person)

Populating the Database

As you begin work in the data mart's database environment, for the next two weeks, forget all about the restocking (data mart refresh) models that have most recently been the focus of that portion of design activity. It's often tempting, while the restocking design is on the radar screen, to develop those procedures and then worry about the initial population.

However, in two weeks, you need to complete construction of a partially operational data mart as an interim deliverable. Therefore, it is imperative that your database activities during the next two weeks be targeted against your mission of populating the data mart with real-world contents from the data mart's sources.

A recommended list of activities to reach this milestone is as follows:

◆ *Create the data mart's database.* Your first activity is to create the data mart's *real* database. Throughout the design phase, numerous databases have likely been created as part of the evaluation and testing process. Throw them all away! (See Figure WK8.2.)

Actually, you may wish to salvage pieces of data definition language (DDL) code from more recent versions that you know will be retained in the data mart's database such as column names, data types and sizes, and CHECK clauses that describe permissible values—to prevent unnecessary retyping, but since you are now beginning construction, don't mistakenly try to build on the database structures and interim contents that were part of the evaluation process. It may be tempting to save time by trying to retain the contents of several database tables, alter the schema definition to add new columns specified in the final approved design, and then add only "delta" contents to the new data elements in each row.

Usually, though, trying to "finesse" the database population leads to a great deal of confusion and data integrity errors that wouldn't otherwise occur (e.g., contents loaded into the wrong rows within a table). As a result, not only have your expected time savings evaporated, but you find yourself behind schedule.

Instead, perform these simple, straightforward tasks: Either drop any existing tables and their contents that may be in the database you'll reuse from your design phase or create a new, empty database.

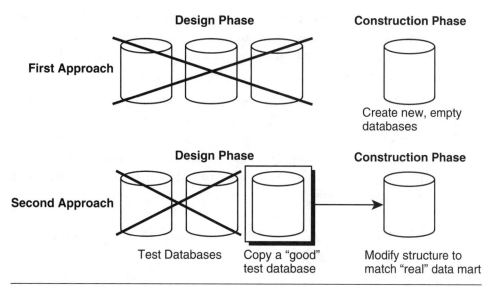

Figure WK8.2 Two approaches to initial data mart population.

You should create the entire database at once, even those tables that you may not be populating immediately.

♦ *Review scripts and business rules from the design phase's evaluation process.* In the area of data mart middleware functions, reuse is a good thing! Many of the transformation business rules, data movement processes (e.g., file transfer scripts), and data quality check rules that you created to evaluate and test products during the design phase can be used intact or with only slight modification (Figure WK8.3). Take an inventory of the components you created during the design phase, noting which ones are likely to be useful during the next two weeks. Separate those from the others that aren't likely to be needed, and quickly create a list of your middleware assets and the source(s) and database contents to which each applies.

♦ *Start with the simplest one-to-one mappings.* Once the database has been created, it's time to begin the population process. It's highly recommended that you begin by concentrating on data extracted from a single source that will be loaded into, and make up the entire contents of, a data mart's database table (Figure WK8.4). For now, forget about any of the more complex source-to-data mart movement models that are discussed later in this section. You want to make sure that you achieve results—complete results—as soon as possible. The database's quality assurance effort will occur in parallel with the initial population, not afterward. Your objective, then, is to present tables to the QA specialist that will be in exactly the same state (including contents) as when the data mart is deployed to the users.

♦ *Begin with archived, historical, offline data (if applicable).* Before you start extracting data from sources' operational databases and file systems, begin with any archived, historical data that is no longer stored online but has been deemed necessary for inclusion in the data mart, as shown in Figure WK8.5 on page 212. (Issues with regard to archived data and your data mart were discussed in Chapter 3.)

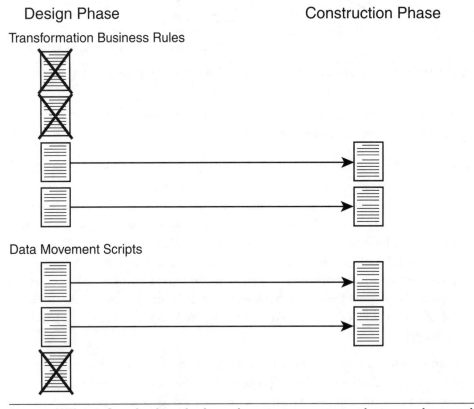

Design Phase

Transformation Business Rules

Construction Phase

Data Movement Scripts

Figure WK 8.3 Cataloging design phase components that may be used to populate the data mart.

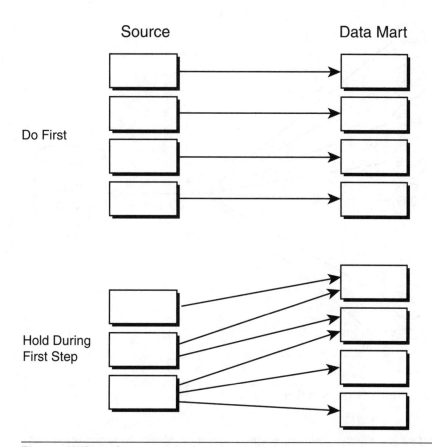

Figure WK8.4 Start with the simplest source-to-target mappings.

The reason for the oldest-to-newest order is simple: you want to intrude into the domain of a production database or file system for your initial load process only once. If there are problems waiting for you—data elements accidentally skipped over when the data mart's database was created, for example—it's best to discover and fix those easily correctable errors and repeat your processes in an environment that isn't impacting the operational systems in the enterprise. By the time all historical data has been loaded, the middleware processes should be "shaken out" enough so only a single pass at each source's operational data is needed.

♦ *Test, test, test along the way.* As soon as you have complete tables in your data mart, turn them over to the QA specialist for testing *immediately*.

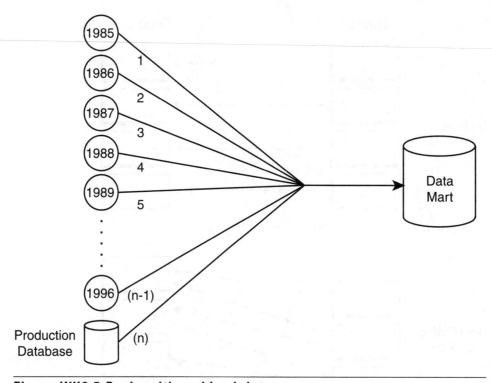

Figure WK8.5 Begin with archived data.

◆ *Add complex mappings.* Once the simple one-to-one, source-to-target mappings have been completed, you need to complete the rest of the population processes. These will include, for example, situations in which two sources converge and are unified into a single source table (Figure WK8.6).

◆ *Test performance and adjust physical design as necessary.* In addition to the QA procedures on the contents of the tables newly created from the complex mappings, database performance should be tested and evaluated. This performance evaluation should occur along the way, also in parallel with data mart population. If you find performance problems, identify the cause(s) and potential correction(s) as quickly as possible.

◆ *If necessary, start over again to take advantage of physical tuning.* The corrective actions necessary to overcome performance issues may require adjustments and tuning to the physical structure of the database. *Don't be afraid to start over!* You are better off repeating your population procedures, which have all been shaken out by now, and trying to make up the time later in the schedule than to stick with a database design that just won't do the job.

The preceding approach by which the data mart is populated might seem odd. Specifically, why should you have to extract data in a piecemeal manner from the sources, ordered by the complexity of the source-to-target mappings? Why not go source by source, staging some of the data if necessary, until you extract companion data from other sources while you load the data that you can?

Actually, you could proceed in a source-by-source manner, and in fact, your data mart restocking procedures will operate that way for reasons of efficiency. However, keep in mind that you are engaged in a one-time mission: initial population of the data mart. In many, perhaps most, situations, you are more likely to run into problems during the initial population effort if you jump right into complex, merge-oriented mappings and transformations. Learn about the data, the tools, and the processes before you add too much complexity to the picture.

TIP Do what's right for *you*! Every data mart situation is different; as long as you reach your objective of a completely populated, quality-checked data mart by the end of Week 9, the steps you take on the road to that point don't matter. Again, initial population of any data mart is a one-time event, so process efficiency is far less important in this domain than it will be for the ongoing restocking processes.

Beginning Front-End Development

In parallel with the database creation, work will now begin on the front-end functionality that will be deployed to the users. This functionality, and the mechanisms through which it will be implemented, will vary widely from one data mart to another. This section presents a general guide to capabilities that might be part of your data mart and the types of activities to be performed during Week 8:

♦ *Database connection and interface.* Front-end tool products vary, but typically you need to establish a connection with, and import data definitions from, the database that you will access using that tool. As soon as you create the data mart's database (as discussed earlier in this chapter), establish the linkage between the tool and the database.

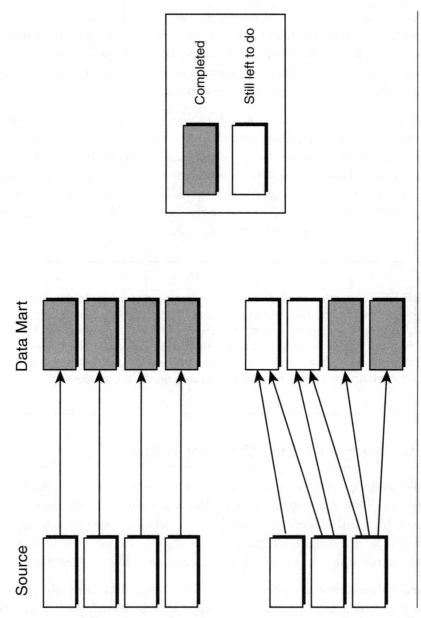

Figure WK8.6 Finishing up with complex mappings.

♦ *Reports.* A good place to start creating functionality is in the area of reports, particularly those that are static in nature (e.g., the same report is regularly run with little or no user-induced variation). When possible, begin with database tables created early in the week (e.g., those populated from simple source-to-target mappings) so that you have real-life data to test the correctness of the reports (see Figure WK8.7).

♦ *Managed queries.* You can also begin creating managed queries, user requests that are bounded by "reasonableness guidelines" that are in concert with the business objectives of the data mart (as contrasted with completely ad hoc, totally unpredictable queries). The work performed by the business analyst and the users during the early weeks of design, when drill-down and drill-up paths, desired data pivot models, and other OLAP and querying functionality were identified, will provide the pool of functionality from which the managed queries can be created (Figure WK8.8). As with reports, begin with managed queries that will access completely populated database tables to check correctness of the queries you create.

♦ *Graphics.* Reports and queries that will generate graphical output (see Figure WK8.9) need special attention. Choices need to be made about the specific graphical representation (pie chart or bar chart?) and the attributes of each graph (colors, styles, labels, titles, etc.). *Don't overlook the complexities waiting for you in this area!* Users are surprisingly passionate about graphical presentations and often spend a lot of time quibbling about the visual properties that have little or no impact on the underlying business information. You don't want your data mart's business value tarnished because users refuse to use graphs that are missing labels or aren't in a preferred output format.

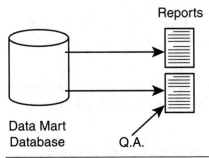

Figure WK8.7 Creating reports.

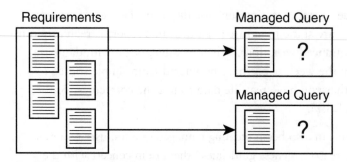

Figure WK8.8 Creating managed queries.

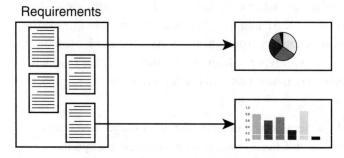

Figure WK8.9 Creating graphical output.

Quality Assurance

Quality assurance during Week 8 should be focused primarily on the contents with which the data mart is populated. Tests should be run to verify the following:

♦ No out-of-range values have been loaded.

♦ Numeric values add up correctly according to "check figures" obtained from the data sources. (Hint: Use scripts and SQL queries developed as part of the source data analysis whenever possible.)

♦ Cross-table data integrity is enforced (e.g., denormalized data, such as department names or product descriptions, that appear in more than one table are identical across those tables).

♦ All identified source data quality problems that were supposed to be fixed as part of the data transformation process have been fixed.

In addition, it's important to conduct data tests to verify the semantic integrity of facts that have been constructed. For example, "total expenses by department by month" may have a business rule associated with the fact: a rolling, month-by-month two-year history of expenses (even if no expenditures were made in a given month) needs to be in the data mart. Therefore, the QA specialist should verify that, indeed, every department does have 24 rows of data, one for each of the past 24 months, containing expense data.

Suppose, though, that the data mart is to contain a fact "expenses by department by expense category by month," again for a rolling 24-month period. What is the business rule that applies in this situation (assume 25 expense categories): 600 rows of data (25 x 24) for every department—even if in any given month a department had no expenses in that category—or 0 to 25 rows of data for each month for each department, which is a totally unpredictable number?

In the latter scenario, QA testing is far more complex than in the former one. You can't just scan the database and ensure that the correct number of rows (24) has been loaded and that the correct range on the time dimension (one and only one entry for each of the past 24 month-year combinations) exists. You now need to create and run a report and then cross-reference that data with the contents of the data source(s) from which expense data has been extracted. To further complicate matters, you need to make sure that any data corrections you made along the way are factored into your testing.

The point is this: QA'ing data mart contents can be a very difficult process.

TIP Don't use the front-end tool for QA yet! It's strongly recommended that you *not* conduct Week 8 QA of the data mart's database using the reports and queries (or variations thereof) that are being run at the same time. Rather, use SQL or a 4GL-like product (e.g., SAS). During Week 9 QA, attention shifts toward the reports and queries, QA'ing the front-end functionality. By having results from SQL-generated queries against which tool-generated queries can be compared, you have a "baseline" to assist the QA process.

How to Achieve the Eighth Week's Goals

Figure WK8.10 illustrates the activities that will occur during the first week of data mart construction.

Project Management During Week 8

Even though Week 7 ended with an all-day meeting—the design review—Week 8 should commence with yet another meeting for the entire team: a morning kickoff meeting for the construction phase. Any weekend thoughts about the design review can be quickly discussed with respect to any impact on the construction phase activities ahead. Then, the balance of the meeting will be taken up by the project manager's discussion of week-by-week, day-by-day objectives and the tactics and techniques that will be used to achieve them.

Make sure that every team member is "on the same page of the data mart play-book" as construction begins. This is particularly important for new team members who weren't involved in the design activity—front-end tool specialists added for additional person-power to assist parallel development, for example—but even if the same team has carried over from the previous phase, the project manager needs to establish a framework and guiding principles of construction, not design and evaluation, and make absolutely certain that all members understand their roles as the team moves ahead.

For the duration of the week, the project manager should pay particular attention to the efforts to populate the data mart's database. If this stream of activity is progressing smoothly, a hands-off approach is recommended; if problems occur, the project manager needs to intercede to achieve as expedient a resolution as possible.

You Know You're in Trouble When

The Week 8 trouble spot is a simple one: populating the database is a dismal failure, or at least way behind schedule. The following may signify more trouble:

♦ Seemingly simple loading scripts continually terminate on a particular row of data, but the error message is cryptic and the data doesn't seem to have any errors.

♦ Data "disappears" from tables after its presence has been verified because of a previously undiscovered serious bug in the fast load utility.

Activity Stream	Monday	Tuesday	Wednesday	Thursday	Friday
Database Population	Review design phase activity; select items for reuse	One-to-one mappings	One-to-one mappings	Complex mappings	Complex mappings
Front-End Development	Establish development environment	Establish database connectivity Screens and scripts	Screens and scripts	Screens and scripts	Screens and scripts
QA Activity			Test along with development	Test along with development	Test along with development

Figure WK8.10 The eighth week's calendar of activities.

219

♦ The duration of the largest data loading jobs is much, much longer than you had expected, even though you had previously tested similar volumes during the evaluation period.

The good news is that you can usually brute-force your way through these types of unexpected problems during the initial loading process; it may take a while, perhaps a long while, and adversely affect your schedule, but you can use a combination of prolonged loading windows and workarounds to overcome product deficiencies to complete the initial population.

The bad news is that the problems you're now encountering will almost always be present also in the restocking process, and you're just getting a taste of what's to come.

Week 8 Spotlight on the Database Developer

The database developer is the "commander in chief" of the database population effort. A flurry of real activity is occurring all at once; unlike in the design phase, this time, results have to be obtained quickly and regularly.

The database developer not only creates the database—the framework into which all the loading activity will lead—but also does the following:

♦ Specifies and controls the order of loading activities (e.g., simplest mappings first, more complex mappings later)

♦ Directs the activities of the QA specialist, but makes sure that they don't interfere with the loading process

♦ Gives a daily status report to the project manager with respect to the initial loading process

The database developer also needs to be involved in the development of user functionality (reports, queries, etc.) in two important ways. First, make sure that the tool successfully imports and coordinates the definitions from the database and that all metadata (data types, sizes, permissible values, etc.) is represented correctly.

Additionally, the database developer will probably need to support the front-end development that will use the database tables already created. Test reports and queries that will access large amounts of data should be coordinated with the loading activity to ensure that no scheduling clashes occur.

What You'll Find in This Chapter

Populating the Database

Beginning the Restocking Processes

Additional Front-End Development

Quality Assurance

How to Achieve the Ninth Week's Goals

You Know You're in Trouble When

Week 9

Delivering the
Preliminary Data Mart Release

A Note to the Reader: Construction has just begun, and already a preliminary version of the data mart will be made available at the end of Week 9.

Too aggressive? Not at all! If Week 8's activities proceeded smoothly, those of Week 9 should be directed toward partial closure, such as making sure that there is a usable subset of functionality that can be deployed on a limited scale.

Note that this initial release is not a full-scale deployment in terms of all data mart users' having access from their desktops to the data mart's contents. Typically, only a few users should be given the initial functionality. Your objective isn't to achieve limited operational capability of the data mart but rather to field test initial functionality in a setting other than the development environment.

At the same time, don't become so consumed in achieving the initial data release that construction activity gets sidetracked during Week 9. The project manager needs to make sure that the team's attentions are appropriately balanced between continued, steady progress toward the real data mart deliverable and the initial release.

Populating the Database

Your data mart's database absolutely, positively must be completely populated by the end of Week 9.

This milestone is driven not by the initial limited deployment coming at the end of the week but rather by the need to turn your efforts to developing the restocking processes by the time the construction phase closes. Given that restocking is usually more complex than the initial population and needs to regularly recur, adequate time must be left for those activities. Therefore, the processes discussed in the previous chapter need to continue to conclusion. Activities include not only finishing the database loading, but also completing the quality assurance efforts.

At the end of Week 9, subject to successful completion of the initial population, the database should be frozen; no more changes should occur until the first restocking cycle after the data mart has been deployed and is in operation (see Figure WK9.1).

Beginning the Restocking Processes

While initial population is completing, it's also time to start work on the restocking processes. These are discussed in more detail in the following chapter (Week 10).

Additional Front-End Development

During Week 8, significant progress was made in the development of the front-end functionality. Reports, managed queries, and graphical output were created and tested.

This week, these activities should continue, and depending on how much additional work needs to be completed (e.g., how many more reports) these development activities should proceed to completion, or as close to completion as possible. Refer to the previous chapter (Week 8) for discussion of these items.

In addition, however, development activities should commence with respect to the following other ways of delivering functionality to the data mart's user community. Depending on the characteristics of your particular data mart, you might begin work on the following:

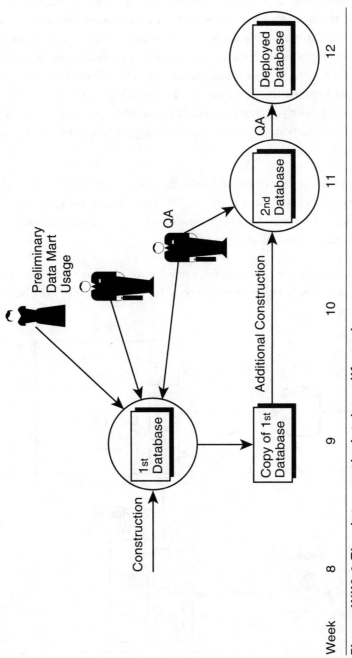

Figure WK9.1 The data mart's database life cycle.

♦ *Report distribution and posting.* Though the concept of data warehousing—and by extension, data marts—is predicated on users' having data at their fingertips, many users have neither the time nor the interest in developing queries, specifying the parameters of a report, or otherwise interacting directly with the data mart. Still, they are interested in and will use the results of standard reports generated by the data mart (see Figure WK9.2). The scope and design processes, if properly performed, will have identified and categorized this segment of the user population and further noted the report-based information desired by each person.

Week 9 is a good time to begin development of the capabilities that will be used for this type of passive data mart use. The exact mechanism(s) you use will, of course, depend on what you have considered in your design; commonly used methods include the following:

◊ Electronic mail (e-mail)-based distribution of selected reports to individual users, based on a report registration service that specifies the distribution policies

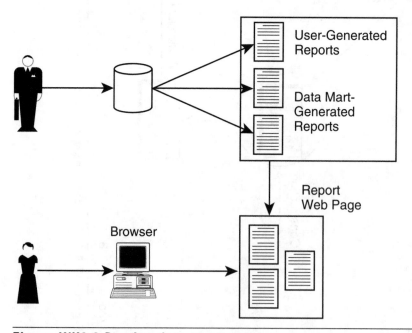

Figure WK9.2 Passive data mart use.

◊ Posting of reports into a groupware environment (e.g., a Lotus Notes database or a Microsoft Exchange folder)

◊ Posting of reports in HTML (Hypertext Markup Language) format on a company intranet

♦ *Results workflow.* If your data mart environment will feature *results workflow*—the transmission of items of interest from one user to one or more others (see Figure WK9.3)—you can begin development of these capabilities. An example of results workflow might be the following sequence of events:

1. An analyst issues a query to receive back a "drillable" report (i.e., the analyst will be able to drill down and up to varying levels of detail, as desired) that will show month-by-month revenues and expenses across the organization.

2. The results returned are compared, "behind the scenes" (i.e., by the product) against prestored thresholds of desirable performance: revenue-to-expense ratios, maximum permissible increase in month-to-month expenses, and so on.

3. Any out-of-bounds results are automatically sent by e-mail to other people in the organization (the analyst's manager, other analysts, the purchasing manager) according to a management directory that details who should be notified of certain events or information.

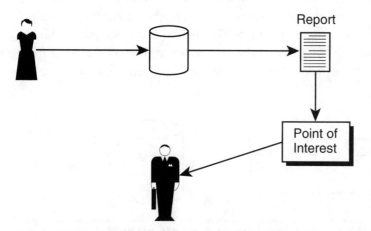

Figure WK9.3 Results workflow in the data mart environment.

4. At the same time, the data mart environment will, based on specified business rules, automatically execute a sequence of queries for supporting information (e.g., what expense categories might also have seen similar undesirable increases in other organizations supported by the data mart) and e-mail the results of that query to the analyst and other individuals who, according to the management directory, should also receive those reports.

TIP Start modestly. Workflow-enabled data mart functionality can be fairly complex. Developing and testing the business rules relating to results distribution, automatic generation of follow-on queries, and coordination of follow-up actions is not a trivial task. If your organization has never developed a workflow-enabled environment before, begin with a few critically important flows that are deployed and used for a while. Workflow-enabled applications (including data marts) often have serious cultural undertones that clash with an individual's work philosophy (and sometimes that of the entire organization). Some people don't like work being routed to them by the system and rebel against the entire concept. Don't overdo your workflow enablement; you don't want an otherwise well-received data mart to fail because of what you anticipated would be value-added capabilities.

♦ *Spreadsheet interfaces.* If some users will access your data mart's contents through their PC-based spreadsheets (remember, spreadsheet programs are the most widely used analysis tool in the world!), you can begin developing this spreadsheet-to-data mart interface. If the spreadsheet will serve as a direct front end to the data mart's database (see Figure WK9.4), you can begin working on the following:

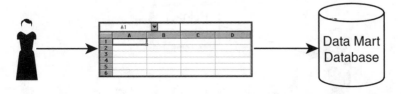

Figure WK9.4 Direct data mart access from a spreadsheet.

- Data layouts on the spreadsheet

- Programmatic code (e.g., Visual Basic controls for Microsoft Excel spread-sheets)

- Macros

- Data filters

- Spreadsheet-based pivot tables

An alternative approach, shown in Figure WK9.5, is to use an intermediate database—PC-based Microsoft Access or NT-based SQL Server, for example—as an integration point in which portions of the data mart (following a regular extraction process) are merged with other data and then accessed through the spreadsheet interface.

TIP Consider live links. You may wish to create an integration point between data mart reports and a word processing package or presentation software using live links, or interfaces that automatically update the representation of the report in the desktop software with the most recent results.

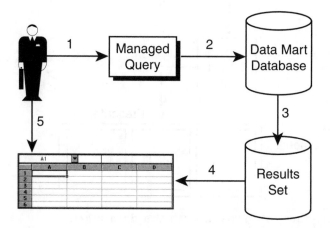

Figure WK9.5 An intermediary database for spreadsheet-based data access.

♦ *Desktop product integration.* In addition to spreadsheet interfaces, your data mart may require integration of reports and query results with other desktop software (a word processor or a presentation program, for example), as shown in Figure WK9.6. You can begin development of these interfaces also during Week 9.

Quality Assurance

QA during Week 9 must be focused on ensuring that the upcoming limited deployment will be usable; The highest data quality possible must be included in the data mart, and all queries and reports that have been developed to date will produce the intended results.

How to Achieve the Ninth Week's Goals

Figure WK9.7 illustrates the activities that will occur during Week 9.

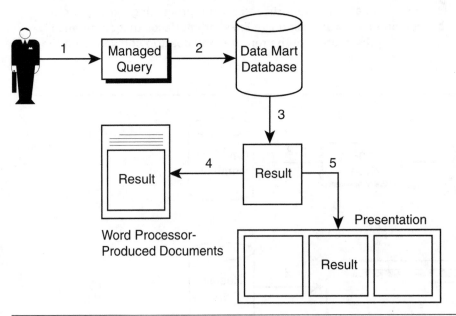

Figure WK 9.6 Desktop product integration with the data mart.

Activity Stream	Monday	Tuesday	Wednesday	Thursday	Friday
Database Population	Complex mappings	Complex mappings	Mid-week test Adjust loading procedures, if necessary	Finish loading	Deliver populated database
Front-end development	Report distribution and posting	Report distribution and posting	Report distribution and posting Spreadsheet and other interfaces	Spreadsheet and other interfaces	Spreadsheet and other interfaces
QA	Ongoing	Ongoing	Ongoing	Ongoing	Ongoing

Figure WK9.7 The ninth week's calendar of activities.

You Know You're in Trouble When

You must have progress by this point!

Achieving the initial release of the data mart makes a very significant political statement to everyone interested in the data mart effort: achieving this milestone tells everyone, from the project's executive sponsor to the lowest-ranking analyst in the user community, that the data mart team can actually deliver what it has promised all along. From here on out, you will have built up political capital that you can call on as necessary for the rest of the data mart's development, planning for additional functionality during subsequent phases or expanding the base of users.

However, failure to achieve the initial release calls into doubt the capabilities of everyone involved in the data mart development effort. Enemies of your data mart effort will chortle, and team morale will undoubtedly sink as the hard work performed by everyone on the team is suddenly tainted.

Failure to achieve the promised level of progress will create tremendous problems for your entire effort and everyone involved in it for the duration of the effort. Make very sure that you have the highest degree of confidence before you begin the construction phase that you will be able to deliver incremental functionality at the point you promise it. Don't commit to unreasonably early deliveries for purely political reasons; your chances for achieving unrealistic commitments are slight, and all you do is add significant risk to your entire effort and jeopardize the delivery of the business value you're attempting to provide.

Week 9 Spotlight on the Data Mart's Executive Project Sponsor

The data mart project's executive sponsor has, to this point, played primarily a supporting role because the project entered the design phase in Week 3. Although the sponsor received regular status reports and periodically met with the project manager and other key individuals, for the most part, design and development have been primarily technical activities. An insightful executive sponsor puts has full faith in the project manager to lead the team through design and construction activities.

Now, in Week 9, an interim release of the data mart, containing real functionality that is expected to be used as part of ongoing business

Continues

processes, is being deployed. In addition, the effort is four weeks away from completion and full-scale deployment. It is time for the project's executive sponsor to become more actively engaged.

For example, the executive sponsor must now do the following:

- Ensure that the workloads of users who are expected to work with the initial capability allow them to devote significant effort to using the data mart as part of their business activities. Too often, early functionality is deployed to selected users who are too busy with other activities to devote adequate time to working with the data mart and providing adequate and timely feedback to the development team.

- Ensure that organizations from which support is needed specifically, the IT department—have assigned personnel to tasks such as database support and desktop software installation.

- Ensure that the support services organization is gearing up for data mart support following deployment.

- Ensure that development of user training is proceeding on schedule and will be available when needed.

- Ensure that project funding isn't jeopardized.

Note the use of the word *ensure* in each of the points above. The project sponsor needs to do a broad-reaching survey of anything that could affect the success of the data mart project. If no problems exist, no action on the part of the sponsor is required. If, however, issues surface, the project demands that all roadblocks be removed.

Unlike the project manager, who typically negotiates necessary support throughout the duration of the project, the project sponsor should be considered to have modest authority that is carefully spent on the most critical items necessary to drive the project to a successful conclusion. Holding this executive weight until the latter stages of the project can be most beneficial.

What You'll Find in This Chapter

Splitting the Database

Restocking Development

    Complete Replacement

    Appending

    Rolling Append

    In-Place Updates

    Additional Complexities

Additional Front-End Functionality

Feedback from the Limited Functionality Deployment

Documentation

    User Documentation

    Data Mart Maintenance

    Data Mart User Support

User Training

Support Services

Preparing for the Next Release

Administration

User Groups

Installation

How to Achieve the Tenth and Eleventh Weeks' Goals

You Know You're in Trouble When

Completing
Construction

A Note to the Reader: As you no doubt know, achieving success in initially populating the data mart is only the beginning. It's an admirable start given that it is now barely more than two months since the project scope began with a discussion of the project's mission statement. However, you now need to address the evolving organism aspect of the data mart: how to address the time, space, and condition aspects of your organization's business needs.

Because a data mart is built exclusively or primarily from previously owned data acquired from other sources, several questions need to be addressed and resolved to ensure that the data mart will remain a viable, valuable corporate asset after its initial deployment. These questions include the following:

♦ When do a data mart's contents become stale? That is, when is the business value delivered by the data mart severely diminished because its contents aren't as up-to-date as possible?

♦ At what point is enough data available to transform the data mart from a stale state of existence back into a condition in which the original business value can once again be delivered?

♦ *Where can the data be found that can negate the stale state, and what needs to be done to acquire that data and include it in the data mart?*

♦ *As part of the data mart's restocking process, what must happen to its current contents?*

The first two questions address the "time" aspect (when) of the data mart's operational viability, and the third question deals with the "space" needs (from where). The last question addresses the "condition" of the data mart: that is, when the time and space aspects are addressed, what else must happen within the data mart to restore it to its optimal operational state?

You already addressed all of these items during the design phase when you designed the restocking processes. From extraction of new data from the sources to the intermediate processes (quality checking, transformation) to database loading, you have well-designed processes that will ensure data mart viability for a prolonged period of time.

But now it's time to transform designs into reality.

Splitting the Database

As discussed in the previous chapter, the fully populated database is now frozen for the duration of the construction phase. If problems that slipped through the QA process are found during the next two weeks, either by the development team or by the user(s) accessing the database for "real work," corrections should be made to the database's contents. Or if performance problems surface, some additional physical tuning may be required. Otherwise, you are done making additions or changes to the database, but you still have significant development work to accomplish, specifically the restocking procedures. How can you freeze your database and still be able to develop and test restocking procedures that will change the contents?

The first task you have in Week 10 is to split your database. Make a copy of the fully populated database, install it on another server, and use one of the servers for continued development while you use the other as the production server.

Resist the temptation to deploy the fully populated database for operational use and then use a scaled-down version with significantly less data for your continued development. You want to test your restocking procedures under real-world conditions, with the data volumes with which you'll have to deal when the data mart is operational. For example, you want to know if you'll have problems with the load windows before you try in vain to squeeze what turns out to be a 36-hour restocking process into a 18-hour window.

Restocking Development

The chapter dealing with Week 7 introduced four models that may be used for restocking part or all of your data mart:

♦ Complete replacement

♦ Appending

♦ Rolling append

♦ In-place updates

The following sections briefly discuss some of the implementation details that you'll deal with.

Complete Replacement

Complete replacement of the data mart's contents is the simplest restocking model. especially if you do a complete replacement of the *entire* data mart, not just certain tables. However, don't overlook some hidden complexities that could cause you problems, such as the following:

♦ The simplest model is to drop the tables that will be completely rebuilt, but what happens if the restocking process fails and there isn't enough of a window left to restart the procedures? If you have enough capacity on your data mart's disks, consider retaining each table until you are absolutely certain that the reloading has successfully completed. You might create a separate database under a new name for the reloading process, with a logical name pointing to the correct database that should be used for the data mart. Upon verification of a successful load, you can then drop the old database (see Figure WK10.1).

♦ Should you perform quality assurance procedures as part of the reload, and if so, what should those procedures be? You are unlikely to have the window of opportunity to perform the extensive QA procedures that you did during initial loading, but you could use record counts, check counts for summary values, and apply other control measures to perform some rudimentary QA (see Figure WK10.2).

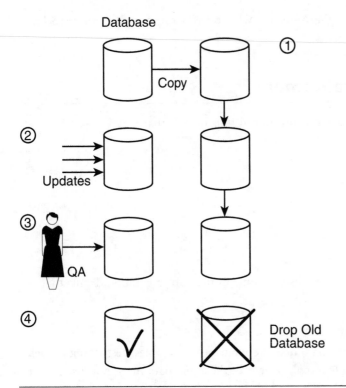

Figure WK10.1 Keeping the old database available during the load process.

♦ Will you have any concurrency control issues? Make sure that you don't schedule complete replacements while users are attempting to access the data mart. You may consider "locking" the database during reloading.

♦ Don't forget to allocate time to rebuild database indices.

♦ If structural changes are occurring in concert with a reload process, you need to ensure that metadata changes are made and the front-end tool's perception of the database's structure is updated and correct.

Appending

Appending data to existing tables can go smoothly, but you need to make sure that the procedures you develop take the following items into consideration:

♦ *Index structures*. Can indices be updated based on the new contents, or do they need to be rebuilt?

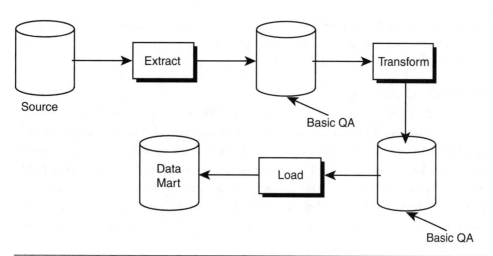

Figure WK10.2 Quality assurance during data mart reloading.

♦ *The exact mechanism by which the appending will occur.* Will you use SQL INSERT statements or a utility? Do you need to turn database logging off for performance reasons, and if so, what recovery procedures do you need to develop if problems occur?

♦ *The exact mechanisms by which you will extract the appropriate data from the source.* Is this extraction being done while the source is off-line? If not, what concurrency control procedures (e.g., database locking) can you use to ensure that your extract is "semantically correct?"

If newly extracted data implies changes to existing data mart contents (e.g., customer-salesperson assignment changes or a corporate reorganization that affects previous expense allocation), does appending need to be combined with in-place updates? If so, what is the exact order of procedures (e.g., do the append tasks first and then make the in-place updates)? What are the recovery procedures if the append operations are successful but the in-place updates fail (or vice versa)?

Rolling Append

In addition to all the appending-related concerns listed above, rolling append restocking models add other complexities, such as the following:

♦ What is the exact mechanism by which now-obsolete data should be removed? Should you remove it using SQL DELETE statements? What needs to be done to keep indices accurate?

♦ Should any data mart archival be done for the data that is being removed (e.g., in case it is determined at a later date that it is needed for other purposes, such as for trend analysis)? If so, how should the archival be done?

In-Place Updates

You may do in-place updates (shown in Figure WK10.3) using SQL UPDATE statements, but you need to take a careful look at potential performance issues. The database overhead usually associated with these statements—starting a transaction, applying a lock, doing a WRITE operation into the database, doing another WRITE operation to the database log, removing the lock, and committing the transaction—can be cumbersome. You need to make sure that you do a very careful performance analysis and develop scripts or programs that optimize your database operations to minimize excessive overhead.

Additional Complexities

You need to consider several other important items as you develop your data mart restocking mechanisms. One is the end-to-end, architected flow of data from the sources to the data mart. You need to ensure that you use as little time as possible to accomplish all the extraction, quality checking, transformation, and loading. The order by which you performed your initial data mart population (see the chapter

	DeptID	ExpenseCategory	Amt
Source Data	NE12	PERS6	3333.55
Data Mart Before Restocking	NE11 NE11 NE12 NE14	PERS5 PERS6 PERS6 PERS4	8888.66 1212.12 4545.67 5730.92
Data Mart After Restocking	NE11 NE11 NE12 NE14	PERS5 PERS6 PERS6 PERS4	8888.66 1212.12 3333.55 5730.92

Figure WK10.3 In-place updates in the data mart.

discussing Week 8 activities) will likely not be optimal for your restocking procedures. You may find yourself needing to have one or more "staging areas" so that your restocking can be efficiently accomplished (see Figure WK10.4).

Another issue you need to consider is cross-platform scheduling. One set of extraction routines may operate on one IBM mainframe, a second set operates on another mainframe, and a third set extracts data from a Unix-resident data warehouse. Your transformation tool runs on an NT server, but your data mart will operate on a Unix server.

You could manually control the systems routines, scripts, and utilities necessary to accomplish all the pieces of the end-to-end restocking procedures. As soon as you see that the procedure on the first mainframe has completed, for example, you could begin a file transfer utility to move the extract set to the NT server and start some, but not all, of the transformation scripts. You can then wait until the rest of the extraction procedures are completed, and copy those data sets to the NT server.

It's easy to see how the interaction of more than a couple of job streams can get very complex to manage. Ideally, you should try to develop scripts using a utility that is capable of managing individual jobs across multiple platforms (see Figure WK10.5).

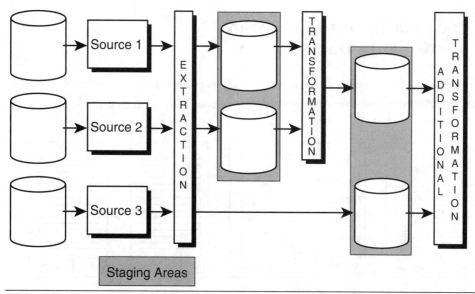

Figure WK10.4 Using staging areas as part of the restocking model.

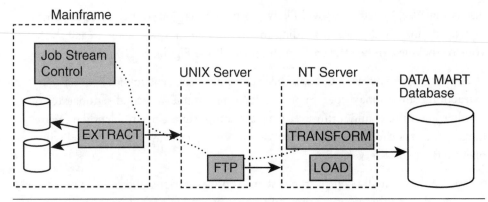

Figure WK10.5 Cross-platform job stream management.

Additional Front-End Functionality

During Week 10, additional development in all the areas discussed in the previous two weeks will continue (reports, queries, spreadsheet front-end interfaces, etc.). In addition, you might begin development of additional types of functionality, such as an executive information system (EIS) front end for "briefing book" access (see Figure WK10.6).

Feedback from the Limited Functionality Deployment

To help ensure that timely and useful feedback is provided from users of the limited functionality data mart that has been deployed, you may wish to provide them with

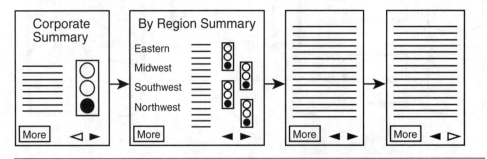

Figure WK10.6 An EIS "briefing book" built from data mart contents.

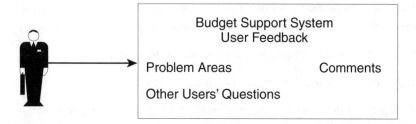

Budget Support System
User Feedback

Problem Areas   Comments

Other Users' Questions

Figure WK10.7 A website for early data mart usage feedback.

a mechanism by which they can provide that feedback. Traditionally, printed forms
have been provided for these purposes. You may wish to consider, however, quickly
developing an intranet-based system that can be accessed in parallel with the data
mart usage (see Figure WK10.7).

Documentation

All documentation should be nearing completion by the end of Week 11, in preparation for the data mart's deployment. Documentation should be available for the
following constituencies:

- Users

- Data mart maintenance

- Data mart user support (support services)

User Documentation

Data mart user documentation is similar to that of any other type of application, but
it tends to contain (or should contain) far more detail about the database environment than that of a production transaction processing application. The reason is that
most or all data mart users will have ad hoc query capability, and it's important that
users understand exactly the data elements to which they have access and that they
have detailed information about the characteristics and properties of those elements.

Though it's tempting, in the interests of expediency, to simply paste database
definition printouts into the user documentation and augment that content with brief
supplemental descriptions, doing so can often lead to a great deal of confusion and
information overload, especially for novice users. Care should be taken to organize
the database descriptions in a manner that is easily understandable: Show facts and

their related dimensions in concert with one another, for example, or perhaps aligned with standard reports (e.g., if denormalized tables are used to generate those reports).

User documentation should include, at a minimum, the following:

- An overall description of the data mart and its business purpose(s)

- A detailed map of all flows within the front-end tool software that covers the entire data mart functionality

- All log-on instructions

- Detailed, heavily illustrated descriptions of all user screens

- Detailed, heavily illustrated examples of all reports generated from the data mart

- Detailed discussions and examples of ad hoc queries

- Illustrations and examples of all drill-down and drill-up paths

- All error and advisory messages as well as the actions users should take when they receive those messages

Data Mart Maintenance

Detailed documentation should also be prepared for the staff members who are responsible for maintaining all components of the data mart, including at a minimum the following:

- The database environment, including the following:

  ◊ The DBMS software itself (overview and description; all environmental conditions, such as physical organization and structure of the database; interfaces with other software)

  ◊ All database table definitions

  ◊ All database metadata

  ◊ Any bugs or problems that were found during development and the current status

  ◊ Backup and restore procedures

  ◊ Any stored procedure code

- The front-end tools, including the following:

  ◊ A complete list of all environmental settings and configuration options

  ◊ All intercomponent connectivity and the mechanisms used

  ◊ Complete listings of all scripts and support code

  ◊ Complete screen-by-screen descriptions of the controls and underlying code: scripts, variables, and so on

- Connectivity and interoperability software, including the following:

  ◊ All open database connectivity (ODBC) or Java database connectivity (JDBC) settings and parameters

  ◊ Any customized interface code (e.g., Visual Basic programs used to integrate the data in a data mart's SQL Server database with a separate decision support system)

- Data mart middleware, including the following:

  ◊ Complete, detailed descriptions of all extraction, quality assurance, transformation, movement, and loading procedures

  ◊ Overviews of the tool(s) used to provide middleware functionality

The maintenance documentation should contain pointers and references to all applicable product documentation and references, including vendor websites.

Data Mart User Support

A separate set of documentation should be specifically designed and created for the support services staff. This documentation should be organized by the types of support requests the staff members are likely to receive, as follows:

- Help during system failures such as with general protection faults (GPFs) and system lockups

- Assistance with analyzing incorrect or uncertain results to queries or reports

- Instructions for performing certain tasks

User Training

User documentation is not enough to ensure that users will use a data mart to the achieve the highest degree of business value from the deployed functionality. A detailed, thorough training program needs to be created and made available to all members of the user community.

Ideally, several different levels of user training should be created as follows:

♦ An *overview course* will explain to anyone in the company—even those who are not direct users of the data mart—the purpose and mission of the data mart, the functionality that is supported, and in as explicit a manner as possible, the ways data mart usage will provide specific business benefit.

♦ A *general users' course* will thoroughly cover the data mart's functionality, using real-world business examples as a framework. The course should cover not only how to access data and run reports but also how to use the results of queries and reports as part of business operations.

♦ A *power users' course* goes beyond the topics and their respective depth in the general users' course. The power users' course will cover subjects such as creating complex new queries, writing scripts, using interfaces not likely to be used by the average user (e.g., exporting report results for use in a data mining environment), and anything else that will help experienced, skilled users obtain additional business benefit from the data mart.

♦ A *support service course* will provide intensive training for the data mart's user support staff.

TIP Consider multiple training courses. If a data mart will be used by an unusually broad constituency—analysts from four or five organizations whose business missions are only loosely related—consider having several versions of the general users' course, each one tailored to the specific functionality used within a specific organization. Doing so will alleviate boredom or attention wandering by attendees, particularly novice users.

Remember that the composition of your user community will change over time, and if your data mart is wildly successful, the community's size will increase dramatically. Training programs should be considered an ongoing process: deliver them as often as necessary, and constantly update them as data mart functionality and contents evolve.

Support Services

Earlier in this chapter, the need for specialized documentation for the data mart's user support staff was discussed. In addition to the documentation, though, an intensive training course should be prepared and delivered to these individuals.

Training and documentation aren't enough, though. For example, if your organization has a call center support environment for internal applications, data mart support should be integrated into the portfolio of systems that are supported. This will enable the support staff to do the following:

- ◆ Log all support requests

- ◆ Look up similar requests and see if the resolution to those applies to the new request

- ◆ Provide a workflow-enabled routing of support requests that can't be immediately handled by the appropriate personnel

- ◆ Track the status of open requests

- ◆ Provide reports and analysis of support requests to guide the data mart maintenance staff

Preparing for the Next Release

It's not too early to start preparing for the next release of the data mart. Features requested during the scope phase that have been deferred can now be considered. Likewise, requests for additional functions by users during design and construction can be looked at for inclusion in the next release of the data mart.

Planning for the next data mart release should include the following items:

♦ *Review of the current release.* This shouldn't be as comprehensive as the "project review" (discussed in the Week 13 chapter), but there should be an open discussion about the following:

◊ The tools and products used: have they performed as advertised, and can you deploy additional functionality using this software?

◊ The development effort: has the schedule been adhered to? How much catch-up has had to occur? Have any shortcuts had to be taken? Has functionality been deferred because of lack of time? Has the QA process let problems slip through that should have been caught earlier?

♦ *Data scalability issues.* Take a quick look at candidates for new functionality to determine the likely impact on the data mart's database environment. Can the current server environment and DBMS software handle the possible data growth?

♦ *User scalability issues.* Determine whether new groups will become members of the data mart user community. If so, how much will the user community grow? Are there any scalability issues (e.g., the front-end software) that could result?

♦ *General data mart receptiveness.* The data mart hasn't been deployed yet, but the prerelease version at the end of Week 9 and the general atmosphere in the company can give an early indicator as to how the data mart will be received. If requests for additional functionality are already pouring in, that is a good indication that the data mart will be well received (assuming it performs as well as envisioned).

♦ *Upcoming systems or infrastructure issues.* Find out if there are any forthcoming wide-reaching initiatives, such as a desktop software migration or an upgrade of the company intranet, that could affect the data mart environment. If so, will the next round of development have to be focused on migrating the data mart rather than adding new functionality?

♦ *General industry trends.* Learn what is happening in the data mart world with respect to cross-data mart integration, distributed access, drill-through access to underlying data warehouse-resident data, and other advances. Are any of these of interest to the next generation of your data mart?

♦ *Additional user interaction models.* If your data mart is used exclusively for OLAP functionality, determine whether it could next be part of a data mining environment. This would augment "tell me what happened, and why" targeted analysis of OLAP with the "tell me what might happen" predictive functionality or "tell me something interesting" digging-around model of data mining.

It's important not to let either the data mart development team or the user community become too focused on the next data mart release at the expense of the task at hand. At the same time, if there is support within the organization for immediate or near-immediate work on that next release after deployment, it's a good idea to begin looking in this direction a few weeks before the current effort is completed.

Administration

The chapter dealing with Week 7 discussed the design tasks related to administering the data mart and ensuring viable operations. As a reminder, these items include the following:

♦ Monitoring data mart usage

♦ Managing data mart security

♦ Managing the user community

♦ Offering data mart support services and assistance

♦ Backing up the database

♦ Scheduling

♦ Managing metadata

Some of the capabilities will be available at the initial data mart deployment; others (possibly usage monitoring and metadata management) may be delivered at a later date. Throughout construction, the appropriate support needs to be negotiated for the capabilities that will be delivered (for example, the database administration organization that will be responsible for the monthly database backup).

User Groups

A good idea is to create some type of data mart user group that can do the following:

♦ Provide ongoing support and assistance to less experienced users

♦ Provide an information exchange mechanism for increasingly dispersed members of the user community (e.g., what new reports have been created recently by power users that can be accessed by others; what's happening on the website where standard report results are posted)

♦ Help achieve cross-organizational agreement as to the relative priorities of enhancement requests

♦ Help ensure the viability of the user community by providing an environment for dialogue and front-line assistance

Installation

In Week 13, deployment week, the data mart software will be installed on client and server machines in preparation for operational use. All the installation procedures and supporting software must be developed during the construction phase to ensure that they are ready at that time. These will include the following:

♦ Zip routines to compress software for more efficient, less resource-intensive distribution (and corresponding unzip routines to bring the software back to an installable state)

♦ All setup scripts that will compile and organize dynamic link libraries (DLLs) and other executable components on the target machine

♦ Any changes to system initialization files (e.g., .INI files, .SYS files)

♦ Any specialized hardware (e.g., floating point accelerator boards needed for specialized data mining software) that needs to be installed, along with associated software

Activity Stream	Monday	Tuesday	Wednesday	Thursday	Friday
Systems Activity	Split the database				
QA Work-first release	QA database	QA database	QA database	QA database	QA database
QA Work-ongoing development	Ongoing	Ongoing	Ongoing	Ongoing	Ongoing
Development	Restocking	Restocking	Restocking	Restocking	Restocking

Figure WK10.8 The tenth week's calendar of activities.

251

How to Achieve the Tenth and Eleventh Weeks' Goals

Figure WK10.8 illustrates the activities that will occur during Week 10 of the data mart project. The calendar of activities for Week 11 will depend on the progress made during Week 10 and, for the development team, will be almost exclusively devoted to software development and unit testing.

You Know You're in Trouble When

You start getting feedback from the three or four users who have access to the initial data mart deployment, and it's not good.

Despite user involvement from the first days of the project; despite consensus as to what functionality should be provided and why; despite widespread agreement about report formats and what user screens should look like . . . despite all this, the feedback you receive is that users unequivocally don't like your data mart.

It's time to start digging for the reasons you're receiving negative responses because chances are it has nothing to do with misunderstandings about business functionality or unacceptable report formats or slower-than-expected response time. Occasionally, as any system (data mart or transactional) gets close to full-scale operability, organizational politics and other disruptive issues start to overtake the teamwork that you've worked so hard to foster. Often, data mart development and deployment are accompanied by changes in business processes. As people start to consider the impact on their particular jobs and career paths, they may very well come to see the eventual deployment of the data mart as a threatening event. Sometimes this "me-first" attitude has already surfaced, and if you've made it this far, you've overcome these issues. Other times, however, it isn't until late in the project—when software is on a desktop or two and data is in the data mart—that users realize the full impact of those process changes.

During Week 9, the project sponsor reappears on the scene in preparation for the initial deployment. During Weeks 10 and 11, it is the project sponsor's responsibility to intercede if suspiciously negative feedback comes from initial usage.

Weeks 10 and 11 Spotlight on the Project Manager

Construction enters the final weeks. Limited usage of the data mart has begun, and feedback is being received. Support activities (defining help desk procedures, creating training materials, etc.) should be nearing completion.

Who holds this all together? The project manager. Perhaps more than at any point in the project, the project manager will be drawn in several directions at once. (Even when a number of parallel streams of design activity were occurring in the first weeks of the design phase, all the activities were dedicated to the design and product selection.)

The project manager may have to resort to a rapid-paced, time-slicing manner of behavior for the next two weeks to keep all the necessary activities moving ahead. Doing so will be challenging and may require assistance from the more senior team members, but it's absolutely necessary. The project is too close to a successful completion to be derailed by preventable problems.

What You'll Find in This Chapter

Data Mart Testing: An Overview
> **The Tools**
> **The Development Team's Activities**
> **Testing Models**

The "Compressed Life Cycle" Approach
> **Team Interaction**

The Certification Process

You Know You're in Trouble When

Testing and Validating
the Data Mart

A Note to the Reader: You may think there's been enough data mart testing already, but it's far from over. The quality assurance testing accomplished during the construction phase—in lockstep with the actual development activities of the database, front end, and middleware—has certainly been valuable in terms of easing your mind about significant bugs and mishaps lying in wait for you. But more needs to be accomplished; specifically, multiple iterations of the data mart's operational life cycle, with each iteration compressed to fit the constraints and needs of the rapid development process that is nearing completion. This chapter's contents will describe how to compress multiple weeks or months worth of data mart restocking and revision into a single week's worth of activity.

Data Mart Testing: An Overview

The recommended data mart testing model is actually a leftover from the waterfall development methodology days of the 1980s, combining development test and evaluation (DTE) and operational test and evaluation (OTE) (Figure WK12.1). The testing activities you've performed to date have been of the former category and are inherently cyclical in nature, dealing with components of the overall system that will be deployed. OTE, on the other hand—the activity you need to perform during Week 12—is oriented toward validating the deliverable that is just about to be deployed to the user community.

For the sake of expediency, your OTE procedures should leverage the activities from previous cycles of DTE activity, when appropriate. For example, the contents of the data mart's database were frozen following the initial population tasks that occurred during Weeks 8 and 9, and significant testing occurred to validate that the contents were correct at that point. Assuming that no database changes have occurred during Weeks 10 and 11, you don't need to repeat the contents testing processes.

If, however, adjustments have been made to the data mart's contents and/or structure over the past two weeks, you absolutely do need to conduct thorough database contents testing.

The Tools

Throughout Week 12, perform all testing functions using the tools and software that will be deployed as part of the data mart's operational state:

♦ Front-end reporting or OLAP products

♦ Desktop office software (word processing, spreadsheet, etc.) with which data mart integration may occur

♦ All middleware products (e.g., a transformation tool)

♦ The mechanism by which users will access metadata about the data mart

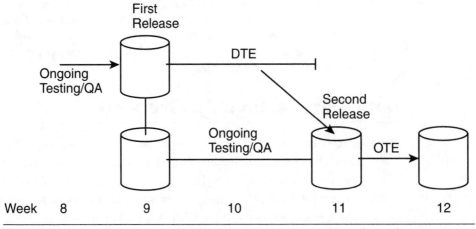

Figure WK12.1 Data mart testing during the construction phase.

♦ Custom code (e.g., a customized extraction routine)

♦ Administration utilities (e.g., for database backup)

♦ A fully populated database with the DBMS configured exactly as it will be during operational use

In addition, you may find it to include an automated testing tool in your Week 12 toolkit, *if* one is available that meets the characteristics of your data mart environment. At present, most automated testing tools are oriented toward transaction processing applications rather than informational environments such as data warehouses or data marts, but if and when tools do appear that can assist you with testing reports, ad hoc query results, the correctness of drill-down operations, and similar capabilities, consider using them if your testing process can be helped.

The Development Team's Activities

During Week 12, the data mart development team—all members who participated in the construction effort—should be on standby. That is, no new development effort should be occurring at this time.

Freezing development is critically important for two reasons. First, there could always be (and usually are) unanticipated side effects of any addition or change on other parts of the data mart. Unanticipated impacts can occur not only in the areas where you might expect them to do so—adding a new data element or two to a table in the database, for example—but sometimes even in areas such as adding a new managed query to a user's portfolio of requests or modifying the parameters of a report. For example, you probably have a number of global variables and parameters, scripts, and environmental settings that are part of your front-end tool environment; even simple changes could cause effects in other parts of the environment affected by these types of linkages.

Also remember that making modifications can introduce outright errors to the data mart, such as the following:

♦ An incorrectly executed drag-and-drop operation as you adjust column placement on a report could cause incorrect rollups of data along a given dimension.

♦ You could accidentally press the DELETE key while the cursor is placed over a particular data element in a query specification and not know it.

The simple rule for everyone to remember is that development has concluded.

Testing Models

Despite the preceding warnings, you most likely will have to make changes to your data mart during the testing period. Therefore, you need to put procedures in place to make changes during the testing phase and decide on the circumstances.

It's imperative that you distinguish real errors—situations whose presence directly and negatively affects the data mart's ability to deliver its mission-directed business value—from other items that don't need to be addressed immediately. Don't underestimate the controversy that can result from making such decisions! It's very common to receive last-minute requests to change report layouts, the ordering of executive information systems (EIS) briefing books, and even significant items such as drill-down paths that can't be supported by the underlying data model.

Every item that surfaces during the testing period needs to be categorized as one of the following:

◆ *Must-fix*. These items, if not corrected, will render the data mart all but useless.

◆ *Postdeployment modification*. These are usually the "look and feel" items, such as report formats and placement of controls on a custom-developed front end, that should be relatively simple to change. However, if no changes occur during Week 12, the data mart's mission is not compromised, and the required functionality can still be delivered.

◆ *Enhancement*. An enhancement could be a new interface or a request to add data from another source. All items that would require significant change to the data mart should be catalogued and eventually prioritized with respect to the next release of the data mart. Hint: Watch out for functionality that was discussed during the scope phase but that the team decided to leave out of the current development effort during the prioritization process.

◆ *Show-stopper*. A show-stopper error is a must-fix item so significant that a real-time correction is not possible, and there is no point in proceeding forward to deployment.

If you encounter a show-stopper error, your entire development effort will be called into question. Not only do you need to go back to the point at which corrections can be made and start over from there, but you also need to thoroughly and candidly address your methodology, your team's capabilities, and everything else deemed responsible for this unfortunate turn of events.

Not quite as serious, but also of concern, are must-fix items that are just now surfacing. As each one is corrected, try to determine how that error was able to be propagated this far along the data mart development life cycle and why it wasn't caught before. You need to do this not for purposes of finding someone to blame, but rather so that you can adjust and tune your processes for each subsequent development cycle.

The "Compressed Life Cycle" Approach

Your objective during the OTE period is to simulate the beginning period of your data mart's operational life. Ideally, you will have three or four cycles of activity, with each cycle typically represented by a restocking process (see Figure WK12.2).

You need to compress this life cycle into the time allotted for your OTE activities: one week, if possible, or more than one week if absolutely necessary. *Don't shortcut this process!* If your original premise is that you will set one week aside for operational testing but as you go through the design and construction process it appears that you would be able to fully test only one or two restocking cycles, extend your testing period by a few days or an additional week. Don't be tied to your original premise purely for the sake of meeting a scheduled end date.

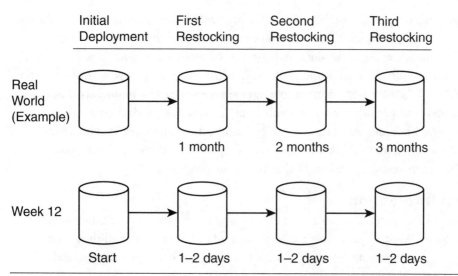

Figure WK12.2 The data mart life cycle and your Week 12 focus.

How can you tell if one week won't be sufficient for OTE? The most telling measure is the window that will be needed for restocking the data mart. The assumption entering the OTE period is that you will be able to fully execute a restocking cycle (i.e., end-to-end extraction through transformation through reloading) in under eight hours. If this is the case, Figure WK12.3 illustrates a sample schedule for Week 12.

Operational testing begins with an intensive, comprehensive one-day period of activity (Monday) that fully tests reports, query frameworks, and interfaces against the data mart's database that will be initially deployed. Assuming satisfactory results, the first restocking cycle should take place the following day (Tuesday), during the day, when it can be carefully observed by all appropriate team members. Assuming no problems occur, the rest of that day and all of the following day (Wednesday) should be devoted to repeating the functionality testing (reports, queries, etc.) and validating that the database's contents have been successfully updated.

As fast-paced as the above steps are, the pace of activity increases from here. The next restocking cycle should be run on Wednesday night, so that you have a fully restocked database—the third iteration, after the initial population version and the first restocking cycle—for testing by Thursday morning. The sequence of nighttime restocking and daytime testing will continue on Friday and, if necessary, into the weekend.

You need to carefully plan how you will evaluate test results, particularly during the latter cycles of Week 12 testing. Since the purpose of this cyclical activity is to simulate the life cycle of the data mart, results of reports and queries will vary each time they are run. You need to have an idea of what the correct results of each run should be. In some cases, changes to a data source happen so frequently that daily extractions can provide you with a sufficient amount of new data from which meaningful life-cycle-based testing can occur. In other situations, in which the actual source contents don't vary quickly enough for meaningful results, you may need to create test data and work that into your processes.

Team Interaction

Despite all the cautions earlier in this chapter about the dangers of making modifications during Week 12, any must-fix items do need to be corrected and then submitted for retest. The following sequence of steps is a framework that you can use and adapt to your particular data mart situation:

	Monday	Tuesday	Wednesday	Thursday	Friday	Saturday	Sunday
Morning	All-Day Test →	Restock Data Mart	Test	Test	Test	(Test)	(Test)
Afternoon	Decision PT	Test	Test Decision PT	Test Decision PT	Test Decision PT	(Test)	(Test)
Evening/ Night	—	Additional (Test)	Restock Data Mart	Restock Data Mart	Restock Data Mart	(Restock)	

Figure WK12.3 A sample Week 12 OTE schedule.

1. *A possible error is found by the tester.* In some cases, the tester should try to immediately replicate the error, with a quickly executing query, for example. In other cases, such as when an error is found from scanning the output from a long-running report, immediate retesting is not desirable. Either way, an error report should be immediately filled out, containing the following information:

   ♦ A description of the possible error

   ♦ The circumstances (what report was run or the exact syntax of a query that was run)

   ♦ An on-the-spot assessment as to the type of error (must-fix or show-stopper)

   ♦ Any other information of importance

   The tester should not attempt to diagnose the error unless there is a very obvious cause (which is unlikely, because if QA has been performed correctly throughout development all very obvious errors have already been caught and corrected). Rather, the tester should proceed as rapidly as possible with the testing sequence that has been defined.

2. *Assign the problem to a member of the development team.* Typically, the person responsible for that portion of development in which the possible error was found would be the recipient, but a "load-balancing" effect needs to occur. If one team member is backlogged with several different errors to fix as quickly as possible, and another team member has the particular skills (product knowledge, subject area knowledge, etc.) to work on that problem, the problem should be assigned to the second member.

3. *Quick Diagnosis.* The assigned developer must make as quick a diagnosis as possible, categorizing the error into one of the following:

   ♦ *Clear cause.* For example, the developer takes a cursory look at the program code or scripts behind a query or report, and the cause for the error becomes obvious. It is likely that modifying a line or two of code, changing a variable assigned to an on-screen control, or making some other simple adjustment will fix the problem.

   ♦ *In domain.* No immediate cause is apparent, but the characteristics of the error indicate near certainty that the problem lies somewhere exclusively within a particular domain of the data mart (i.e., code used for the report in which the error was found; a particular business rule on a transformation process; etc.).

♦ *Cross domain.* Not only is a cause not readily apparent, but there is a high likelihood that the correction would require changes to several components.

♦ *Platform.* A product bug may be responsible for the error.

♦ *Unknown.* At this point, there is little understanding of the possible reasons behind the error.

4. *Determine if the error is repeatable.* Based on the description provided by the tester, can this error be repeated? If not, it needs to be set aside for further analysis. Also, determine if the error produces different results—all of them erroneous—on subsequent attempts to repeat it.

5. *Fix it.* Based on the information determined in the previous steps, the assigned developer needs to do whatever is necessary to correct the error.

6. *Place the correction into the configuration control process.* At the end of each testing cycle, the team member responsible for configuration control needs to collect all the fixes, apply appropriate versioning rules to the software, and perform whatever tasks are necessary to apply the corrections and rebuild the data mart system.

7. *Document.* The developer will close out the error report by documenting the correction, describing the results of preliminary retesting and other appropriate material as required by your organization's QA processes.

Not every reported error will be fixed immediately and quickly. Therefore, at the end of each day's testing period, hold an all-team meeting to discuss the state of the data mart with respect to the whether the next cycle of testing should proceed. Or, more precisely, determine whether the data mart's database needs to remain frozen in its current state so that the correction and retesting process can commence or if the next restocking cycle can begin.

It's important to note that the decision with respect to the next restocking cycle does *not* require every outstanding error to be fixed. There may be some errors that, upon initial research, the developer determines will be relatively easy to correct but just hasn't addressed yet because of other corrections in process. If there is a high degree of confidence those fixes can be applied and verified in the next cycle—

that is, the state of the database's contents is immaterial with respect to what needs to be done to effect the corrections—you may decide to proceed with the next restocking sequence. The outstanding errors should be the ones fixed and retested first, but your goal should be to keep the testing process moving ahead as quickly as possible.

The Certification Process

Following completion of operational testing, you absolutely need to formally certify your data mart in accordance with any organizational policies you have in place. If none exist, strongly consider creating a formal statement of certification for your data mart.

You want every direct user and everyone else in the organization who will rely on results and output from data mart activity to have absolute, 100 percent confidence in the accuracy of the information being delivered. It is not uncommon for a data mart to have been deployed and in operation for a short period of time and then to have its quality called into question by users who claim that query results are wrong.

Keep in mind that business rules associated with your data mart may not be the same rules in effect before the project began. And, along with evolving business rules, you often are faced with changing data. Definitions change; for example, "expenses" may have previously included capital expenditures on month-by-month reports but now include only operating expenses. A user who looks at a given time period in the previous year and sees a different value for expenses for a given business location for a given month will instinctively question the results coming from the data mart.

Having a formal certification process, with detailed explanation about the data testing and report format testing and all the other activities that have occurred throughout the development process to ensure the highest quality and correctness, will help alleviate any postdeployment challenges to the data mart's validity.

You Know You're in Trouble When

There's one simple answer to the question, "Are we in trouble?" for Week 12: If show-stopper errors are found, that answer is *yes*. It isn't only that you've found severe errors that will cause some, perhaps, much, backtracking and rework. It's *when* you've found these problems and *why* they weren't found earlier.

Somehow, somewhere, there has been a failing in your rapid data mart development plan of execution. Perhaps technology selection wasn't as diligently accomplished as it should have been, or some team members didn't have the right qualifications for their respective assignments. More ominously, the QA processes may have been your failing. Perhaps it wasn't your fault; facing schedule constraints, the project sponsor directed that development proceed and that all QA be delayed until the designated testing period in Week 12 instead of occurring in parallel along the way, which may have caused schedule slips. You're facing schedule slips now, as well as possible morale problems, a crisis of confidence in your team's ability to deliver, and other possible unpleasantness.

Week 12 Spotlight on the Configuration Control Specialist

Configuration control takes on new significance during Week 12. The rapid turnaround necessary for error correction described earlier in this chapter means that the team member responsible for this function needs to be absolutely certain that corrections are applied correctly, that code isn't accidentally overwritten, and that in general, new problems aren't introduced as the team tries to fix other ones.

Configuration control is usually an unglamorous role, but it is an important one at all stages of development. During Week 12, configuration actually takes center stage as the central point into which corrections are sent. It is the responsibility of the configuration specialist to hold off any of the restocking cycles until all of the day's corrections have been properly applied to the appropriate component(s) of the data mart.

In addition, the configuration control process itself needs to be checked. Typically, another team member can observe all activities, but not be involved in applying the actual changes, to help ensure that in the frenzied pace of activities, errors aren't accidentally introduced.

What You'll Find in This Chapter

An Overview of the Deployment Process

Client Software Installation

Client Software Check-Out

Server Software Check-Out

Support Software and Network Connectivity

Other Week 13 Issues

    Training

    Replacing Functionality

    Conducting the Project Review

How to Achieve the Thirteenth Week's Goals

You Know You're in Trouble When

Deploying
the Data Mart

A Note to the Reader: Even though your data mart development has proceeded along at a rapid pace, chances are that to the development team, the past 12 weeks have seemed more like 12 months (or maybe even 12 years!) because of the intensive, no-downtime efforts everyone has had to put forth.

At last, though, success is really in sight. Construction has been completed, the comprehensive testing has successfully concluded, and the data mart has been certified as ready for operation. Now comes the deployment of the data mart.

Data mart deployment is often overlooked as business analysts focus their efforts on the way functionality relates back to data sources, and the technologists concentrate on matters such as star schema design and the way key fields should be handled.

This chapter presents a concise discussion about the data mart "end game" matters. The discussion will be of particular interest to data mart project managers and team members who are responsible for deployment.

An Overview of the Deployment Process

The activities you need to need to consider during Week 13 include the following:

♦ Installing front-end tool(s) on each user's client machine

♦ Checking out the software to ensure that installation has occurred correctly

♦ Installing the database and supporting software on the data mart's server

♦ Ensuring that server installation has occurred correctly

Client Software Installation

During the construction phase, you created (and verified the correctness of) the installation scripts you will need to install the tools on all of the users' client machines. Traditionally, data mart client systems have been desktop-based PCs, but increasingly, laptop computers are also serving as client machines.

When connected to a server over some type of networking connection (local area network, dial-up, remote network access, etc.), laptop clients will behave almost exactly like static desktop PCs. However, mobile users may be making use of your data mart by periodically accessing the server-resident database, downloading portions of the data mart to the laptop, and manipulating that slice of data in a remote, detached manner (see Figure WK13.1).

If your data mart will support laptop-based clients operating in a detached manner in addition to fixed-station desktop machines, your installation procedures for client software need to be augmented to support this model of operation. Specifically:

♦ A database storage area needs to be allocated and configured on each laptop machine.

♦ Adequate storage space for data, according to system specifications, needs to be available; this must be verified as part of the installation procedures.

♦ Any database management software that needs to be resident on the client machines must be installed.

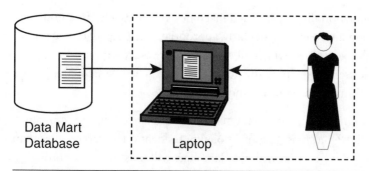

Data Mart Database

Laptop

Figure WK13.1 Detached data mart clients.

♦ Software used to establish and manage a remote connection, effect the data download, and handle all communications protocols must be installed.

The list of very specific items serves to emphasize this point: don't overlook the complexity of client software installation. Don't assume all client systems will be identical in configuration or use. Before the deployment phase begins, you must take an inventory of all members of the user community and their respective hardware system(s) from which the data mart will be accessed.

Among the issues you need to consider for client software installation are the following:

♦ *Type of installation.* Will it be active or passive? Perhaps users will arrive at their desks to find fully loaded, data mart-ready PCs or receive data mart-ready laptops back after the installation process (passive installation, with no action required by the users). Or perhaps your installation model will require users to log onto a data mart website, download an executable SETUP procedure, and manually start the installation process on their client systems (an active installation procedure). Either model is acceptable, but there will be differences that need to be considered as part of your deployment plan. Have all users who are actively performing their own software installation performed those functions, and successfully? Have all laptop-based data mart users turned their existing laptops in to the team for software installation?

♦ *Type of software distribution.* Will it be automatic or manual If data mart software will be installed for users without their assistance, your team may install it manually (one or more data mart team members performing CD-based or diskette-based installation directly on each machine). Alternatively, an automatic software distribution approach, particularly appropriate for large data mart user communities, might be used, in which all client software is stored on a LAN-based software and transferred over the network to each client system along with self-running and self-monitoring installation scripts.

♦ *Type of data mart interface.* If your data mart will be deployed on the company intranet with an OLAP and reporting functionality resident on a server rather than client machines, users' interaction with the data mart will most likely be through their respective Web browsers (Figure WK13.2). You need to ensure that all plug-ins or controls, Java or ActiveX support code, and anything else particular to the intranet environment is included in the client installation procedures.

Client Software Check-Out

Even though Week 12's operational test and evaluation (OTE) processes have verified that all possible client configurations work correctly, you still need to verify during Week 13 that each individual's client software has been correctly installed and configured.

A mix of reports and queries should be run to verify database connectivity and the correctness of presentation controls (e.g., default fonts, screen placement). Verify any client software interfaces (e.g., spreadsheet or word processor) with the data mart as correct through performing functions that use those interfaces. In short, never take it for granted that completion of installation automatically equals successful installation.

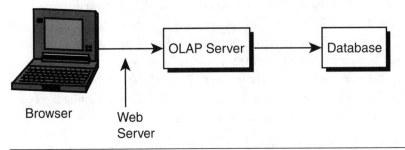

Figure WK13.2 Intranet-based data warehousing and software installation.

Server Software Check-Out

Your server environment should already be in place, having been completely built and populated prior to the Week 12 testing period. Every time a client machine is checked out for correctness after its software installation, though, the data mart's server(s) can be further exercised.

Note, though, that large, complex data mart environments could feature multiple server instances: multiple databases, or perhaps multiple OLAP servers (in the case of intranet-based data marts), with each "server set" serving a portion of a sizable user community (Figure WK13.3). Data marts of this variety typically have had their testing accomplished against one server (or group of interacting servers). If that is the situation for your project, the additional server software needs to be installed during deployment week and validated for correctness.

Support Software and Network Connectivity

Any yet-to-be-installed support software and network connectivity needs to be installed and deployed as appropriate. These might include the following:

♦ Network cards in servers or client systems that aren't currently connected to the organization's infrastructure

♦ Hooks into the organization's security infrastructure (e.g., user authentication services)

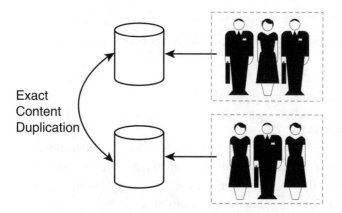

Figure WK13.3 Dual-server data mart environments.

♦ Remote data mart access over the company's connection to the Internet

♦ Data mart performance and usage monitoring software

♦ User access to an online data mart problem reporting system

♦ Support service software installation (e.g., the call center support system)

♦ Computer-assisted training software for the data mart

♦ Supplemental online help guides (including intranet-based rather than local help systems)

Other Week 13 Issues

In concert with the deployment tasks, Week 13 will also find the following activities occurring:

♦ Training users

♦ Replacing retired functionality

♦ Conducting the project review

The following sections briefly discuss each of these activities.

Training

Every user should go through data mart training during Week 13. The training should include instruction in the following:

♦ Running reports and queries

♦ Using the results of reports and queries as part of business operations

♦ Reporting problems

Training was discussed in the chapter on Week 11.

Replacing Functionality

Occasionally, a data mart is being deployed as part of a functionality migration. That is, home-grown extract files equipped with rudimentary data access tools are used in producing a set of standard reports. Functionality is being subsumed into and replaced by the data mart's more robust OLAP front end.

The business side of functionality migration has long since been discussed as part of the project's scope and has been manifested in the features and capabilities of the data mart. Consensus has been reached that effective with the deployment of the data mart, those reports will no longer be provided by the extract file.

But how exactly is the cut-over to be accomplished? When do users stop performing their about-to-be-retired tasks? Sometimes it isn't as simple as telling users not to run old reports anymore. Very often, report batch jobs are preset to run from users' PCs, and these presets need to be removed.

Any time your data mart will be replacing existing functionality, you need to take a comprehensive, end-to-end look at what needs to be done to effectively perform the cut-over.

Conducting the Project Review

The data mart project isn't quite completed yet, but now is the time, during Week 13, when the "highs and lows" of the project are still fresh in all participants' minds and the team is still together, to conduct a detailed project review. This review should include:

♦ In the final operational configuration, have products still performed as advertised and as expected based on the extensive analysis the team performed during the design phase?

♦ What portions of the project's methodology and approach broke (i.e., didn't occur on schedule because of inadequate preparation or issues that the team somehow missed)?

♦ What compromises had to be made during the project because of real-world constraints (e.g., budget cuts, loss of one or more team members, etc.) and how was the project affected?

♦ What were the lessons learned that can be applied to other upcoming data mart projects or, in many cases, other general application development projects?

How to Achieve the Thirteenth Week's Goals

Figure WK13.4 illustrates the activities that will occur during the 13th week of data mart construction.

Activity Stream	Monday	Tuesday	Wednesday	Thursday	Friday
Client software installation	Installation	Complete installation			
Server software installation	Verify installation correct				
Support software installation	Installation, as necessary	Installation, as necessary	Installation, as necessary		
First usage and feedback	Ongoing	Ongoing Training	Ongoing Training	Ongoing	Ongoing

Figure WK13.4 The thirteenth week's calendar of activities.

You Know You're in Trouble When

At this point, you should be well past the point at which serious problems would unexpectedly surface. You may have a bump or two during deployment week—installations go more slowly than expected, or perhaps you have to make a last-minute adjustment to the client software setup procedures—but for the most part, everything within your control can be managed fairly easily.

But how about items outside your control? You might find that the database administrator assigned to support your data mart has resigned, and there is no replacement available; as a result, the IT organization is recommending that deployment be postponed for several weeks, perhaps longer, until support can be lined up from a contractor or a new hire.

Or perhaps a company reorganization suddenly occurs, and the business organization that sponsored the data mart project has now been subsumed by another group. Deployment is put on hold because the new director wants to spend the next two months taking a comprehensive look at combined business processes.

Even if such circumstances occur, the fact that they are out of your control doesn't mean that you and your team have problems proceeding toward successful development of a data mart. You've done your jobs, successfully. Chances are the organization-induced delays will be lifted; if not, you still have accomplished what you set out to do.

Week 13 Spotlight on the Data Mart Team

Throughout the 13 weeks of data mart development, a period that encompassed four distinct phases of activity (scope, design, construction, and deployment), hundreds, perhaps thousands, of interdependent tasks have been done. There is absolutely no way that a data mart project can succeed in this time frame without the highest levels of cooperation among team members, from the first day of the scope until the business community begins to use the data mart as part of regular analytical and decision-making processes.

The true spirit of teamwork has been at work throughout these weeks. Team members have accomplished their respective tasks in a timely manner, always keeping an eye on other activities that depend on their

Continues

Week 13 Spotlight on the Data Mart Team

(Continued)

specific deliverables and accomplishments. Problems have been resolved expediently and effectively, with a minimum of disruptive organizational politics or posturing.

Now it's time for the party. Everyone involved in the data mart effort deserves it.

Enterprise Data Marts:
An Introduction

A Note to the Reader: The discussion in this appendix and the following one will guide you through an emerging trend in the world of data warehousing and the emphasis is definitely on the word "emerging."

One of the knocks against rapid development of business case-focused data marts—the approach presented in detail in this book—is that organizations are typically left with "silos" of non-integrated data marts, each one developed to support the business needs of a given organization or set of business processes or some other subset of the overall corporate mission. There tends to be duplication of effort across these projects, such as multiple data extractions from the same sources, multiple product evaluation and selection efforts, and so on. More troublesome from an enterprise perspective is the long-standing problem of multiple definitions of key corporate concepts—customer and product are the ones usually mentioned—with these multiple definitions leading to an inability to gain an enterprise view of a corporation's operations, opportunities, problem areas, and so forth.

The "natural" answer to this quandary is to coordinate data mart development efforts across organizations to eliminate duplication of effort and gain economies of scale through component reuse, commonly agreed-to definitions, and other areas. This sounds good, at least conceptually, but how exactly should this coordination be approached?

Much of what I see discussed in the area that has come to be commonly known as "enterprise data marts" is troubling. For example:

> ♦ *Vendors are trotting out many of the same marketing pitches used to sell the concept of distributed database management systems (DDBMSs) in the mid- and late 1980s.*
>
> ♦ *Corporate data warehousing and data mart directives and requests for proposals (RFPs) are increasingly based on enterprisewide data models, with phrases such as "provide a single common definition for customer that will be used by all organizational data marts" a prominent part of the stated "requirements."*
>
> *To repeat the assertion from above, the idea of enterprise data marts is an emerging one. This appendix highlights what has worked—and what has failed—in this area, along with the reasons for success.*

Introduction: The Philosophy Behind Enterprise Data Marts

"Quick-strike," tactical data marts deliver business value *very* rapidly. However, this business value is typically provided to a relatively small group of users, those within one or two closely related departments, only those individuals across the enterprise who are part of the annual budgeting process, or some other cohesive group that is closely aligned with whatever the data mart's *content model* (see Chapter 1) happens to be.

When viewed in isolation, the idea of a tactical data mart makes a lot of sense. The data mart is up and running, delivering business functionality and value as quickly as possible with as little interruption from other aspects within the enterprise that don't directly contribute to the specific mission of that data mart. Given the backlash against data warehouses that was discussed in Chapter 1, the idea of a focused, mission-driven data mart appears to be the best of all possible worlds: rapid, tailored business intelligence with as little overhead and interference as possible.

What has typically happened in most organizations, though, is that tactical data marts have proliferated very rapidly across the enterprise. This proliferation is not necessarily undesirable, and if each data mart were serviced by its own subset of data sources with little or no source-to-target overlap, a collection of individual, nonintegrated data marts would be an optimal direction for the enterprise's IT and business planners.

In reality, there is a tremendous amount of overlap among sources and their respective flows into the domain of data marts throughout the enterprise. For example, a catalog order-entry application has data that is needed by a data mart focused on customer loyalty and retention, and another data mart dedicated to analyzing profitability from the organization's various marketing channels, and yet another data mart that analyzes the effectiveness of customer reacquisition campaigns (e.g., targeted e-mail and direct mail to customers who have not ordered any of the company's products in more than one year), and other data marts across the enterprise as well.

It is easy to see where a proliferation of many-to-many relationships among the enterprise's source applications and target data marts will lead to a confusing spider's web of data flows that will almost always become impossibly unmanageable. Clearly, if an identified set of data marts needs a common set of data elements from the catalog order-entry application, it would be desirable to be able to leverage data extraction, transformation, movement, quality assurance, and loading processes to the greatest extent possible.

At the same time, however, introducing the idea of cross-data mart leverage represents a swing back from tactical, focused, and *isolated* data marts toward the real-world inefficiencies and complexities of classical data warehousing, which are the very problems that have driven the focus of organizational planners toward data mart development and away from cross-organizational efforts.

The quandary, then, is to achieve the optimal degree of balance across the enterprise with respect to the architecture and processes through which source applications and data marts can be developed *and maintained* in an evolutionary manner. In other words, the goal is to achieve the optimal balance between *leverage* and *empowerment*. The "leverage" side of the equation typically means combining data acquisition processes (e.g., extraction, transformation) to eliminate duplication of effort. "Empowerment" means that organizations can, for their respective data marts, choose the most appropriate tools for their business needs and, more important, not be constrained by delays or problems with either corporate data warehousing initiatives or lack of progress with other data mart initiatives across the enterprise.

The following section discusses approaches to data mart integration that have usually failed.

Approaches that Do *Not* Work

Most organizations that have embarked on enterprise data mart initiatives have tried one or both of the approaches described below. These two approaches—the "big bang" and the "loose confederation"—represent the extremes on the spectrum from extreme centralization and absolute decentralization. And, as discussed below with respect to each, both approaches are extremely susceptible to problems that compromise their effectiveness.

The "Big Bang" Approach

Enterprise planners concerned about the proliferation of overlapping source-to-target data flows usually turn to the "big bang" approach, as illustrated in Figure A1.1. A single data warehouse will serve as a "clearinghouse" for all data that will be acquired from all sources that will feed all data marts. Then, the data warehouse will supply data to all data marts, where that data will be accessed by each mart's users. Basically, this model is one that mirrors a wholesale-retail set of flows that would commonly be used for the movement of physical goods from manufacturers to consumers.

The big bang approach is a highly logical one that seems to feature the best of all possible worlds:

◆ Maximum data extraction leverage is achieved on the source side of the architecture. Each data source is accessed only one time, and all elements that are needed by any of the data marts are acquired at the same time and made available for any and all of the enterprise's "knowledge workers."

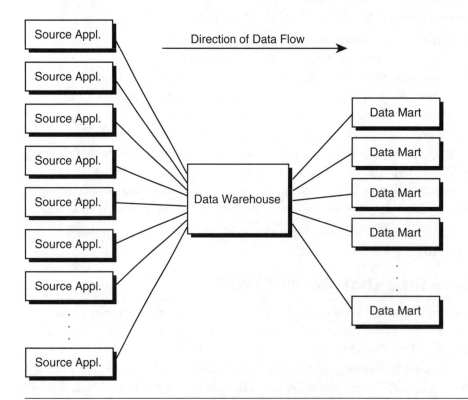

Figure A1.1 The "Big Bang" approach to enterprise data marts.

♦ The highest degree of source-neutral information abstraction is provided within the data warehouse environment through its transformation processes, and there will be one definition of "customer;" one definition of "product;" and so on.

♦ A single, enterprisewide metadata model based on source-neutral information can be created, with all appropriate links back to the sources and forward to the data marts to provide a consolidated picture of the enterprise's data assets and their respective end-to-end flows.

♦ Users will access data primarily from the data marts, which will contain *only* the information that is part of the mission being supported. If additional data is needed that is not resident within the data mart, it can be obtained from the data warehouse through remote data access facilities or "drill-through" access for increased levels of detail.

Unfortunately, there is one weak link with the big bang approach: The monolithic data warehouse in the middle of the architecture. All the data warehousing problems that have driven the rise of the tactical data mart are suddenly back in the picture again, including the following:

♦ *Cross-organization cooperation.* The level of cooperative work required across many business units and various IT organizations is extremely difficult to achieve, resulting in project delays, conflicts, and in most situations, a failed initiative.

♦ *Technical complexity and infrastructure problems.* From the large number of database load windows in the data warehouse to high network traffic volumes and bottlenecks, the seemingly straightforward hub-and-spoke architecture shown in Figure A1.1 rarely works in real-world corporate settings.

♦ *Data semantic issues.* As discussed in detail in Appendix 2, it isn't always desirable or valuable to provide an enterprise with one and only one definition of main concepts such as *customer* and *product*. For example, in the banking world, retail customers (i.e., individuals and small businesses) and wholesale customers (i.e., large corporate clients) may share some common attributes such as *name* and *address*, and all customers share some common behaviors (e.g., payment histories). However, the products and their respective attributes applicable to each class of customer are different enough that providing an integrated view of *all* customers and *all* products has no business value.

♦ *Delivery time.* Whereas a tactical data mart can be developed and deployed very quickly (as discussed throughout this book), adding a sizable data warehouse in the middle of the architecture will *dramatically* lengthen the time until which users can begin receiving business value from their respective data marts.

The "Loose Confederation" Approach

On the other end of the spectrum from the big bang model is the approach built around a universe of data marts that an organization attempts to tie together in a *federated* approach, building what might be termed a "loose confederation" of data marts. This approach is illustrated in Figure A1.2.

The idea behind this approach is that each data mart is planned, architected, designed, and built in the manner most appropriate to the business needs of the organization(s) it supports. At the same time, the contents of each data mart will be "open" and accessible by individuals who aren't part of the data mart's primary user base.

The philosophy behind creating a bottom-up federation of data marts is to avoid the data warehouse-in-the-middle deficiencies of the big bang approach yet, at the same time, avoid creating an "islands of data marts" problem. Using remote access techniques (see Figure A1.3), users have access to information outside the realm of their "official" data mart(s) on an as-needed basis with a sort of "universal" data mart access.

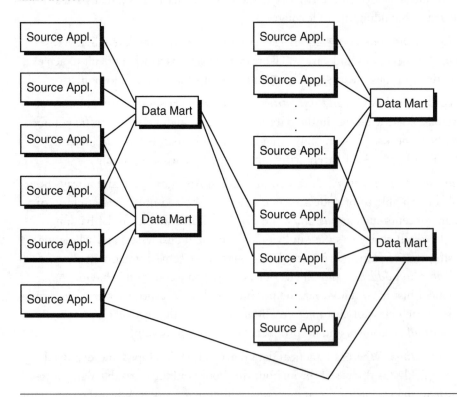

Figure A1.2 The "loose confederation" approach to enterprise data marts.

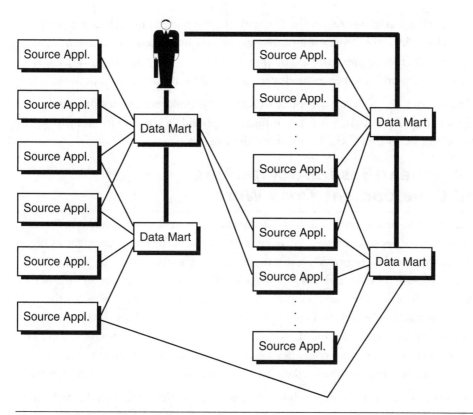

Figure A1.3 Universal data mart access.

Though the data warehouse-driven deficiencies may be overcome, an entirely new set of problems is faced by organizational planners and architects who decide to pursue this approach, including the following:

- *Lost leverage.* If each data mart is developed in a bottom-up manner, the opportunity to achieve extraction leverage from the data sources (i.e., reducing the duplication of effort) fades away.

- *Unclear objectives.* Most organizations have only a vague idea of what they expect to achieve by "integrating" data marts, resulting in difficulties obtaining funding above and beyond what would be needed to develop a tactical, organization-specific data mart.

- *Technology challenges.* Universal access from any client to any data mart database is, with the current state of technology, barely achievable, and such environments are susceptible to performance and interoperability problems.

- *Organizational cooperation.* Just as with the big bang approach, attempting to develop a loose confederation of integrated data marts requires a much higher degree of cross-organizational communications and cooperative work than if each data mart were being developed in a focused, nonintegrated manner.

The bottom line is that with today's technology, building a series of loosely integrated data marts that, when taken together, provide a sort of virtual distributed data warehouse is more wishful thinking than reality.

Component-Based Architecture and Development *Does* Work

The component-based enterprise data mart architecture achieves a balance between the two approaches discussed above, overcoming most of the major deficiencies of each. As illustrated in Figure A1.4, this model features a data warehousing layer that provides insulation between the organization's collection of data marts and the many different applications that serve as data sources. A major distinction between the component-based approach and the big bang model, though, is that instead of trying to build a single monolithic (and usually overly complex) data warehouse serving as the middle layer, you instead construct a *series* of components—typically three to five—that when taken together make up a distributed data warehouse environment.

As is the intention with a monolithic data warehouse that would feed a collection of data marts, the components act as a data clearinghouse and a buffer between the sources and targets. Each component, however, can be viewed as a "mini-warehouse" in which *highly cohesive* pieces of data will be managed, stored, and made available for whatever organizations across the enterprise that need to make use of them.

Data mart projects, in turn, will draw from one *or more* of these components as determined by the business needs of each data mart. In practice, a series of one-to-many, many-to-one, and many-to-many relationships will exist between the components and data marts. What is critically important to understand, though, is that the *cardinality* of each relationship (i.e., the number of points on either side of a component(s)-to-data mart(s) relationship) is a relatively low number, usually five or fewer. In contrast, the model shown in Figure A1.2 for the loose confederation approach shows that a given data source may supply contents to upwards of a dozen data mart targets, and likewise any given data mart may have its contents provided by many different sources. With the cardinality of the component-to-data mart relationships kept relatively low, initial construction of the enterprise environ-

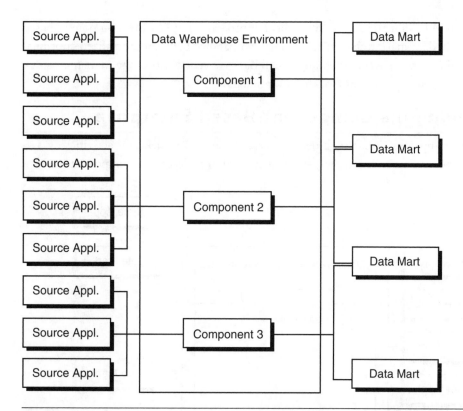

Figure A1.4 The component-based enterprise data warehouse and data mart architecture.

ment *and maintaining and modifying that environment over time* is much more achievable than without the middle layer of components being part of the architecture.

Flexibility as a Fundamental Property

Proponents of the big bang enterprise data mart approach discussed earlier usually mandate that data marts receive their data *only* from the data warehouse, the rationale being that only through centralized control and coordination of data assets can "data mart chaos" be avoided. Recall that in Chapter 1, the following three data mart source architectures were presented:

- Data provided solely by the data warehouse
- Data acquired directly from one or more sources
- A hybrid approach of the above two

Figure A1.5 illustrates how the hybrid approach is applied to a component-based enterprise data mart architecture, achieving a balance between centralized coordination and time to delivery when additional data is needed within the mart that isn't currently available from any of the components.

Building the Component-Based Enterprise

The next appendix discusses in detail the recommended sequence of activities by which you can architect, design, and construct all the pieces of a component-based

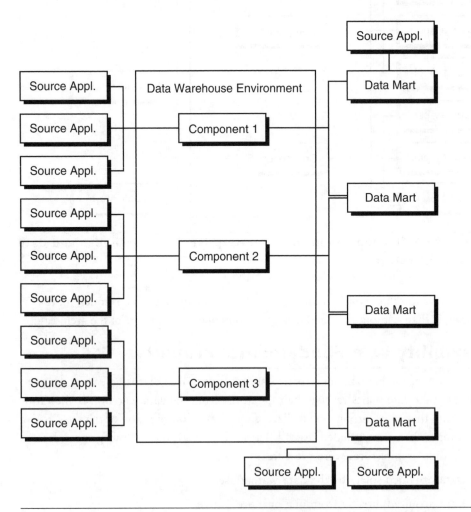

Figure A1.5 Hybrid data source architecture and data warehouse components.

enterprise data mart: the data marts themselves, the components, the source-to-component flows, the component-to-data mart flows, and so on. IT planners who have had experience with component-based architectures (e.g., object-oriented transaction processing systems built around object broker services) are likely to be concerned about adding "unnecessary" complexity to the data warehousing environment and the associated risk that results from multiple layers of source-to-target data flows.

This risk is mitigated by embarkation on a series of 90-day phases, beginning with a data mart strategy effort to determine the scope and issues of what the organization will embark on. Successive phases will cover different cycles of architecture, design, and construction for both the data warehouse components (the middle layer) and the target data marts.

Your goal is to use this sequence of quick-paced phases to deliver a series of incremental capabilities on a steady schedule. The overall pace will naturally be slower than that of tactical, quick-strike data marts, but the risk of doing little else than architecture and design and never delivering business functionality (i.e., the "big project failure syndrome") is mitigated. Schedules and other details are presented in the next appendix.

The Data Warehouse Layer Components

The chapters that discussed Weeks 1 and 2 of the rapid data mart development approach presented discussion and illustrations of how data mart functionality should be closely aligned with the facts needed to support each required capability. The end-point data marts that will receive their contents from one or more components are still developed in this tight, functionality-driven manner.

The challenge, though, is how to determine what should be in each of the data warehouse layer components. Given that any given component is likely to support up to five different data marts, it is likely to be an exercise in futility to try to synthesize the exact functionality-to-fact details of all data marts (particularly since yet-to-be-defined data marts will almost always be waiting around the corner and will need information from that component).

Complicating the challenge is the always tough task of avoiding turning the data warehouse component into a "data dump"; that is, the recipient of thousands of attributes and large volumes of data that are acquired from sources "just in case they might be needed."

A technique you can use to achieve an appropriate middle ground between the extremely precise business functionality of the data marts and the myriad of candidate

The "Market Forces" Analogy

An analogy that helps explain why the component-based approach is preferable to the "big bang" approach when conceptually, the opposite would seem to be true, is a centrally planned economy compared with a market economy. It would appear that a group of powerful, insightful leaders of a country with near-absolute control over policies and the way they are implemented could create a multiyear economic plan with formally defined, finely tuned flows of goods and services across the land. Certainly, such an economy would be superior to the chaotic, inefficient, do-pretty-much-what-you-want philosophy of a free market economy.

In reality, a centrally planned economy fails because of any number of unforeseen factors to which the rigidly structured flows and mandates cannot react. At the same time, in a free market economy the components (companies and individuals) are empowered to take advantage of opportunities as long as they adhere to a general set of norms and guidelines.

The analogy is that the component approach to enterprise data marts, like a market economy, responds to "market forces" within the enterprise. Organizations with unique information needs are free to act as quickly as possible within the constraints and guidelines (e.g., budget, infrastructure). At the same time, information delivery needs with a broader constituency usually propagate into the data warehouse component layer, and the desired efficiencies are achieved.

data attributes is to focus the contents of the data warehouse components on *concepts*, or higher-level, cohesive groups of attributes that have a *high* likelihood of providing business value.

As a lead-in to the enterprise banking example in the next appendix, examples of concepts might include the following:

♦ "Retail customer borrowing and payment behavior" with attributes drawn from the checking account application (average account balance, average overdraft usage, average monthly payment on overdraft, etc.), from the consumer loan application (types of loans, average beginning balance, average prepayment amount, average number of days delinquent, maximum number of days delinquent, etc.), and from externally provided credit bureau data (credit bureau score, last credit bureau score, total outstanding debt from all sources, etc.)

♦ "Wholesale customer borrowing authorizations and usage" with attributes acquired from the corporate loan management application (maximum amount borrowed, average outstanding credit balance, authorized loan instruments, collateral, etc.), from the wholesale customer management application (subsidiaries authorized to borrow on a master account, changes in ownership, bond ratings, etc.), and from other applicable sources.

Issues and Tradeoffs

Time Until Delivery of Business Functionality

A successful tactical data mart development effort will provide usable business functionality in approximately 90 days. It takes about three times as long to deliver the first usable business functionality (270 days, or 9 months) under an enterprise component-based approach. Figure A1.6 illustrates the respective functionality availability of the contrasting approaches. (The details of each phase in the enterprise approach are discussed in the Appendix B.)

Over the expected life cycle of an enterprise data mart initiative—approximately two years—the "delivery gap" will narrow near the end of this period, and you will have a much more maintainable, evolutionary architecture through which business intelligence is delivered throughout the enterprise.

However, funding policies, budgetary and staffing issues, earnings pressures, and all the rest of the realities IT planners and architects constantly face will undoubtedly factor into the decision-making process and the strategy that any given organization chooses to pursue (or not to pursue).

Adding to the complications is the reality that enterprise data mart initiatives—no matter what approach is considered—are relatively new, and those who control

Tactical Data Marts

	X	X	X	X	X	X	X
Start	3 Months	6 Months	9 Months	12 Months	15 Months	18 Months	21 Months
		X	X		X		

Enterprise Data Marts

X = Deployed Data Mart Functionality

Figure A.6 Contrasting time frames of functionality delivery.

funding and expect real and measurable business value will *absolutely* be reticent to trade off near-term receipt of business intelligence for significant delays in hope of down-the-road data mart maintainability and evolution. (IT professionals may view this philosophy as short-sighted and bottom-line-driven, but the realities of organizational funding are what they are. That's why there are so many difficult-to-maintain legacy applications still in existence.)

Tools and Infrastructure

An additional complication is that data warehousing and data mart tools (e.g., middleware, desktop tools,) tend to be focused on "classical" data warehousing (e.g., point-to-point movement of data data access from a single database). A new generation of tools is emerging (tools from new vendors as well as enhancements to market-leading tools), but it's still early in the game for next-generation tools capable of supporting a component-based architecture.

Complicating matters is that the vendor hype machines have turned their attention to the idea of enterprise data marts, and product messaging is already heavily focused on this area. As we all know, though, there is (to put it delicately) a not-so-insignificant lag time between product messaging and the ability of products to efficiently and consistently deliver upon those messages.

Art vs. Science

Make no mistake about it: this area of enterprise data marts is much more of an art than a science. There is no such thing as "the correct model" for structuring components and the flows of data across the enterprise. The Appendix B presents some examples of component-based enterprise data mart architectures from various industries; these are only representative and intended to serve as examples. Any given organization's environment is likely to radically alter what such an environment would look like for its enterprise.

Cross-Organizational Cooperation

The need for cross-organizational cooperation was identified as a significant complication and risk factor at several points in this appendix. *Any* attempt at an enterprise data mart initiative, regardless of the approach you select, will require levels of cooperative work that are unprecedented in most organizations. In effect, they negate the support-yourself benefits with minimized external dependencies of tactical data mart development.

T I P It is absolutely essential that an enterprise data mart initiative be driven by the highest levels of the *business* organization (i.e., the chief operating officer, chief financial officer, or even the chief executive officer) and fully supported by the chief information officer. Large multinational companies with several international divisions need to have support at these levels from *all* organizations that will participate. Otherwise, stick with the tactical quick-strike data marts because you have little chance of succeeding with an enterprise initiative.

Summary

Consultants, analysts, and commentators in the data warehousing world typically have an opinion about whether or not data marts should be tactical, "dead-end" efforts. Those with an IT philosophy and background typically advise against tactical efforts because of IT-related issues (e.g., the duplication of data extraction procedures and other areas discussed earlier). On the other side, those whose background is from the line-of-business area tend to be skeptical about any enterprise-scale initiatives (not only data mart integration, but also widescale workflow-enabled applications, case-based reasoning, a knowledge management infrastructure, etc.).

There is definitely an organizational cultural aspect to the path you should consider with regards to your data mart initiatives. If your organization embraces the leading edge of new technologies and has had a string of successes in doing so (e.g., early adopters of client/server technology or early users of relational database management systems) and if there is a from-the-top-down emphasis on business intelligence and knowledge-driven work processes across the entire company, certainly consider an enterprise-scale data mart initiative that you build in a manner described in this appendix and the next.

If, however, projects of any type tend to be painful, and if cross-department cooperation is not one of your organization's strong points, you will likely be extremely disappointed in the results of anything other than tactical, departmental data mart development and deployment.

It's your choice; both paths are achievable, but select wisely.

Who Should Lead an Enterprise Data Mart Initiative?

It is dismaying to see marketing messages and hype that are recycled from the mid- and late 1980s days of distributed database management systems, CASE-driven automated software development, artificial intelligence, and vendor-driven enterprise architectures. In particular, the enterprisewide data model, the all-encompassing framework offering one and only one definition of *customer*, *product*, and other major concepts seems unsuitable. These models would then provide universal definitions that would be standardized across all applications.

Nearly every attempt to develop such a data model either failed outright or, if common definitions were actually developed, was only sparsely used by newly developed applications (and a legacy application's data definitions could not be retrofitted to accommodate newly defined ones from an enterprise data model effort).

Someone who has been through the earlier generation of enterprise data management initiatives is particularly suited to steer through a new generation of recycled interoperability messages with questionable product support and to be able to relate to project sponsors an authoritative "been there; tried that; it doesn't work" reply in response to directives that seem conceptually sound (e.g., the big bang approach driven from a monolithic data warehouse) but often fail in real organizational settings.

A Blueprint for Your
Enterprise Data Mart
Initiative

A Note to the Reader: The previous appendix introduced the idea of enterprise data marts and presented a direct, to-the-point discussion of alternative models from which you can choose and reasons to proceed along the component-based path. This appendix adds the "how" to the "what" and "why" aspects of enterprise data marts, should you choose that approach over tactical, nonintegrated data marts.

A Banking Example

Banking is one of the industries in which there is a very strong business case for enterprise data mart as contrasted with tactical, standalone efforts. The discussion in the sections below about architecture and project phases should present a clear explanation of how, over time, to build an evolvable environment that can adapt to changing information access needs across the enterprise.

The Business Case

Most large banks have several lines of business, such as the following:

♦ *Retail banking* (sometimes known as consumer banking) that focuses on individuals and provides services such as checking, automobile and other consumer loans, mortgages, and so on

♦ *Wholesale banking* (also known as commercial banking) that serves large corporate customers and provides high-volume, high-dollar services such as letters of credit and overnight loans

♦ *Brokerage services*, such as those provided through a subsidiary organization

♦ *Private banking services* for individuals or families with a high net worth

A number of analytical and information access needs that are common—at least conceptually—across several or all of the above lines of business, include the following:

♦ Profitability

♦ Risk management

♦ Customer service

♦ Cross-selling and other marketing functions

♦ Customer retention and loyalty

♦ Organizationwide financial performance

A major complication to determining how these analytical services should be provided is that the end-to-end flows will *not* be common across all the service areas. Organizationwide financial performance, for example, draws data from all lines of business. Other services such as risk management and cross-selling might be performed in both the wholesale and retail sides of the bank, but the two sides use entirely different sets of data and are implemented in totally different manners by each organization.

Conceivably, each line of business could develop its own set of data marts, as illustrated in Figure A2.1. As you can see from the figure, though, there is a high degree of overlap and inefficiencies among the various source data acquisition services. Therefore, an operating premise is that an enterprise approach to data mart development should be considered.

The Enterprise Data Mart Architecture

Figure A2.2 illustrates a component-based data mart architecture through which source-to-data mart flows are supported.

Several points are worth noting:

♦ The data warehouse components are aligned with the bank's lines of business. The primary reason (in this example) is that very few business processes and data needs cross multiple lines of business. Most data marts will draw from only one component of the data warehouse layer, which in turn is built primarily from source applications and external data that deals only with retail customer performance.

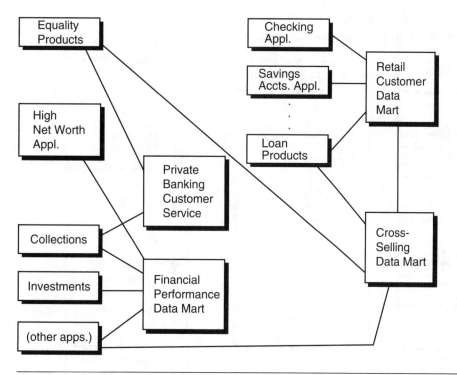

Figure A2.1 Independently developed data marts.

- Some functions do cross the entire enterprise, such as financial performance; the data mart dedicated to this area will draw selected data from all components.

- Business processes and functionality are very important factors in the way the components and the data marts will be organized. If, for example, retail customer cross-selling is solely for loan products, a data mart that supports cross-selling will likely draw data exclusively from the retail component that is built from retail applications. However, if cross-selling extends to securities products, that data mart would draw appropriate data from the brokerage services component.

- If an environment of data warehouse components and functionality-focused target data marts is built, changes in business policies and processes can readily be accommodated. Following the example directly above, an initial cross-selling policy focused exclusively on loan products can evolve into one featuring securities products in a rapid, straightforward manner by "tapping into" the ready-to-go data from the brokerage services component of the data warehouse environment.

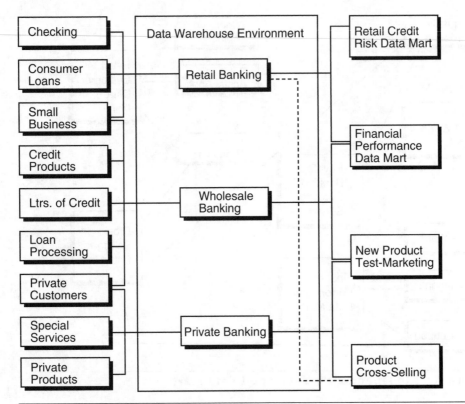

Figure A2.2 A banking industry enterprise data mart architecture.

Architecture and Development Phases

Enterprise data mart development is, of course, *not* a 90-day process. As explained in the previous chapter and discussed in detail below, a recommended approach is to embark on a series of 90-day cycles, starting with an initial scope and architecture phase and leading to a series of design and development cycles.

Phase 1: 90-Day Enterprise Scope and Architecture

How many components should be in your data warehouse environment? How many target data marts need to be built? How can the greatest degree of source data acquisition leverage be obtained?

These questions, and many others, need to be addressed very early in the enterprise data mart process. The first 90-day phase is purely conceptual and architectural; no development or hands-on activity is accomplished. A blueprint for this phase is as laid out in the following sections.

Week 1

The first week needs to be devoted to achieving consensus about the objectives of the enterprise data mart initiative. Whereas the consensus-driven process of tactical data mart development (discussed in the Week 1 chapter) focuses on a very specific, high-value business mission, the enterprise data mart effort needs to initially operate at a higher level. Questions such as, "Why are we even considering this approach?" and "Do we have the funding to see this through, or will the initiative be put on hold after six months without delivering any functionality?" need to be addressed.

It is important that representatives from across the enterprise—all major organizations and lines of business that are expected to be within the realm of the data mart initiative—be part of the team to get as complete a picture as possible.

Week 2

The focus of Week 2 (assuming consensus toward this approach is reached) shifts to developing a conceptual picture the collection of data marts. At this point, the middle layer (the data warehouse components) should be disregarded; the group should proceed as if availability of necessary data to all data marts is guaranteed.

For example, a bank may decide that the following data marts should be implemented:

- Retail credit risk
- Wholesale credit risk and exposure
- Bankwide financial performance and profitability
- Retail customer retention
- Private bank customer service
- Securities trading performance analysis
- Consumer cross-selling

Week 3

During Week 3, additional high-level detail is provided for each of the identified target data marts. The team will focus on the major types of functionality that will be provided by each (representative mission statements) and identify major concepts necessary to provide each data mart's expected functionality (e.g., retail customers' complete asset and loan product profiles).

Week 4

Week 4 is a continuation of the work begun in Week 3, the goal being to achieve a first-draft conceptual picture of all the data marts.

At the same time, part of the team will split off and begin looking at the current environment: The source applications across the major business lines that are likely to supply data to one or more data marts, current extract files and the way they are used, external data that is used throughout the bank (e.g., credit bureau scores and supporting data), and other material as relevant.

Week 5

During Week 5, work continues on the analysis of the current environment. The team's goal should be to complete this thread of activity by the end of the week.

In parallel, other team members begin to look at the degree of overlap of major concepts and similar functionality across the identified data marts. It is important to recognize that the concept of "retail customer complete asset and loan product profiles" is needed for the following data marts:

- Retail credit risk
- Retail customer retention
- Consumer cross-selling

Week 6

The team will complete the conceptual analysis of the way concepts map to data mart usage. At the same time, another group will begin to look at the mapping between the identified candidate sources and the concepts that have been identified.

Week 7

Week 7 will be a checkpoint for the viability of proceeding with the enterprise data mart approach, following completion of the source-to-concept mapping. At this point, the middle layer of data warehouse components is still undefined; the focus is to determine that there is enough overlap among the source-to-target flows that a sequence of independent, tactical data marts is inefficient and impractical.

Week 8

The focus during Week 8 shifts to looking at a number of alternatives for organizing the data warehouse middle-layer components. In the architecture illustrated in Figure A2.2, the bank's lines of business drive the organization of the components. The team should arrive at this conclusion by exploring other alternatives, such as basing the components upon geography; that alternative might be suitable for a multinational conglomerate but would be inefficient for a domestic bank with limited international operations.

Week 9

By the beginning of Week 9, a preferred component model will have emerged. Work during this week will be oriented toward applying end-to-end, sources-to-targets flows of data into and out of the components. The team should focus on keeping the cardinalities of all the flows at a relatively low, manageable level (see the discussion in the previous chapter) but at the same time, achieving a greater degree of leveraged data flow efficiency than if a "loose confederation" approach (also discussed in the previous chapter) were being explored.

Week 10

The first part of Week 10 will be focused on completing the detailed data flows begun in Week 9. By midweek, this work having been completed, the focus needs to shift toward applying real-world detail to the model. How exactly is data likely to be extracted from the database that contains credit bureau-provided information that is updated monthly? What are the details (hardware, operating system, data management layer, etc.) of the application that manages commercial loan payment processing?

Week 11

Week 11 will see the completion of the detail work begun in Week 10; by the end of the week, a first draft implementation-specific model, with references to specific platforms and products, will be available.

Week 12

During Week 12, the entire team will conduct an end-to-end walkthrough of the entire source-to-target model, looking for issues and alternative strategies and, to the greatest extent possible, determining if there is a high enough likelihood of success if the initiative were to proceed on schedule into subsequent phases.

Week 13

Week 13 features a combination of performing "cleanup tasks" (going back over any loose ends or open items) and finalizing consensus as to the data marts that will be tackled first. The objective is to select two closely related data marts (e.g., cross-selling and retail credit risk) upon which a pilot effort for the enterprise initiative can be developed and the concept validated before moving into additional areas.

Phase 2: Create Partial Enterprise Architecture and Design

Phase 2, like Phase 1, has a focus on conceptual, nonimplementation activities. The team will focus on architecture and design tasks for a portion of the end-to-end environment (see Figure A2.3) that is necessary for the first data marts to be built and delivered. Most of the tasks that will occur during this phase are identical to those of the scope and design phases of a rapid data development effort, as detailed in the chapters for Weeks 1 through 7; refer to those respective chapters for additional details about the techniques you should use.

Weeks 1 and 2

During the first two weeks of this phase, two teams will work in parallel to identify and define the functionality details of the two initial data mart implementations (in this example, cross-selling and retail credit risk). Each team will do the following:

♦ Discuss and achieve consensus on a mission statement

♦ Create a functionality-fact matrix

♦ Do preliminary analysis of the likely data sources (using the work completed during the enterprise scope and architecture phase described earlier)

♦ Create a fact-data source matrix

♦ Synthesize the two matrices to map functionality to data sources

♦ Analyze material about source platforms and infrastructure from the first phase that is applicable to its efforts and perform additional research as necessary to provide more details

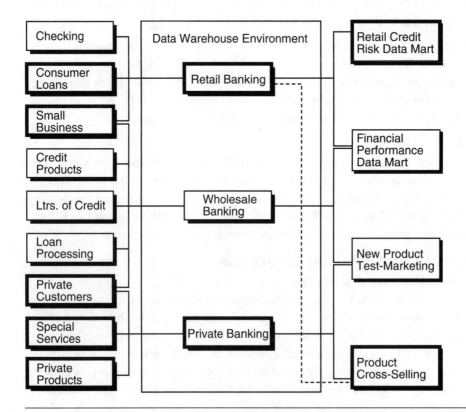

Figure A2.3 Selecting the first data mart components.

At the end of Week 2, the teams should be at the same stage as if they were pursuing a tactical, standalone data mart initiative.

Week 3

During Week 3, the two teams will recombine their efforts and look at their respective data marts as a system, noting the facts common to both (or facts that should be common but are slightly different in their current form) and similar functionality.

One of the first major decision points of the effort will occur at this point: deciding whether these two data marts should remain as separate projects or be combined. The group will be guided by the degree of overlap of functionality and facts that the two teams have developed during the first two weeks. If there is relatively little overlap—a handful of facts that have been identified for use in both data marts or only a few items of functionality that are common to both missions—the team can confidently continue down the path of dual data mart development. If, however, there appears to be a higher degree of commonality than had been previously thought (a large number of common facts and very similar functionality), it is likely that these efforts should be combined to support one larger, multi-organization user community.

Also during Week 3, team members will begin evaluation of front-end tools, middleware products, and DBMS engines. It is possible that the two data marts will wind up using common products (i.e., the same OLAP tool), but it is just as likely that their respective business needs will lead to separate sets of tools. Accordingly, the product evaluation and selection process can be combined across the two data mart implementations or done separately, whichever makes more sense.

More products will likely be evaluated than in a tactical data mart effort, not only because of multiple target data marts but also because of the data warehouse component layer (additional source-to-target data flows, an additional DBMS engine, etc.)

Week 4

Design of the data warehousing component(s) will begin during Week 4, based primarily on the synthesized data needs of the two target data marts. This task is a complex one because the components serve as an intermediary between the sources and the data marts, and there are two sets of data flows and transformations that need to occur. Additionally, data quality assurance needs to be accomplished not only for data as it is acquired from the various sources, but also to ensure that the quality is retained as data is sent downstream to the target data marts.

To best manage this complexity, Week 4 component design activity should be driven by the data mart facts that were already defined during the preceding weeks, and for now, the data sources should be ignored. Basically, you want to design the portions of the enterprise over which you have control and that don't currently exist: the target data marts and the components of the data warehouse layer. Once you've designed those pieces in an optimal manner, you can concentrate on the interfaces into that controlled environment from the areas you don't control (e.g., the source applications), as illustrated in Figure A2.4.

Package evaluation also continues, eliminating those products that don't seem suitable and adding effort to further test those that do.

Week 5

During Week 5, component design should be completed, as should the flows from the components to the data marts. Discounting the data sources for the moment—work in that area will commence during the following week—there should now be a complete conceptual picture of all data that is needed for business intelligence purposes and the mechanisms through which that data will be made accessible.

At the end of Week 5, a small-scale design review of this work completed to date should be conducted to ensure that the effort is still on track. Likewise, product evaluation should continue, moving into cross-product integration testing, high-volume test loads, and other testing to emulate real-world environments as closely as possible.

Week 6

Architecture and design work now shifts to the realities of dealing with the data sources. Tasks will include the following:

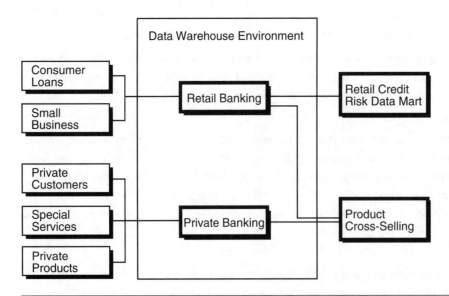

Figure A2.4 Designing the controlled portion of the enterprise.

- *Source data analysis.* Content analysis, quality evaluation, potential data gaps, and the other items discussed earlier in the book
- *Platform analysis.* Built on the work from the first phase, determining requirements to extract and move data from the source environments
- *High-level transformation design.* Focused on the transformations needed to move data into the *component layer*, not the end-point data marts

Package evaluation work also continues, shifting focus to extraction and transformation tools necessary to bring the source environments into the end-to-end enterprise.

Week 7

By the end of Week 7, the end-to-end architecture should be approximately 90% complete, with only a few minor details left (e.g., how data gaps will be handled or what approach to database partitioning will be used within the components).

Package evaluation proceeds, leading to the following two weeks' intensive end-to-end testing. Preliminary selections in each of the categories (front-end tool, middleware, etc.) are made.

Weeks 8 and 9

Any remaining uncertainties about the end-to-end architecture need to be resolved early in Week 8. Then, the entire team's efforts will be devoted to the detailed product evaluation described in the Week 6 chapter (e.g., representative data samples and volumes, end-to-end movement of data and access through the front-end tool).

At the end of Week 9, official selection of all products will occur in preparation for the product-specific design.

Weeks 10 and 11

Two weeks of intensive, product-specific design for all pieces of the end-to-end enterprise will be conducted during Weeks 10 and 11. All extraction scripts, transformation controls and callout code, cross-platform data movement scripts, and other facets of the enterprise will be developed as necessary to support the two data marts for which construction will soon begin.

Whereas architects of quick strike, tactical data marts may choose to forego system administration and metadata management functions because of budgetary pressures or in the interest of rapid delivery, these areas can't be ignored in an enterprise-scale data mart environment. Therefore, you need to dedicate adequate resources and time to designing these areas.

At the end of Week 11, another preliminary design review should be conducted, this time focused on the implementation details of the past two weeks' work.

Weeks 12 and 13

The detailed design is adjusted during Week 12 and, if necessary, during the first part of Week 13. The architecture and design phase then concludes with a final, end-to-end detailed design review. Expect this review to take at least two days, perhaps longer, depending on the complexity of your particular environment.

Phase 3: Construct and Deploy First Components

The third 90-day phase is devoted to the construction and deployment of the data warehouse layer components and the first data mart that has been designated for initial use within the enterprise. You need to strike a balance between the extremely aggressive construction schedules that you would use for a tactical data mart (i.e., the five-week schedule detailed in the chapters for Weeks 8 through 12) and a more cautious pace of activity that you would use for a larger-scale, distributed computing environment (such as a multitier client/server transaction processing application, for example) because of far-reaching dependencies.

Ideally, multiple teams will work in parallel on both the data mart and the components, their work interleaved with multiple interim deliverables and checkpoints as appropriate.

It is critical that all data warehouse components and the data mart be led by project managers and that their work be coordinated by a multiproject program manager. The person designated program manager should be versed in coordinating work across multiple projects, in quickly dealing with development issues in one project that can adversely affect other projects, and in ensuring that multiproject quality-assurance procedures are rigidly followed.

Phase 4: Construct Second Data Mart

Phase 4 sees two major occurrences:

- Construction and deployment of the second data mart
- Enhancement and tuning of the components in the data warehouse layer to support the additional data needs of the second data mart

It is *essential* that as the data warehouse components are modified and enhanced, and source system extractions and data flows are adjusted to include the new data requirements, regression testing be at the forefront of all project activities. That is, it is imperative that the initial data mart's functionality—which is now being used operationally—will not be adversely affected by modifications made to the environment that are necessary to support the second data mart.

Again, the exact sequence of development activities will vary from one environment to another.

Phase 5: Complete Enterprise Architecture and Design

At this point, approximately one year has passed since the beginning of the enterprise data mart initiative. Two data marts are operational, and a growing layer of (hopefully) well-managed data warehouse components is available for further enhancements in support of additional business functionality.

The next step is to take the lessons learned from the first year's activity and, coupled with any changes in business processes or overall mission of the data mart initiative, complete the blueprint for the remainder of the initiative. This should take place over yet another 90-day cycle, mirroring the activities of Phase 2 as described above.

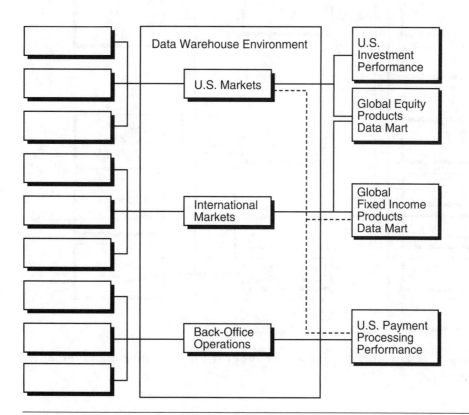

Figure A2.5 A brokerage example.

Your objective should be to designate pairs of phases—90 days of architecture and design, followed by 90 days of construction and deployment—over which the remainder of the data marts and their supporting infrastructure can be built in a controlled, manageable manner.

Other Examples

Figures A2.5 and A2.6 illustrate additional examples of enterprise data mart architectures. Figure A2.5 shows an environment from a brokerage and investment firm, and Figure A2.6 illustrates a model of ways customer management initiatives (customer retention, customer reacquisition, etc.) can be supported through interrelated data mart initiatives.

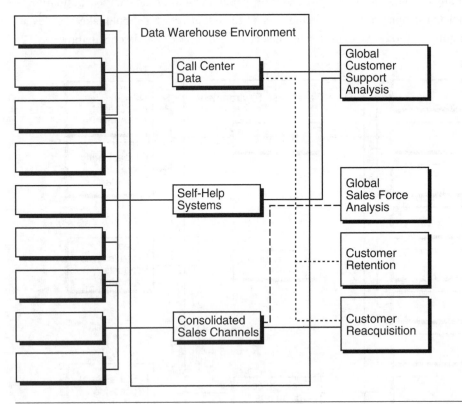

Figure A2.6 Enterprise data marts supporting customer management initiatives.

Summary

This appendix presented a blueprint that you can adapt to the specifics of your particular organization to develop an enterprise data mart environment. The details will naturally vary from one organization to another, just as they do in tactical non-integrated data marts.

Regardless of the exact path you will take, remember the following:

♦ *Proceed cautiously.* As discussed in the previous appendix, the enterprise data mart is very much an emerging area with a very small body of practical knowledge.

♦ *Proceed in a phased manner.* The 90-day cycle approach presented in this appendix helps you gain a handle on the overall business case for pursuing this approach (as contrasted with a series of independent data mart projects) and gaining the consensus and support you'll need.

♦ *Modification and enhancements are essential to every design and construction phase.* Existing data extraction processes, database definitions, load scripts, and the other parts of the environment will constantly be upgraded to meet the new requirements of each phase. Make sure that regression testing and intensive quality assurance are integral parts of your project plans in each phase.

✓ Data Mart Week 1 Checklist

❑ *Determine a confidential beginning-of-week risk rating.*

You almost always have a "gut feel" at the beginning of a project about the level of risk and the project's likelihood of success. By understanding and confronting that risk, you can better deal with issues that develop during the early days of the project. This rating should, for the time being, be confidential—that is, do not tell the business users what you believe may cause trouble even before you begin.

Use the following risk ratings:

♦ *Green.* Few risks, high level of cohesion among team members and users

♦ *Yellow.* Some moderate risks, but with an expectation that all will be overcome very early in the project

♦ *Red.* Significant risks that are likely to jeopardize the project

Ideally, you will never start a data mart project when the risk rating is *red,* but organizational realities (e.g., timing and budgeted funding) often dictate that projects begin before risks are mitigated and managed or projects that really should be shelved move forward anyway. In these situations when you find yourself "forced" into an undesirable project situation, you should at least know what you're dealing with.

❑ *Make sure business users are available during the entire week.*

You need to ensure that all key business users are available throughout the entire week; the ability to effectively and rapidly achieve consensus across business lines and organizations will depend on consistent communications and give-and-take among these users.

❑ *Ensure that project team members are available during the entire week.*

The team leader, facilitator, and scribe must be available throughout the entire first week; interruptions from prior projects or other job commitments need to be minimized to ensure that everyone is focused on the needs of this new data mart project.

❑ *Catalog all your data mart project prerequisites and make the documentation publicly available.*

Chapter 3 listed a number of data mart project prerequisites: technology (e.g., early product evaluation), organization and personnel (e.g., training), and methodology (e.g., agreement on the processes and deliverables that will be part of the project). The data mart project manager should catalog all the work done (including any work from earlier projects or company research initiatives being leveraged) and make this information readily available for use throughout the project.

TI P Use the company intranet or groupware (e.g., Lotus Notes databases) to create the project's documentation knowledge base and to make it readily and widely available.

❏ *Create the mission statement.*

Some data mart projects begin with a mission statement having already been created, and the work during the first week of the scope is oriented toward tuning and validating that mission statement. In other projects, there is no mission statement in existence at the beginning of the scope, and the statement needs to be dynamically created by the group. The time allotted during the first week of the project for the mission statement should reflect its existence, or lack thereof, and adequate time should be allotted for the exact activities that need to occur.

❏ *Build the business case on a "hard" return on investment (ROI).*

Some data mart projects are driven by "hard numbers" with a quantifiable financial benefit; other projects are based on "softer" benefits that are much more difficult to quantify. Discussion throughout the scope—and particularly during the first week—regarding functionality must be framed by the business case. To keep discussion focused and on track, there needs to be consensus for, and a clear understanding about, whether that business case is ROI driven or based on intangible, difficult to quantify factors.

❏ *Determine the overall project time frame and composition.*

By the end of the first week, you will have a good idea of whether the data mart's functionality will be delivered in a single set of project phases (e.g., design, followed by construction and deployment) or multiple phases (e.g., several design-construction-deployment cycles). Based on this determination, you can appropriately request funding, staffing support, IT assistance, and so forth.

❏ *Determine the most difficult data sources and platforms with which you'll have to deal.*

Initial Week 1 analysis of data sources and platforms will reveal the areas that are likely to present you with the most difficulty. Identify these and handle them appropriately (e.g., plan for additional resources or work to overcome resistance by a data source's "owner" that will be detrimental to the data mart project).

❏ *Determine—and make known—an end-of-week risk rating.*

How has the project risk rating changed from that of the beginning of the week? If the risk rating has worsened (e.g., gone from green to yellow), corrective action must be taken as quickly as possible before Week 2 turns into a nonproductive, confrontational exercise in futility.

☑ Data Mart Week 2 Checklist

☐ *Determine how complete the functionality-fact matrix is.*

Your objective during Week 1 was to complete the matrix that aligned data mart functionality with the facts needed to support the functionality. How far did you get in this process? How much catch-up work remains to be done at beginning of Week 2? How is your Week 2 schedule affected by these catch-up tasks?

☐ *Find out if enough is known about the data sources to build the fact-data source matrix.*

During Week 1, a fast-paced high-level analysis of data sources was conducted, building upon the work done before the data mart project was begun (see Chapter 3 for a discussion of project prerequisites). Now, during Week 2, you must build upon that knowledge and match the sources you've identified with the facts that will be built from the contents of those sources. Is enough known to be able to efficiently and effectively build the fact-data source matrix?

TIP An "80–20 rule" can be used to guide your comfort level with respect to the data sources. That is, there will always be gaps and questions while you are mapping facts to the contents of data sources. The data mart team should keep moving through the facts and the sources, building a list of facts for which there are open questions and possible data gaps. As long as this list remains at approximately 20% or less of the facts that you've looked at thus far, you can proceed through the list until the end and then go back and fill in the gaps. If the number of facts for which there are questions and issues rises above that level, it will be necessary to go back and look at the data sources in more detail to learn about their contents and respective contributions to the data mart.

☐ *Establish the way functionality prioritization will be done.*

By the end of Week 2, identified functionality must be prioritized to guide the order of design and development, particularly if multiple iterations of data mart development (i.e., multiple deliverables) will be necessary. The techniques and processes used to accomplish the prioritization must be determined and communicated with enough lead time to achieve consensus in the business community. For example, you may choose a weighted voting technique with the following rules:

- Every business community member receives 15 votes that can be allocated among the identified features and capabilities.

- Each person can allocate multiple votes to a given capability.

- A person can give no more than five votes to any one feature.

Then, at the completion of voting, all features with a minimum of (for example) 20 votes will be included in the initial release of the data mart; all other capabilities will be deferred until a subsequent release.

❏ *Establish a plan to handle identified gaps.*

If data gaps—that is, facts that are needed to support high-priority functionality but cannot be built from the available data sources—are identified, what is the plan to handle those data gaps, and how is the project's schedule affected? Does design need to be delayed until external data can be acquired? Can design proceed because a supplemental data source has been identified and made available prior to the beginning of construction?

❏ *Determine the "budgetary realities."*

Is the available funding enough to proceed all the way through design, construction, and deployment? Is funding sufficient for the project staffing levels that are needed? If adequate funding is not available, what changes (e.g., delays, reduced functionality) should be made to the project plans?

❏ *Determine and make known an end-of-scope risk rating.*

If the project's risk rating at the end of the scope is not *green*, corrective actions should be put in place before you proceed with design.

☑ Data Mart Week 3 Checklist

❏ *Make sure the entire data mart design team is in place.*

There are only five weeks available for design activity; it's imperative that all team members are in place and all activities begin on schedule. It's not impossible for someone who joins the team a few days or a week late to catch up. However, because the schedules are so tight and with such a quick pace of activity that shifts from one task to another with minimal downtime, any team member who is not in place will undoubtedly affect the progress of others simply because precedent tasks aren't completed.

❏ *Determine how much knowledge the user community has about OLAP functionality.*

The Week 3 schedule should reflect the OLAP background and knowledge of the users with whom the business analyst will work. That is, business community members who have made use of drill-down, stoplighting, and other advanced online analytical techniques don't need to be grounded in the basics of those capabilities; they are more likely to get beyond the "dazzle" of tools under consideration and focus on areas that will be directly tied to the business functionality that must be delivered. If, however, the user community has received information primarily through reports on large printouts, the business analyst needs to steer analysis in such a way that the users can be quickly grounded in basic OLAP techniques yet still make the necessary progress in selecting a tool that will serve their needs.

❏ *Establish issues-resolution processes for the design phase.*

Unlike during the two weeks of the data mart scope, when the majority of the project's decision makers from the business and IT communities work side-by-side, during the design phase, most of these individuals have gone back to their "real" jobs. Still, access by the data mart project team to these stakeholders must be possible to achieve timely resolution of issues, answers to new questions, and clarification of decisions made during the scope. The project manager needs to establish the ground rules and processes for these communications at the outset of the design phase to keep activities moving smoothly.

❏ *Determine the state of the company's intranet environment.*

The company's intranet will almost always be used as the mechanism to support passive data mart users, or those users who will primarily access reports and query results created by others. There should be a clear understanding of the intranet capabilities available and the processes and procedures that the data mart project team will have to follow to create reporting home pages, add necessary plug-ins to users' browsers, and so forth.

❏ *Figure out how much offline data will become part of the data mart.*
During the first week of the design phase, all offline data (e.g., data stored on archived tapes) that needs to be loaded into the data mart will be identified. This offline data is particularly suitable for use during tool evaluation with minimal impact on production databases, and provisions should be made as soon as possible for access throughout design and development.

❏ *Make sure everything is in place for acquisition of external data.*
If external data will be part of the data mart and that external data is already being used within the organization (e.g., in extract files), nothing in the contracts or agreements should prohibit the new usage of the data in the data mart. If newly acquired external data will be used, all agreements need to be in place, as discussed in Chapter 3.

❏ *Determine what vendor support is available for product evaluation.*
Vendor support during product evaluation can range from "here's an evaluation copy; call us if you want to place an order" to an onsite analyst (typically a presales consultant) who will be assigned to your organization throughout your evaluation process. Put plans in place to most effectively use whatever levels of support you have from the various vendors' representatives, whether onsite or through telephone support.

✓ Data Mart Week 4 Checklist

❑ *Even if you been unable to get a product successfully installed and working, continue work on the project.*

Whether product failure is due to vendor problems or incompatibilities with your organization's environment, you simply don't have time to repeatedly install and debug products that you can't get working. Vendors may promise to send the patch within the next few days and have the product working then, but time is of the essence. Move on!

❑ *Determine if anything in the scope of functionality or data has changed by the end of the week.*

Two weeks into the design phase is an ideal time to checkpoint the alignment of data mart functionality, facts, and data sources that was determined during the scope. Minor adjustments should be expected; major overhauls and changes are indicators of continued uncertainty as to the business scope of the data mart and the likelihood of serious project problems ahead.

❑ *Establish the viability of the data warehouse as a source to the data mart.*

Often, a data mart project is predicated upon receiving some or all of its data from an organization's data warehouse. And just as often, that data warehouse turns out to be a "project in process"; in other words, the contents that have been identified for transmission to the data mart aren't currently stored in the warehouse. By Week 4 of the project, the reality—or lack thereof—of the warehouse-to-mart data flows will be clearly understood. If the data mart project team has operated under a premise (or pressure) of having the data ready when it needs it but finds this is now highly unlikely, the project needs to go back to the drawing board to acquire data directly from the transactional sources. (See Chapter 1's discussion of the data source architecture for a discussion of these two models.)

❑ *Count the number of dimensions in your data mart model.*

Models with more than 10 dimensions are more likely to run into implementation difficulties than those with a smaller number of dimensions. Large dimensional models should be carefully evaluated for product suitability with an eye toward potential performance issues.

❑ *Determine how closely aligned your fact definitions are with the levels of your model's dimensions.*

The functionality-fact matrix (see Week 1) and the related fact-data source matrix (see Week 2) are built around specific levels of detail for each dimension (e.g., budgeted revenues by store by product family by week). Most of your candidate dimensions (e.g., customer, product, time, geography) could easily have 5 to 10 levels of detail (often more); supporting query capabilities at all possible combinations of levels can lead to storage capacity and performance issues. Therefore, as you prioritize the levels your data mart will support, you need to be able to closely tie what levels you do and do not support to the business functionality and the facts that you need to support.

❏ *Find out if the project plan is still being used.*

This checklist item serves as a reminder: it's one thing to create a project plan at the beginning of a project or the beginning of the design phase of a project, but it's another thing to continually enter task completion data, new tasks, revised time frames, and so on. It's imperative that the project manager continue to make use of the project plan rather than shuffle it off to the project's archives, never to be used again.

❏ *Deliver reality-based project status reports to the project's sponsors.*

As with the project plan, status reports are important communications vehicles. They should not only be completed and delivered on a regular basis (e.g., weekly), but they should also reflect the reality of the project (successes, issues, new risks, etc.).

✓ Data Mart Week 5 Checklist

❏ *Make sure you are really ready to select products.*

The likelihood of making intelligent choices for the various products is dependent on the progress you made during the previous two weeks. Even if you entered this project with an operating premise of a given OLAP tool and middleware product, based on company standards or pre-project research (see Chapter 3), there is always a possibility that Weeks 3 and 4 have been totally unproductive in the area of product evaluation because of installation problems, incompatibilities with your organization's infrastructure, or other reasons.

If you're not absolutely confident that you have enough information to select the products upon which you'll base the success of your data mart project, pay careful attention to your progress (or lack thereof) during Week 5 before proceeding with the following week's product selection.

❏ *Ensure that the data mart's data permissions model is well understood.*

You could simply grant all users of your data mart access to its entire contents, particularly if all the users are part of the same organization and perform relatively similar functions with the same types of information. If, however, people in a variety of roles and at a variety of different organizational levels will make up the data mart's user community, it is likely that some degree of data access authorization is a must for your data mart's implementation.

TIP In most organizations, the answers to, "Who can see what data?" are fairly well understood, if not formally documented. If a permissions model for the data mart needs to be implemented, the guiding principles should be driven by current and/or projected job function rather than technology. Since nearly every commercial DBMS product supports rudimentary data access control (as implemented by the SQL GRANT statement or an equivalent), you can assume that the technology will be available to support basic permissions.

❏ *Make sure the infrastructure is ready to go.*

Any augmentation to the organizational infrastructure necessary for the data mart's operational environment—additional network connectivity, new database server hardware, and so on—must be in place by this point in the project.

✓ Data Mart Week 6 Checklist

❏ *Resolve any product interoperability issues and questions you still have.*
Remember, product evaluation and selection are not done in isolation. You must make sure that products that need to work together in your production environment do so in your evaluation environment.

❏ *Ensure that your middleware testing and evaluation procedures reflect the operational model of your data mart.*
If your data mart will require in-place data updates as part of your restocking process, make sure that you conduct end-to-end testing of the extraction, transformation, and updating processes that will have to occur in the production environment. Don't just test bulk loading and replacing. Likewise, rolling updates will require bulk deletions to be made in the data mart's database, so make sure that the middleware product(s) and the data mart's DBMS work together to accomplish this restocking model.

❏ *Determine if you will be going against company or organizational standards.*
If the company's DBMS recommended standard is Product X and you've selected Product Y based on your evaluation, what is the impact likely to be? In many situations, you will have complete freedom to use the product of choice (subject to budget considerations) for your data mart project. In other situations, however, you may have to delay further work to justify your choice to an internal standards board or other organization. Make sure that any justification is built into your project plan and that you consider the impact of nonstandard decisions.

❏ *Be prepared for reactions from vendors whose products were not selected.*
Data mart project managers and architects are often surprised when they select OLAP Tool X over OLAP Tool Y based on their evaluation process and then find Tool Y's sales representative "going over their heads" to the project sponsor or division director, or even the CIO, attempting to override the team's product choice. Be prepared with detailed descriptions of your evaluation and selection process, and stand your ground!

TIP Vendor "counterattacks" often occur when outside consultants (either individuals hired to augment the data mart team or an organization to which development has been contracted) take the lead on the evaluation and selection processes. If you're a consultant, be prepared for your vendor "friends" to turn on you if you recommend a competitor's product. More important, *don't* let this type of confrontation affect your relationship with your client or the progress you've made on the data mart project.

❑ *Make sure the team is adequately trained for implementation-specific design.*

Following product selection, design activity shifts from a conceptual focus to the "physical" level—that is, modeling the specific functions and features of various products and exactly how they will be used. It's important that the team members working with these products understand the most expedient, efficient ways the products should be used. Any team members who need additional training must receive that training as soon as possible.

TIP Training in the middle of a project's design phase is not the most desirable turn of events, but it is often a reality. Fast-paced product training can usually be obtained over a two- or three-day period. This time away from the project can be made up over the following weekend to keep the project on schedule.

✓ Data Mart Week 7 Checklist

Before beginning the design review, make sure you're ready to discuss items below.

❑ *Functionality.*

- ◆ Any changes to the data mart's functionality made during the design phase (e.g., features that have been eliminated or postponed to a subsequent phase)
- ◆ The reasons those changes were made
- ◆ The impact on the overall data mart project

❑ *Your top five technical challenges and remaining uncertainties.*

❑ *Any deviation from company or organizational standards and guidelines and the reasons you made changes.*

❑ *If your data mart will be built around a dimensional database model.*

- ◆ Why you chose the dimensions you did
- ◆ What dimensions had been considered but eliminated, and why
- ◆ What levels you've selected for each dimension, and why (along with those you have chosen not to support, and why)
- ◆ How you will implement the dimensions of your data model (e.g., through a multidimensional cube or through a ROLAP metadata layer with all the interfaces from the tool's data model through the underlying database schema)
- ◆ Which areas regarding performance and response time are of greatest concern

❑ *If your data mart will be built around a nondimensional model (e.g., using denormalized tables).*

- ◆ Why you've decided not to create a dimensional model (e.g., developing a data mart solely to support a handful of standard reports with no ad hoc query capability)
- ◆ The impact on storage requirements of the denormalization (i.e., the duplication of data)
- ◆ The impacts on data mart restocking and reloading due to denormalization (e.g., what happens when a customer's address changes, how many tables are affected, how will the updates be done, how long will they take)

❑ *The data mart's initial loading model.*

- ◆ The details of each source-to-target flow, including all "sub-sources" (e.g., a production database plus data from archived tapes)
- ◆ The exact transformations that need to occur
- ◆ The quality of the source data and any transformation-related issues that you are likely to encounter (e.g., unpredictable data values for which automated corrections can't be created)

- ♦ Any availability or accessibility issues to source systems (e.g., extraction windows)

❑ *The data mart's repopulation/restocking model.*
- ♦ The details of each source-to-target flow, with a particular emphasis on extraction windows
- ♦ The exact transformations that need to occur and any variations from the initial loading model
- ♦ Any target-to-source feedback loops for data errors that are found and the way they will work
- ♦ The quality of the source data and any transformation-related issues that you are likely to encounter (e.g., unpredictable data values for which automated corrections can't be created)
- ♦ Any ongoing availability or accessibility issues to source systems
- ♦ Loading of windows into the data mart and the *details* of the model(s) by which the data mart will be updated (complete replacement, rolling append, append, and/or in-place updates)

❑ *System and infrastructure review.*
- ♦ All applicable network links
- ♦ All interoperability drivers or software that will be used
- ♦ All job or process control (e.g., JCL, Unix scripts, DCL) that will be used
- ♦ Utilities and facilities for metadata management (e.g., an enterprise repository) or data mart usage monitoring (e.g., database performance tracking software)

❑ *Security architecture and model.*
- ♦ The details (if applicable) of all data mart security capabilities (simple data access, authentication, network infrastructure capabilities such as encryption, etc.)
- ♦ The expected impact on performance of the security capabilities

❑ *User environment architecture.*
- ♦ All locations at which data mart users will reside and the method by which they will access the data mart's contents: single-building local area network (LAN) access, campus-based LAN access, metropolitan area network (MAN) access, remote access over a private network or the Internet, and the impacts on performance and response time at all locations
- ♦ Mobile user access models, such as data caching architecture, and the means by which stale data will be detected and refreshed

❑ *User assistance facilities (e.g., online help, intranet or Internet website access for help, "wizard" tools).*

❑ *Software distribution models for updating client-side and server-based software (e.g., OLAP tools).*

Data Mart
Week 8 Checklist

☐ *Make sure the user community is ready for a Week 9 limited initial deployment of the data mart.*

The data mart project's success is predicated upon timely feedback from "the real world" with regard to usability, previously undetected product problems, and related factors. Before the scheduled initial deployment, the selected members of the user community *must* be ready to put the software to use as soon as they receive it.

☐ *Verify that all additional hardware and software is ready for the Week 10 environment split.*

At the point initial user capability is provided, it is imperative that construction activity proceed on course. Any separate hardware (e.g., a database server) and software (e.g., a separate DBMS license upon which the still-in-progress database development will continue) needs to be ready to go at that point. Two weeks' lead time (at a minimum) is essential.

☐ *Conduct a brief but thorough review of the last evaluation database version from the design phase to determine if your production database building (the initial data mart population) should continue from that point or from a clean (e.g., empty) database.*

See the discussion in Week 8.

☐ *Make certain all developers have copies of coding and naming standards.*

The data mart development team has no time to go back and rename data fields or adjust hyphens, capitalization schemes, and so forth. Any standards with which components of the data mart must comply need to be communicated—and readily available—to all developers and the quality assurance team member.

☐ *Determine whether any reports have changed.*

If the initial charter of the data mart is to create (or, more accurately, recreate) standard reports that are currently being manually created or are built by a mainframe application or some other means, verify that the format or content of those reports has not changed since the last time the team reviewed them.

☐ *Identify and make readily available to the entire team all preferences related to graphical items.*

Time cannot be wasted developing bar charts when the users want pie charts, selecting blue as the color for the company's data across all graphs when the "official" color is green, and so forth. Make sure all developers are aware of these preferences and all output complies with the standards and guidelines.

❑ *Ensure that all QA procedures are ready to go.*

The team member responsible for QA must have all procedures and tests identified *and tailored* to the particulars of this data mart project.

✔ Data Mart Week 9 Checklist

❑ *Determine what development "problems" have developed and make a plan to overcome them.*

Even though you've been through product evaluation, end-to-end integration testing, and a detailed design phase (and review), there will likely be development problems that surface: product bugs, features that work differently from the description in the documentation, or areas of product-to-product interfaces that had been overlooked during the integration phase of the product evaluation. To keep the project on track, you need to have plans in place.

❑ *Ensure that vendor support is still in place and sufficient.*

The critical weeks of construction are directly ahead: Has vendor support during the first two weeks been satisfactory? If not, you need to elevate issues.

❑ *Determine whether capacity or performance issues are surfacing.*

At the end of Week 9, the data mart is initially populated and data volumes will reflect those that will be part of the production environment. Performance and response time must be satisfactory before you proceed.

❑ *Make sure all interproduct interfaces are in place.*

If data will be accessed through a spreadsheet, for example, all the necessary hooks and linkages (e.g., an ODBC driver) need to be in place and ready to be used.

❑ *Have a team offsite outing!*

At this point, everyone on the data mart project team has been working long hours. The initial deployment should be cause for an offsite outing. Everyone should get away from the project for an evening, perhaps even a long afternoon (if things have gone especially smoothly).

✓ Data Mart Weeks 10 and 11 Checklist

❏ *Determine what lessons have been learned from the initial data mart population that will affect restocking.*

Chances are that issues and workarounds were discovered during the first two weeks of construction in the area of source-to-target data movement (e.g., features that haven't worked as well as had been thought, resulting in callout code having to be written and accessed from your tool). If you need to adjust the detailed design of any of your restocking procedures, you must do so quickly before proceeding with development of the additional code.

❏ *Make sure user documentation is being created!*

It's tempting to bypass documentation tasks while frenzied development and real-world deliverable dates are at the forefront of your team's attention. Don't neglect the documentation tasks, and get assistance if necessary to make sure these tasks are completed.

❏ *Ensure that the training program for data mart usage is nearly completed.*

The training course must be ready when the users are.

❏ *Determine if the initial deployment is being used.*

By the end of Week 10, it will be clear if the initial data mart usage is actually occurring. If not, you need to find out why users aren't accessing their initial capability (data mart system problems? lack of support? no time?) and handle the issues accordingly.

❏ *If there will be a subsequent release of the data mart with additional capabilities, determine what will be in that version.*

It's not too soon for the project manager and the project sponsor to spend a few hours—but not much more—looking at the next release of the data mart. Discussion should include the following:

♦ Functionality that was removed from the current release and deferred to a subsequent version—is that functionality still considered necessary?

♦ Additional features and capabilities that hadn't been discussed during the scope but have surfaced during design and development (and have been deferred under the "no scope creep" edict).

❏ *See if the restocking models need to be modified.*

As development proceeds during Week 10 and into Week 11, you need to make sure that the model(s) you've selected for data mart restocking (e.g., complete replacement, rolling append) are working as efficiently as you would expect from your product evaluation. If unforeseen problems are occurring during development, you may want to quickly—*very* quickly— look at an alternative model to see if those problems could be overcome (e.g., if a rolling append is taking too long because of database DELETE statement problems or inefficiencies that you can't overcome, you may want to see if a complete replacement works better, even though logically, the rolling append is the preferred approach).

❑ *Establish that the operational test and evaluation (OTE) procedures are prepared and ready to go.*
OTE needs to begin as quickly as possible at the beginning of Week 12; the procedures must be created, reviewed, adjusted (if necessary), and completed by the time they're needed.

❑ *Make sure all deployment procedures are ready to go and the appropriate people are available when they are needed.*
If the IT organization will be responsible for deployment and rollout (as is usually the situation), the staff members need to be assigned and adequately briefed and trained for these tasks.

✓ Data Mart Week 12 Checklist

❑ *Make sure the development team is available to fix problems as quickly as possible.*

Ideally, the development team should be "on standby," as discussed in the Week 12 chapter. If the team is developing last-minute functionality, the fix-it-rapidly processes will likely be compromised. Under these circumstances, the operational testing is unlikely to be completed within the one week allotted and the schedule for the remaining steps (including the following week's deployment) should be adjusted accordingly.

❑ *Ensure that the time windows allotted for database extraction, movement, and loading are adequate.*

Figure WK12.3 illustrates the recommended sequence of rapid stocking and restocking cycles surrounding the testing period. For most data marts of "moderate" size (e.g., 25–50GB) that aren't doing complete database replacements, this model of daily refreshing should be adequate. If your data mart environment will have significantly more data volume and complex source-to-target movement processes (e.g., several staging areas where data is merged as part of the transformation process), these windows may not be sufficient. Your schedule should be adjusted accordingly.

❑ *Determine if immediate vendor support is still available.*

It is highly recommended that *each* vendor whose products you are using have either on-site or callable support throughout the construction phase. This should carry through to operational testing *and* to the last week of the project when deployment occurs.

❑ *Make sure you have consensus as to whether problems will be corrected.*

The Week 12 chapter discusses a recommended model in which problems that are discovered are immediately tagged as one of the following:

♦ Must-fix

♦ Delayed for modification until after deployment is completed

♦ An enhancement (i.e., declared not part of the current scope)

♦ Show-stopper

There needs to be consensus among all IT and business community members about the use of the above model (or one very similar to it) during the testing period and the general criteria by which identified problems will be placed into one of the above categories. Agreeing to these parameters *before* testing begins will save valuable time by avoiding unnecessary conflicts.

❏ *Determine if IT infrastructure support is available.*

It isn't uncommon to have problems surface that can't readily be traced to the front-end tool, the middleware product(s), or the DBMS. Adequate levels of infrastructure support from the IT organization must be available to help compartmentalize the end-to-end environment and identify "nonspecific" problems as quickly as possible.

❏ *Ensure that adequate version control procedures are available and that the team is adequately trained in their use.*

Ideally, the entire construction phase of a development project (data mart or otherwise) has been predicated upon "proper" software version-control processes. In reality, rapid development efforts (again, data mart or otherwise) often forego these practices, particularly when the effort is more of a package installation effort than custom coding (e.g., in Visual Basic or C).

Whether or not construction has made use of version control processes, it is essential that at least some rudimentary processes be put in place to keep the rapid find-and-fix cycles from corrupting the data mart's software environment. Even if version control software (e.g., PVCS) isn't used, some manner of directory-based version control (e.g., separate directories designated for production code, to-be-tested code, code that has been tested but not yet released for production) should be used.

✓ Data Mart Week 13 Checklist

❑ *Determine if the user desktop environment has changed since product evaluation was completed.*

During the design phase, when packages were being evaluated, one of the criteria to be considered was product compatibility with users' "standard" desktop environments. Even though only a short period of time (approximately two months) has passed since that testing occurred, users may have had updates made to their PCs, such as the following:

♦ Patches to existing software

♦ New utilities or tools

♦ New applications

♦ Software downloaded from the Internet

Any such changes could inadvertently affect the operation of OLAP or reporting tools. In the case of installation problems or abnormal termination of queries or scripts, first, check to see if the desktop environment has changed since the intensive product evaluation and testing occurred.

❑ *Make sure that software distribution mechanisms are fully tested.*

If you will be using automated software distribution capabilities to load PC-based software products (as you might for large user populations), make sure that those mechanisms have been fully tested. Better yet, see if they were previously and frequently used to distribute software into the same environments you need to access.

❑ *Ensure that user support facilities are fully available.*

The organization's help desk or call center needs to be completely capable of quickly resolving user questions and issues as they arise. This means that all support personnel must be fully trained and have access to the appropriate data mart software.

❑ *Schedule the party!*

Arrange for a well-deserved party, congratulating the entire data mart development team for a job well done as soon as possible after the data mart is rolled out and operational.